RANGE OF THE POSSIBLE

CONVERSATIONS WITH CONTEMPORARY POETS

TOD MARSHALL

EWU
P·R·E·S·S

EASTERN WASHINGTON UNIVERSITY PRESS
SPOKANE, WASHINGTON

Cover by Scott Poole
Book Design by Joelean Copeland

Acknowledgements

Foremost, all of the writers with whom I've spoken deserve my deepest thanks. Their vision and talent have served as illumination. A generous grant from Rhodes College helped with travel expenses for several of these interviews. Chris Howell, my editor, should be recognized for his faith and patience. Friends and fellow writers—Nance Van Winckel, Greg Dunne, Rob Carney, Don Revell, Claudia Keelan, and Nick Twemlow—have been instrumental in keeping me motivated and providing suggestions; Rob, Nick and Greg also helped with a few of the actual interviews. I'd also like to thank Marshall Boswell—thanks for so much, Boz. Lastly, I'd like to thank Paulette Burgess for her support while this collection was coming together.

I'd also like to recognize the editors of the following journals in which some of these interviews first appeared: *The American Poetry Review, Cutbank, The Denver Quarterly, Five Points Review, The Kenyon Review, Quarterly West,* and *Willow Springs.*

Library of Congress Cataloging-in-Publication Data

Range of the possible: conversations with contemporary poets / Tod Marshall.
    p. cm.
ISBN 0-910055-78-5 (pbk.)
    1. Poets, American--20th century--Interviews. 2. American poetry--20th century--History and criticism--Theory, etc. 3. Poetry--Authorship. I. Marshall, Tod.

PS325.R37
811'.509--dc21

2002001169

Range of the Possible

For Lincoln and Henry—
you've asked the questions and provided the answers.

TABLE OF CONTENTS

A Note on the Interviews

Although these interviews were conducted over the course of a decade, I've attempted to maintain consistency and focus in the discussions. Methodologically, I've asked some of the same questions—usually framed a bit differently—of the poets. Of course, my limits and obsessions—poetry and religion, Modernism, the shaping of a poetic line, to name only a few—have certainly guided the questioning.

INTRODUCTION

Born between 1941 and 1959, the poets in this collection have lived within a variety of compelling contexts. For some, the Second World War and its attendant images and realities shaped their childhoods; for others, the post-war boom and ideological recoil from that consumerist transformation were formative contexts; for all, the images of protest, violence, and unrest sparked by the civil rights movement and the Vietnam War defined the decades of their early years. Further, the aggressive rhetoric and political polarity of the Cold War guided foreign policy for a good portion of their lives (Korea, détente, the Cuban missile crisis, "star wars"). Nuclear holocaust's looming specter darkened all of their childhoods and, despite the dissolution of the Soviet Union, has continued to shadow their days. Just as ICBM's and other weapons of mass destruction multiplied in the latter decades of the twentieth century, this list of historical contexts proliferates: environmental devastation; overpopulation; numerous "small" wars in "third world countries" such as Nicaragua, El Salvador, Argentina, and Afghanistan; continued conflict in the Middle East; the emergence of terrorism as political tactic; *glasnost*; corporate colonialism; and the obvious impact of the oil industry on everything from United States' foreign policy to recent elections. These are but a few of the national and global backdrops, all of which say little about the influential technological developments of the period: from television and the polio vaccine to "the web," cell phones, and the prospect of species ending biological warfare. Although not defined by a series of specific conflicts or events like the writers of modernity, this generation of American poets has lived in an era of hyperbolic change, ongoing globalization, ever present tension, and, for the intellectually and emotionally engaged, palpable anxiety.

Of course, another development during these writers' lifetimes has been the emergence of a pervasively consumerist American culture. To put it in different terms, these writers lives have chronologically overlapped with the crystallization of much of American culture around the salty core of selfish consumption—conspicuous, yes, but probably more grotesque than Thorstein Veblen could have ever imagined. From commercials and infomercials to the cancerlike expansion of fast food chains and every possible saleable product (made in China) at the ubiquitous Walmart (Kmart, Shopco, and/or Sears), all aimed, in many ways, at easing the life of the oh-so-fragile, oh-so-devouring, and oh-so-neurotic self: as the pie graphs of *USA Today* tell us, the latter half of the twentieth century in America has been as defined by this consumptive gluttony as the frequently "distant" grindings of history.

The possible contextual angles which have impacted these poets stretch even to employment: one might argue that American prosperity and the attendant consumerism coupled with the "opening up" of the American university admissions system in the early seventies have led to the institutionalizing of a great deal of American poetry and, along with all of the "legitimization" of academic standing, taken away what was previously one of the primary difficulties of the poet: how to pay the bills. Although some critics have written disparagingly of such a partnership, the comprehensive effects are still rather uncertain. That American poetry and academia are conjoined is not; among the poets in this collection, all but Lee and Addonizio teach at a college or university, and even these two poets teach part-time for support.

These are merely a few observations; I am neither economist nor historian nor psychologist nor pomo-pop-culture-Americanist. However, I feel confident asserting that the historical and cultural contexts in which these poets grew up and in which they've written were myriad and influential. Certainly, many of the writers discuss these contexts with more exacting detail, precise elaboration, and engaging specificity in regards to their own lived experience than any introductory note. Whatever the case may be, poetry is at the center of these discussions, and I am more confident describing the literary milieu in which these writers have found their voices— even if such literary contexts are equally divergent.

The great modern American writers—Eliot, Moore, Hughes, Pound, H.D., Williams, and Stevens—all died during the lifetimes of the poets in this collection. As one generation passed, a "mid-century" generation moved to the fore, and a third, of which the poets in this book are representative, emerged. Born in the first decades of the century, Lowell, Bishop, Berryman, Olson, Roethke, Rexroth, Bronk, Duncan, Everson, Rukeyser, Oppen, and Niedecker published their first significant work primarily during the forties and fifties. Further, Sexton, Dickey, Ammons, Merrill, Plath, Hall, Rich, Ashbery, O'Hara, Kizer, Hayden, Wright, Levertov, and Kinnell—the "younger siblings" of the older mid-century poets— began to write and to publish their enduring work during the same time period. Hence, when the writers in this book began reading poetry, many of the mid-century's generation had already begun to have a shaping influence on the work that the next generation was to write. However, what's most astonishing to me about this partial yet representative list of poets who rose to prominence during the forties, fifties, and sixties is the wide range of writing: the aesthetic leaps from Lowell to Olson to Roethke to Merrill to Niedecker to Ashbery to Sexton to Wright are lengthy. Consequently, just as the historical and cultural contexts toward century's end are diffuse, when one really tries to understand the shaping literary influences— not to mention those of music, painting, sculpture, and, even, literary theory—well, the anxiety of influence becomes more of a stressful tension on the tenuous claims of critics than a clear connective thread in the works of the writers.

In the last decade of the twentieth century, the younger of the mid century generation entered its twilight, and the work of the poets born mid-century announced a diasporic rather than lineal legacy. To put it another way, in hindsight, much of the poetry of the mid-century and even into the sixties and seventies was written out of a reaction against Modernism. The "giants" still walked the earth, and their monoliths—from *The Waste Land* and *Spring and All* to *The Cantos* and *Trilogy*—loomed like challenging peaks; hence, for that generation of writers, models of influence and anxiety, the notion of precursors makes some sense—we see Lowell struggling with his two fathers, Eliot and Williams; we see Bishop trying to move away from Madame Marianne; Olson and Creeley extending the lineal experiments of Doc Williams; Ashbery pushing Stevens into and through a Hoonian box, and so on.

Of course, weaknesses with such generalizations hold true of any generation of writers (What of the effects of literary theory? Translation? The other arts?), but for contemporary American poetry at the beginning of the twenty-first century, the tendentiousness seems especially apparent. For example, think about a few of this century's poetic lineages, isms, movements, and such: Eliotic, Poundian, Stevensian; Imagism, Objectivism, Projectivism, Confessionalism, and deep Imagism; the New Agrarians, the Black Mountain School, New York poets, San Francisco's Renaissance, New Formalists, neo-Narrative Writers, and the Language poets— to name just a few. Now take a look at a specific poet; let's say, Robert Hass. Hass has asserted that Pound and Wordsworth are formative poets for him—the Wordsworthian posture toward nature and the Poundian license of inclusion are certainly elements in his work. However, can one discount the influence of his famous formalist teacher Yvor Winters? Or of the Bay poets: Snyder, Rexroth, and Palmer (three very different threads)? Further, Hass's grappling with translating Milosz and the haiku of Basho, Buson, and Issa has certainly shaped his poetics—not to mention his familiarity with literary theory, his struggles understanding the writing of Rilke and Lowell, his interest in the relationship between the novel and middle-class consumption (the subject of his doctoral dissertation), his engagement with environmentalism, and even his taste for exotic cooking. And then, of course, what does one do with biographical facts? The historical and cultural clatter—from J. Lo's newest love interest, M.J.'s most recent comeback, and "The Weakest Link" to terrorist attacks, genome research, and AIDS pandemics in Africa?

Simply, as a tool for making generalizations about contemporary poets, the vortex of influence cycles out of control. Consequently, an interview with each writer is a valuable interstice through which to glimpse a writer's work and to begin to understand various perspectives on the century in which he or she began to write.

In this collection, I have chosen a list of poets that seem to me representative of a "range of what's possible" in contemporary American poetry. Borrowed from the interview with Brenda Hillman, my title phrase speaks to one of the primary strengths of American poetry, a strength that is directly connected to the multiple energies fueling the artistic practices. Again and again, these interviewees speak to a nonpartisan vibrancy, an enthusiastic call to the art that generously invites pluralistic traditions, numerous practices, multiple approaches; I find such expressions invigorating and encouraging.

In fact, if I were to identify recurring threads in my discussions with the writers, then one of the most significant is the emphasis on the need for variation in the art. From Addonizio to Wrigley, these writers emphasize again and again how sectarian divisions based on lines in the sand lead to little good for the art. "I don't approve of any restriction that would limit American poetries, especially when it involves throwing out other aesthetics," Edward Hirsch gently cautions. Many of his peers agree: writers who have studied beneath different teachers, championed radically alternative poetics, come from diverse backgrounds, and offered varying visions on the art, religion, and politics echo this same theme of inclusion.

Another repeated thread involves what might be called a meticulous devotion to craft. Recently, some poets and critics have described sloppiness in much of contemporary American poetry— a failure of form due to the loose boundaries of free verse. The writers with whom I spoke articulate a different reality. Whatever shape the poems ultimately take—from the more "mainstream" use of the line and page by a writer like Dave Smith to a radical use of space and margin by Brenda Hillman—these writers are devoted to meticulous shaping of the page. Further, although meter and traditional form may not be as prevalent in their practices, each of the poets articulated an intense fluency with such matters. As a side note to the this observation, though, I should mention that even in the most "traditional" of the poets with whom I spoke, there was an awareness of the more experimental aspects of contemporary writing. Robert Wrigley, for example, may write in what appears to be a fairly "regular" line, but his emphasis on percussive musicality coupled to strong metaphoric imagery bespeaks an awareness of the most experimental and nonreferential work of his generation.

Yet another recurring thread—perhaps the most significant one— is what I might call a Shelleyan faith in the power of the art. Nearly all the writers in this collection speak passionately to the cultural importance of poetry, to *the need* for poetry. Cynics might decry such a refrain as an obvious outgrowth of the project; get a group of poets together and of course they're going to talk about the importance of poetry! Perhaps. However, I'd like to think that this refrain speaks more to the poets' attentive engagement with the political, social, cultural, and spiritual fabrics surrounding them, engagement that has given them hope that the art they create reaches ears that hear and eyes that see. "The generosity of these artistic practices broadens the available reality," Claudia Keelan argues in regard to the artists who have affected her. The same is true of the musing, rumination, and speculation of the writers included herein: because their visions make us ask important questions about poetry, reexamine our thoughts on aesthetics, as well as consider the political, spiritual, and cultural contexts in which we live, make us—how else to put it?—equally attentive and present, they have provided a generous gift. They show us that the range of the possible is boundless

—Tod Marshall, 2001

RANGE OF THE POSSIBLE

PHOTO BY JEANNE C. FINLEY

Kim Addonizio was born in 1954 in Washington, D.C. Her three books of poetry articulate a unique vision rooted in stark worldliness yet driven by a lyrical desire to transcend this broken world. The Philosopher's Club, Jimmy & Rita, *and* Tell Me *(a finalist for the 2000 National Book Award) also exhibit a dynamic formal range; from variations on the sonnet to a muscular free verse line, Addonizio's formal repertoire is flexible and wide ranging. A recipient of National Endowment for the Arts grants, as well as many other awards, she lives in the San Francisco Bay area and teaches in the low residency M.F.A. program at Goddard College.*

KIM ADDONIZIO

Kim and I conducted this interview in the early fall 2001.

Many mid-century poets were shaped by Modernism; many contemporary poets reacted to the reaction of the mid-century poets. How did you come to poetry? How does it connect to your understanding of literary history in this century?

I have to say that I was shaped very haphazardly. My formal literary education was sketchy, so I have all the quirks and deficiencies of the autodidact. I started late—around twenty-seven, twenty-eight. I had no background in poetry, didn't read it until I found myself writing it. At that point I went to get a Master's in English/Creative Writing, but I wasn't particularly shaped by any historical period, I don't think. I managed to evade entirely a requirement for nineteenth-century literature, and had to catch up later, on my own. In graduate school I read the Modernists, some of whom I liked very much, some of whom I found merely interesting. The "Language" poets were dominating ideas of poetics at the time, and I was interested in those ideas, but as a poet, I found myself pursuing a kind of writing that was considered outdated and was certainly unfashionable. It was hard to find my own territory at first, but once I did, I pretty much lost interest in other people's definitions of poetry and pursued what compelled me. I'm not very cerebral; I mostly don't like academia and its categorizing. Theories of language make me nauseous, though I'm aware that every writer still operates under some theory, whether consciously examined or not. But I think it goes deeper than language; what you think the projects of language and of poetry are have a lot to do with who you are in other ways.

Which of the Modernist poets did you like? Why?

Well, I read those poets fifteen to twenty years ago. I don't often go back to them, because I don't teach modern poetry classes or anything. I suppose that's a way of saying, I don't generally look to those writers for sustenance. Though sometimes I'll encounter a fragment of, say, Eliot's *Four Quartets* and like it a lot. And I think "Prufrock" is a great poem. I remember I liked Eliot in graduate school, and some of Stevens for the music of his language in poems like "Sunday Morning." My daughter had to read *The Waste Land* for high school a couple of years ago, and I kind of enjoyed rereading it after I went through the process of figuring it out again.

All of those wonderful notes. Tell me about some of the poets to whom you look for sustenance. Specific poets and even poems and why.

Right now I'm finding a lot of sustenance in Rumi. It's helpful to remember the eternal, when civilization seems so fragile—here we are at war again, and there are real dangers to our survival. There are certain Jack Gilbert poems that I love, poems like "Tear It Down," where he writes, "Love is not / enough. We die and are put into the earth forever. / We should insist while there is still time." When a student and friend of mine was dying, I read her Jack Gilbert's poems. They don't have any bullshit in them; they're full of the core issues of being human—love, loss, loneliness, how to live authentically. Then there are poets I go to for other reasons as well. C.K. Williams, say, whose syntax is ravishing and who captures the minute turnings of consciousness on the page. Neruda's love sonnets. Philip Larkin for his formal skills and that great edge of bitterness. Merrill and Komunyakaa and others for sheer language. Elizabeth Bishop for her imagery. Whitman for his expansiveness and Dickinson for her depth. Donne and Herbert for their questioning and soul-searching. Keats I love going back to for companionship. I feel him so strongly through his work—that presence and imagination there on the page. I guess that's what draws me.

You said that "it was hard to find your own territory" but once you did, everything else seemed sort of inconsequential. How would you describe or define your poetics?

Here is what I believe, if this constitutes a poetics: I believe language was developed over millions of years as a way to communicate. Personally, I'm not interested in destroying meaning or multiplying it *ad infinitum.* I believe in narrative, in story. I believe in the lyric, that it is possible to sing. I believe that poetry is an act of consciousness and that most critics miss the point completely. And I'm a little tired of hearing how naïve that position is, and that poetry isn't self-expression. Of course it is! That doesn't negate its being an art and a craft. Artists create out of their ideas, their obsessions, their interests, their passions, their lived and imaginative experience. If that isn't self-expression, I don't know what else to call it. Art is a function of the human spirit. To play intellectual games with language is interesting, but it doesn't take you anywhere. I'm not saying that I feel writers shouldn't fracture meaning, but there are certain kinds of writing that seem to me a real dead end because the writers are operating completely from the intellect. That's a dead end. Then there's a writer like Anne Carson, for example, who is an interesting mix of what I'd call Modernist or Postmodernist techniques combined with some rather traditional emotional territory. That's a lot more appealing; it's not bloodless. I think poetry has to negotiate with the *duende.* Any poetry that does that I am happy to read, and I respect it, whether or not I understand it.

You've written in both "closed" and "open" forms. How do traditional forms fit into this "poetics?"

I use whatever tools are available. I like using traditional forms as a template, the way African tribal rhythms and traditional features like call-and-response singing were a template for so much that came after—field songs, spirituals (which mixed in Protestant hymns), jazz, gospel, the blues, and from the blues, rock and roll, soul, and R&B, on to rap, hip-hop, and whatever else is happening musically now. And classical composers like Bartók and Copland used folk songs and incorporated those forms. Poetic forms are useful in that they put a certain kind of pressure on language, and also there's a dialogue that a contemporary poem can have with the tradition through the use of a previously established form. Free verse does it too, of course. Whitman used the structure of Biblical verse. And there are other ways to have that dialogue that don't have to do with structure, that have to do with subject matter or presentations of the self. I don't feel compelled to stick to the "rules" of the form if the poem works better by violating them, but I like sometimes to have those rules to lay out the territory. And anyway, all traditional forms are experimental. The English sonnet, for example, didn't spring forth fully formed in the sixteenth century. It's more than the migration from Italian; it took about three hundred years to develop, from the time someone probably added a couple of tercets to an eight-line form. So there's been a constant evolution of poetic forms along with poetic language—a constant interplay of tradition and experimentation and various influences, as in all the arts.

The sonnet, in particular, is a form that you've done some great things with. Can you say more about how you see that particular form functioning—the idea of the volta, *the rhyme scheme, the balance between lyricism and rhetoric?*

What I like about the sonnet is that there's a great jolt of energy in it, because you have to make your argument in a short space. I like the idea of the *volta*, but I don't always follow it. I'll keep in mind that the poem wants to shift gears in some way around the transition from octet to sestet, but I rarely hit it; usually, in my sonnets, the *volta* occurs a bit later or only in the last two lines. Or not at all. Again, I see the form as a template, as something useful to take off from. If I have to mess it up, I will. It's more interesting to me to follow the poem, ultimately, than to follow the form. The point of form is to release the poem, not inhibit it.

And the sonnenzio?

It was really an accidental thing. I'd given my students a pretty standard writing exercise—to take the first line of someone else's poem as theirs. I had a list of first lines, all in iambic pentameter (they got existential extra credit for following the meter in their own poem). I used a line from a well-known sonnet by Michael Drayton that begins, "Since there's no help, come let us kiss and part," and about three lines into it, I realized I had repeated the word "part" a couple of times. I was trying to decide if I liked it or not, whether I should get rid of the repetition, and instead, I decided to push it. That started to get fun and interesting, and I figured I might as well try to do it in fourteen lines, like a sonnet. Then, when it looked like that might work out in terms of the poem, I thought, why not add a closing couplet like an English sonnet? It wasn't meant as an invention of a form, but once I'd written it, I wondered if it was a viable form or just one that had worked out for this material. So I wrote a second one, which didn't go very well, and then a third, which I thought was more successful. And the rules are what I developed as I wrote: begin with a line from someone else's sonnet, repeat one word from that initial line in each succeeding line of the poem, make it fourteen lines, and close with a couplet. I know David Lehman, who edits the *Best American Poetry* series, wrote some with his students, and some of them were pretty good. It can be a little gimmicky, I suppose, but it's a great challenge to have to repeat a word fourteen times and not have it become a dead space in your poem. And immediately you have to resort to all sorts of other tricks to use the idea of repetition sometimes without the actual repetition of the word. That interests me, the echo in the mind without the echo of the actual sound. I've also always wanted to write a conceptual sestina, where the end words are all repeated concepts or associations rather than literal repetitions. But I actually hate writing sestinas, so I probably will never do it. There are some forms I seem to have an affinity for, like the sonnet and pantoum, and others I can't seem to use at all at this point.

Many writers have written about the relationship between poetry and politics. How do you understand the two to intertwine?

I feel very resistant to considering that issue right now. At this moment—a month after the WTC and Pentagon bombings—I'm too exhausted from talking and thinking about the world. And I just went to a museum exhibit on torture that threw me into complete despair about the innate evil of our species. About all I can muster right now is the belief that poetry is a force on the side of light, however practically ineffectual it may be at this time in this country. Our government for the most part doesn't need to suppress poetry because it's managed pretty much to marginalize it, to make both poetry and poets invisible or trivial to the average citizen. Anyway, I don't feel I can speak with any special authority about the relationship of politics and culture. I'd rather hear from someone who has deeply studied those relationships, as I have not. One thing that struck me about the exhibit, though, was the statement, "The soul of torture is male." I believe that. And the soul of war is male, too. Why is that so? And what can we do about it? I think a lot about our relationship to suffering and evil, and that's one of the recurrent subjects of my work. I do think that poetry, some form of art anyway, is essential for our survival.

Many have also cast poetry as a spiritual endeavor, one counter, perhaps, to the masculine soul of torture. In a primarily secular age, how do you understand poetry's relationship to the spiritual?

You know, before the events of September 11, I would have taken as axiomatic the idea that we were living in a secular age. Now I'd question that, given so-called Muslim terrorists, given that quite a few people in this country seem to be intoning "God Bless America" at every opportunity. Religion seems more present than ever, and a spirituality that is not particularly based on religion—or maybe is based more on Eastern religions like Buddhism—is also a part of American culture. The Psychic Friends Network is, on some level, a manifestation of American spirituality. All that stuff: the UFO cults, the TV shows on near-death experiences. All of that speaks to some sort of belief in, or at least longing for, more than the material. So that's one thing. It's axiomatic, too, to say that the arts historically split off from their religious function. But it seems to me that art has always trafficked in the spiritual. It may confirm the doctrine of some religion or may transgress it, but it is interested in ultimate reality, in the sacred. Anyone who deeply practices an art form connects with that. From the outside, though, art has been secularized, commodified, trivialized. I experience the writing of poetry as a spiritual practice, and I bet any other poet would say a version of the same thing, even if he or she didn't use the word "spiritual."

Some critics have written disparagingly about the academization of poetry—in a nutshell, since it's been taken in by the university and subsidized, so to speak, by creative writing programs, American poetry has lost a meaningful edge, a truly radical avant-garde. What do you think about such assertions?

I don't want an academic job, personally, but such jobs have provided a livelihood for a number of poets, and I don't see that as necessarily a bad thing. A lot of the so-called "avant-garde" is in the universities, with tenure. I don't see American poetry losing its edge. The thing about separating the academy from everything else is that you can't. All sorts of people pass through universities and especially community colleges, where creative writing has also found a strong foothold as part of the curriculum; there's been a trickle-down effect from all the M.F.A. programs. So you have at one level the critics and scholars trying to categorize everything and take it apart— which is fine if they're the right kinds of critics and scholars, i.e. lovers of the art, who get it (and unfortunately too many of them don't). And then you have the poets, some of whom are stifled by the academy, some of whom are trying to subvert it; and then all kinds of students being exposed to poetry, reading poetry and trying to write it, being taught often by practicing poets. There's a great diversity in the supposed Ivory Towers of learning, I think. And beyond that, again the trickle-down effect: poetry is being taught in high schools, in elementary schools, in senior centers and prisons and battered women's shelters. Why? Because all these creative writing programs in colleges and universities have nourished people with an interest in and passion for poetry who then take it out into the community since most of them aren't going to get those tenure-track positions. There's a whole climate now for poetry to be appreciated that wouldn't exist, I think, had there not been this "academization" of poetry. Of course, there's a lot of bad poetry being written now, possibly fueled by all that, but so what, really? There are a lot of terrible musicians in the world, but that doesn't take anything away from the good ones. People do it because they enjoy it. If they get a chance to read great poetry, and study with poets, and try to improve, that's a good thing. And you can't kill the edge, anyway. You can't kill poetry, or the impulse to art, or the imagination that is going to try to take it to places it hasn't yet been.

I'd like to talk a little bit more specifically about your poetry. What shapes your determination of line? What are the sound qualities that you find most compelling, the rhythmical qualities that when

you're composing begin to take over and let you know that you're
working on a poem?

A line is a unit of rhythm and a unit of meaning. I consider both, but what I think dominates often, in my case, is rhythm. A line is a rhythm that can work with or against the rhythms of the sentence. It's pacing. And yet I think you hear it internally; when I read a poem silently, my own or someone else's, I hear the silence of the white space. But when I read poems aloud, I may run roughshod over that silence for the sake of the sentence, or I may pace the poem dramatically some other way—say, a long pause after a period, which isn't at all indicated on the page (but may be called for, come to think of it, by the meaning). Still the music is there on the page if you listen with your inner ear. I got interested in very long lines after steeping myself in C.K. Williams, because the long line seemed able to accommodate a different kind of thinking, a more discursive language. But I want a sense of pulse in my writing, whatever the length of the lines; for me, a poem is very much a way of singing. I think I feel about poems the way Poe felt about the short story— that idea of it being apprehended as a whole, being something that you take in all at once that produces an effect. Or I should say, I aim for that in the poems that I write. I want them to be felt immediately. That's not achievable with a novel, I don't think. It's possible in poems and stories because of the usual brevity of those forms. Of course, a longer poem may be up to something else entirely. But with short poems and some stories, the reader can have a sort of peak experience. Maybe it's the difference between romance and sustained relationships. The romance is the glimpse, you know? You glimpse some deep beauty in the other person. You grant the other person a kind of perfection of soul that you long for. And it's real and not real. Poetry for me is a kind of romance and also a long, sustained grappling with what is glimpsed in that moment of the poem.

When I'm writing, I generally fool around at a different level of language—a duller, more pedestrian level. Then something happens, that I liken to dousing for water. I hit the underground stream of a richer kind of language, and then I'm just trying to keep up with it. Sometimes it'll turn into a trickle, and I'll have to wander around looking for it again. I don't know how else to describe it; it's not a very willed thing, but all my knowledge and study is required to follow it.

Some poets look back at their earlier work with a feeling of discontent. How do you feel about The Philosopher's Club *and* Jimmy & Rita?

I'm fine with those books. I don't think they're brilliant, but I think I achieved my vision with whatever ability I had to achieve it. It took a long time for *The Philosopher's Club* to see print, which was fortunate, because it turned out to be a much better book than it would have been otherwise. As it went around and around to various contests and got rejected by each of them, I kept taking old stuff out and revising, and I was learning more about how to write, too. So when it finally got taken, it was a stronger book. I'm happy about that. And *Jimmy & Rita* is very close to my heart because it started from a scrap, really, a moment between two people shooting speed in a parking lot, and I got a flash that I could tell their story. And actually going from that first vague apprehension of a story to a realized book really helped me as an artist. It helped me to trust my creative impulses, to let them go and not shut them down because of fear. I used to sit at my computer writing "Rita, Rita, speak to me" at the top of a page, or "Jimmy, where are you?" because I was so afraid I couldn't realize their story, afraid that whatever I'd glimpsed was going to disappear, and I didn't know what else to do but appeal to the characters themselves. And now I'm working on a novel that takes up their story where that book left off, and I've gone through the same feelings of doubt and inadequacy. But I've realized that I just have to go forward anyway, and if I end up writing a shitty novel, that's what happens. I don't think it's a shitty novel at this point, though. I hope it will be published, and I also think that five or ten years from now I will see things that I'll wish I'd known how to do better.

What do you think are the primary changes in your writing since you've published your first book? To put it another way, do you think that becoming a "validated" poet has changed your attitude toward publication and even the route of your work?

If I weren't published I'd still be writing, still be reading and studying. It's what I love to do. For the past couple of years I've also been passionate about learning blues harmonica, and I'm now at the stage where I can get up at a jam and play with people and feel like I've got something to offer. But I'm not interested in making CD's or headlining clubs or anything; I'm interested in playing. I love the blues; I get high standing in that section of a music store being surrounded by the evidence of so much great music. I love to play along with CD's, and it's exciting to play with live musicians. That's where the satisfaction is. Of course, the other part of it is that I'm making progress. Being able to bend notes I couldn't bend or to play a lick I couldn't play, that's a great feeling. I think that *Tell Me* is a progression from earlier work, too, that I'm able to do more in a poem, that I have a greater range tonally, that I'm learning more about metaphor. The route of my work is what it's always been; the recognition I've gotten has given me more confidence in it.

Is there a difference in your approach when you're writing prose as opposed to poetry?

I think of it this way: when I'm swimming, I'm not taking a bath. There's a relationship between them, but they're different activities. If I'm reading prose I generally want to write it. Same with poetry; reading triggers some possibility of language or story. When I wrote *Jimmy & Rita*, I was writing poems, but then as a whole they had to fit together in a more novelistic way. And now the novel I'm writing is a continuation of their story, in prose. I know whether I'm involved in a poem or a story or a prose poem, though. And ultimately I don't think it matters. Who cares, really, what you call it? What matters is that you have an experience with it, as a reader. I've seen several pieces by various writers that were published in one anthology as prose poems and elsewhere as short-short stories. Those are definitions, not the work itself. Maybe this contradicts my analogy about swimming, but maybe not; in either case, you're immersed in the water. The important thing is to be in the water. As a reader and as a writer.

I've spoken with Brenda Hillman and Gillian Conoley, and both of them have praised the presence of a vibrant community of women writers in the Bay area. Can you talk about how such a community has affected your work?

I don't personally feel this big presence of a community of women writers affecting my work. I had a writing community at San Francisco State consisting of other graduate students, and we met after graduating, and started a literary journal, *Five Fingers Review*, and organized benefits for a few community and political causes. Then I met some other writers, and we got together for years to workshop our stuff. I consider my community to be my writer friends, wherever they are, and my other friends, and my students and family. I'm not really friends with many writers in the Bay Area right now. I mean, I see people now and then at readings; I like them fine, but we're not calling each other up and hanging out. My three closest women friends, though, are writers.

In a recent poem, "Round Midnight," you wrote, "Now I feel a misery / only violence could cure." Describe the impulse behind that line—it's different from the idea that "the soul of torture" is masculine, but it speaks to a need for extremity that seems to be on the same continuum—if that makes sense—and whether or not it might reflect an aspect of your poetics.

That poem is (I think) about the relationship between life and fiction, the stories we tell ourselves, our need for drama. I'm not sure how to relate it to a poetics. What it makes me think of is that saying about the first rule of fiction: "Only trouble is interesting." It seems to me that poetry, fiction, all art, comes out of some sort of psychic disturbance that needs to be addressed. Maybe, if we were perfectly evolved beings, we wouldn't need art at all. But then again, maybe we'd make it all the time out of the energy of being completely alive.

Linda Bierds was born in Wilmington, Delaware, in 1945. The author of six books of poetry, including The Ghost Trio, The Profile Makers, *and, most recently,* The Seconds, *Bierds is a meticulous crafter of highly original work. Working line by line and never shaping more than a single poem at a time, Bierds has written an enduring and highly acclaimed body of poetry. The recipient of numerous awards, including the distinction of a MacArthur Fellowship, Bierds' poetry frequently calls upon both well-known and obscure historical figures and events to propel her work. Bierds is currently a professor of creative writing at the University of Washington.*

LINDA BIERDS

Linda and I spoke during summer 2001 on Bainbridge Island, Washington.

Many mid-century poets were shaped by Modernism; many contemporary poets reacted to the reaction of the mid-century poets. How does your reaction to what you read connect to your understanding of literary history in this century?

I had a typical, large-state-university education, both for my bachelor's and master's degrees in English and Creative Writing. We read in historical periods, and in our twentieth century readings, we were guided, as most were, into thinking about the forking between Eliot and Williams or Eliot and Williams/Whitman. I approached this division initially as a student of literature, and then as an apprentice poet. As I've watched the twentieth century close, I've watched that division, that wall that seemed so defined in the century's first half, gradually become more permeable. Oftentimes I think that in fifty or seventy-five years the distinctions between the legacies of Stevens or Pound or Eliot could seem less significant, finally, than those between all of the above and the Postmoderns.

Can you tell me more specifically what you understand that division between Modernism and Postmodernism to be?

Volumes are being written about this! But briefly—and with acknowledged over-simplification—I feel that the majority of poets writing before the birth of the postmodern sensibility believed that language could be crafted to produce a poetry whose path-work of lines could lead to the ineffable. And that path-work was often laid down as a trackable progression—whether linear (moving forward or backward), circular, or arcing. It resulted in, or strove for, a condition of wholeness. Because the Postmoderns question not only the concept of wholeness, but language's ability to represent reality at all, I'm curious about what impact the resulting poetry will have in terms of literary history. But finally, to return to your first question, I'm really less interested in the separate lineages of poets than I am in their individual achievements across the centuries. Less interested in following schools of thought and influence because that ultimately and unavoidably would result in my enrollment in one.

As an undergraduate taking courses on Elizabethan or Romantic verse, I was reading contemporary poetry on my own, primarily in the journals, and I began photocopying my favorite poems and pasting them into a scrapbook. I did that both for the journal poems and the poems I was reading in my classes, without regard to century or theme, and the scrapbook contained juxtapositions that I'm certain would be nauseating to scholars: Thomas Wyatt's "They Flee From Me" next to Philip Levine's "They Feed, They Lion"; Coleridge's "Frost at Midnight," a page from Stevens' "Anecdote of the Jar." I didn't care. I was storing individual examples of what seemed to me, at the time at least, extraordinarily successful poems. Well, the scrapbook has grown for over thirty years, and I realize now that I have assembled a kind of private anthology-as-Bildungsroman, one that I use to study the individual poem. I rarely read more than one at a time, though recently I tried a few pairings: Herbert's "Easter Wings" and Hollander's "Swan"; Blake's "Holy Thursday" and Amy Clampitt's "Meadowlark Country."

Tell me a little bit more about the poems that make it into your book. What commonalities do they share?

Remember, I've kept this scrapbook for over thirty years. The only commonality they share is the consciousness that selected them! At nineteen, in love with lost romance, I'm sure I was drawn to those naked feet stalking in Wyatt's chamber. At fifty-plus, I'm drawn to the metrical reversal in that second line!

You mentioned the ineffable a moment ago. How does poetry express the ineffable?

I share Richard Wilbur's feelings about poetry: "The poem is an effort to express a knowledge imperfectly felt, to articulate relationships not quite seen, to make or discover some pattern in the world. It is a conflict with disorder." And when it's done well, it takes us to a place that is perfectly unseen or unseen perfectly. How that happens, of course, differs from poem to poem. Wilbur's "The Death of a Toad" is one of the finest examples of this phenomenon I know.

But the ordering of chaos isn't isolated to the physical making of the poem for me—it's also the subject of many of my poems. And the perfectly unseen is always preceded by the precisely seen, by my dependence on the visual image. I'm certain, in thinking more about my scrapbook poems, a commonality shared by the majority would be the luminosity of their visual images.

Which poets did you find most fulfilling in that respect?

Oh, so many. But I've been guided not only by poets, but also by the visual arts and film. I suffer from degenerative myopia, and I have from the time I was a little girl. I understand, much more completely than I did several years ago, that my vision is slowly failing. The doctors tell me that I won't be blind, but that in time I won't be correctable to twenty/twenty and that, in a much greater amount of time I hope, I may not be able to read well at all. Consequently, the visual image has always been of supreme importance to me—so I'm naturally drawn to the visual arts and to film and have learned so much from both. In the first poem of *The*

Stillness, The Dancing, for example, I focus on Fellini's *Amarcord*. In the closing half of that poem, I describe how the film moves inside itself, photographs its own making. Suddenly, a peacock walks across the set within a set, and its appearance introduces a moment of seeming spontaneity when an image outside the ongoing narrative is allowed predominance—a moment when Fellini trusts that all of us will wait—as the outer and inner cameras do, as an image outside the narrative rises into symbol.

I was so moved by that moment, that great fanning of feathers against the snow, that I took it into my poem's first half—in reverse: the fanned white bones of the skeletons of a woman and child. And, thinking of direct influences, I'm remembering Ermani Olmi's *Tree of the Wooden Clogs*—how it opens with the image of a bird, with a bell around its neck, fluttering above the heads of a group of peasants. They're trying to hit the bird with sticks, and the cacophony of that erratic ringing is painful. Suddenly the bird breaks away, lifts off toward the hills, and the steady rhythm of its wings changes the bell's cacophony to music. Chaos had been ordered in such an original way! I borrowed and reversed that image in my poem "Erebus": a small bird with a red patch under its wings washes itself, and the motion of the washing interrupts our appreciation of the steadiness of that red. Chaos from order.

> *Letting go of intentionality seems important to what you're talking about. Letting go of the narrative and allowing for the possibility of accident.*

Certainly in these examples and many others. An interruption in expectation. A trust in the orphaned image.

> *I understand what you're saying about film; have any poets used similar methods that have influenced you?*

Bly, of course, and James Wright—except for those poets, the singular image is more sire than orphan, the entire poem its progeny. And W. S. Merwin, of course. And Norman Dubie, in relation to this issue, because his imagery is singular but not solitary, so often interwoven with, yet brilliantly apart from, the anticipated narrative.

In the early twentieth century, Pound is usually associated with the turn toward the image. When I think about Pound and your work, I think of his collection, Personae. *He uses so many different voices in that book.*

Yes, but the great difference between us, in terms of our use of the persona, is one of intent. Pound's seems—in *Personae*—exorcistic to me. When he wrote about that book, he stated that one dons mask after mask in pursuit of some ultimate self—and that the moment one says, "I'm really this, or I'm really that," one ceases to be that thing. By completing the poems in *Personae*, he tells us, he repeatedly cast off complete masks of the self in his journey toward a pure consciousness. The poems there, like many of Browning's, are ultimately "self"-striving or -revelatory, either within their contexts or as a result of the act of their composition. Their focus is the self, and their inquiry is primarily psychological; my focus is, quite often, communal—that is, how the individual character is representative of the larger community—and my inquiry is primarily spiritual.

Do you try to enter into the consciousnesses of the figures?

I try to be true to the situations they inhabited—their biographies. Generally, I'm less interested in complexities of personality or character within my figures—as subject—than I am in the metaphoric or symbolic significance of their private or public achievements—those achievements as they influence a spiritual inquiry. In this way, I feel a kinship to many of the war-persona poems—adult and child—of Randall Jarrell. They too are less interested in the individual self as subject; their focus is ultimately communal, though the poems are housed in the most vulnerable voices.

This isn't to say that I'm not drawn to characters who have deep psychological complexities. I've written about Robert Schumann and Zelda Fitzgerald, Kafka, Clover Adams, Dorothy Wordsworth. But I'm drawn to them because of the ways in which their psychic pain allows them to achieve an extraordinary vision of the world and not from any desire to understand the origins of that pain or to interpret its significance in an analytical fashion. When I was much younger, in my late teens, I was terribly troubled and began an extensive psychotherapy. I went twice a week for five years—and I think I mined into dust the self as subject! I removed so many masks and examined them so carefully. I'm certain that that early education has so much to do with my attraction to lives other than my own and the ways in which that attraction becomes poetry.

What makes you want to write about certain figures?

For the majority, sympathy and admiration. Increasingly, I have conceived of books of poetry as unified statements. If you look back at *The Profile Makers*, the central metaphor is photography or, perhaps more accurately, the captured image. That book began when I read that the glass plate negatives of Matthew Brady—the lesser ones—were held in surplus and used to replace broken greenhouse windows. What an evocative image! It kept me going for three years! Once I realized that it would sire a book, it wasn't difficult to find characters throughout the centuries—the captured visual image is held in common by all of them. What was more difficult was finding people to give a depth and variety to that central focus. So, someone like Clover Adams was a godsend; she added a dimension to balance that of Edison and Daguerre and Matthew Brady.

The Ghost Trio began when I learned that Charles Darwin was married to Emma Wedgwood—and that their families were united through friendship for generations: Erasmus Darwin was Josiah Wedgwood's physician. I've always been interested in miners, so my trio—the Darwin family, the Wedgwood family, the "family" of miners throughout the centuries—was born. I thought of each as "visiting the soil" in unique ways, physically, scientifically, artistically, spiritually. Other characters in the book were selected for their unique "visitations."

If there is something that many of these characters hold in common—across the books, at least until *The Seconds*—it has to be their perseverance. Let me put it this way: if, being fully aware of one's own mortality, one not only chooses to get out of bed in the morning, but to stand for hours trying to bake just the right amount of luster into the slope of a teacup—or to tip the perfect filament to a fleeting spark of electric light—they're worth consideration, if only as examples of how far our attempts to order chaos can lead us, negatively and positively.

The hold on the image, the hold on reality, the hold on shapeliness which propels The Profile Makers *is much firmer than the poems in* The Seconds, *where everything seems much more provisional. Does that make sense?*

Yes. *The Seconds* doesn't have that tidy, umbrella-image that *The Profile Makers* uses. It is much more complex in its structure and in what unites its characters. They hold in common that spiritual inquiry I mentioned, a commonality that unites their voices. In fact, at one time I have Marie Curie say, "I think we are one harmonious voice, one set of days circling."

Your use of voices hinges on the use of allusion, which raises some issues with your work. What if a reader doesn't know anything about the photographer, the painter, the historical figure to whom the poem alludes? What if the reader isn't familiar with the piece of music you mention? Do you think that that creates a certain level of difficulty or even an exclusionary dynamic in some of your poems?

A certain level of difficulty? Yes, of course. I've struggled for years over whether or not to use footnotes. I've resisted them because I want the poems to be freestanding. I want their world to be pure poetry, not poetry with an addendum of prose. I try to imbed within each poem—or, as a concession to footnoting, within a tight epigraph—all that the reader needs to know to experience the poem with, I hope, some satisfaction. I try to imbed rewards that might compensate for missed allusions: an interesting narrative line, startling imagery, idiosyncratic phraseology, perhaps some snippet of information—how bees behave in the hive, or how that ancient, magical document, "The Doctrine of Signatures," instructed people to cure their throats or hearts by ingesting throat-shaped or heart-shaped plants!

But "exclusionary dynamic" is a political phrase, and the rhetoric that surrounds it has elements that are chilling to me. I write about what draws me passionately. I have no sense of myself as a visionary—I'm a questioner—or that my poetry will, or should, appeal to thousands of people—or that it should be required reading for anyone. Certain allusions will make some of my poems inaccessible to some people, just as certain components in, say, experimental poetry or poetry birthed by the hip-hop culture make some of that work inaccessible to me. So be it. Art thrives on diversity, not conformity. I'm troubled when I hear people speak of poetry as a walled unit—"Poetry should do this, or shouldn't do that, or should be here and not there"—as if poetry has the finite borders of a runner's baton. Because someone's possession of that baton necessitates another's loss, even if, in terms of activity, we're all on the same team.

Recently a woman told me after a presentation that I should feel a responsibility "to bring my poetry down a few notches," because of this issue of exclusivity. I was uneasy with her hierarchical language, but, of course, I understood the origins of her concern. For so many years, the only door to a validated poetry was in the academy's wall. But so much is changing now, on the street corners, in private homes, on the lawns, in theaters, in bars—and in the classrooms. I truly believe that every person moved by words can find a poetry that enriches his or her life. A problem occurs only when that person says, "This is great; from now on, all poetry must be like this."

What you've said makes sense—and is generous. No hierarchies. The last decade has seen so much energy dedicated to division.

When people say "this is poetry and this is not poetry," they invalidate all sorts of avenues of expression.

You've mentioned several formal concerns in your shaping of the poem. Could you talk more about these?

For me, the complexity of the line, of the patterning, is something I'm becoming much more devoted to studying during what I think of as the second half of my career as a poet. I'm, of course, influenced by Williams' theories and especially by critics writing about Williams. As a practitioner, I'm interested in the ways that the counterpoint of sentence across line enhances a poem, how it did so for Williams and others. Most specifically, how counterpoint influences enjambment and how that influence differs from the lyric to the lyrical narrative to the narrative. I'm thinking of poems like Williams' "Iris." Do you know it?

Not off the top of my head.

I'll recite it for you with conventional pauses:

> A burst of iris
> so that come down for breakfast
> we searched through the rooms for that sweetest odor
> and at first could not find its source
> then a blue as of the sea struck
> startling us from among those trumpeting petals

But here's how he wrote it:

> a burst of iris so that

come down for
breakfast

we searched through the
rooms for
that

sweetest odor and at
first could not
find its

source then a blue as
of the sea
struck

startling us from among
those trumpeting
petals

It's so interesting to me how the "oral version" enhances the poem's narrative elements and how the true poem suppresses them. I think that the short, highly enjambed lines interrupt the poem's linear progression through time and space and emphasize its synesthetic progression through the senses. Its major focus isn't "story" but perception. Its goal isn't to tell us that people rose, went downstairs for breakfast and looked for iris, but to take us with them as seas strike and an iris bursts and petals trumpet and the mind steps here and there, trying to unite stimulus and source.

But counterpoint and enjambment in the longer-lined narrative or lyrical narrative—which is how I think of many of my poems— have a different effect. In my work, at least, I use them to enhance the narrative elements rather than suppress them. My enjambment after a verb, for instance, often hastens the reader's journey into the next line, eases that journey, rather than interrupts it, because of the velocity of the lines and their narrative contexts. I'm not saying that enjambment between those longer-lined "narratives"—after an adjective or transitive verb, perhaps—can't be used to create tension or anticipation, but that tension often stems from dramatic concerns rather than lyric concerns.

When I think of your poems, the first poet that comes to mind is not Williams. And yet there are some powerful enjambments in your poems, and so I can see that bridge now. Now how do you keep the longer lines musically engaging?

Well, my lines really aren't that long; it would be better to look to poets like C. K. Williams for that talent. When I was referring to longer lines I meant in comparison to short, contemplative, say one-syllable to five or six-syllable lines in lyrics like "Iris." My lines generally hover around twelve syllables, though they're frequently shorter. The longer ones stay buoyant—I hope—because of their musical qualities—a little two-step exchange of anapest and iamb at times, an energetic shove from counterpoint, assonance, alliteration, most of the techniques that keep language afloat.

When you talk about these poems, you use the language of metrical poetry. Yet this is "free verse" poetry. So, to borrow Eliot's phrase, you're very aware of there being a "ghost meter" behind your poetry.

Oh, yes. In my persona poems, the predominant rhythm is anapestic or dactylic—one can't really make that determination in verse that's not formally metrical. When I use the third person point of view, iambs predominate. The voice within my persona poems is more malleable with the cadences of anapest and dactyl. Everyone argues that the rhythm of familiar speech is iambic. Evidently not for my characters.

How do you draft poems?

I don't draft poems. I have an absolute fear of letting a poem close, even by draft, before its time. I write line by line, and so I might spend a day and have two lines and then the next day add two more. When I have the first two lines, I have a distant, preverbal shadow of the rest of the poem; I feel it there, an entity beyond language. So, the next day two more lines come, or three. And I feel that preverbal shadow a little more distinctly until it becomes three-dimensional and the poem closes. I've never been able to write a draft and then say, "Okay, let's start over again," because that draft would have reached a provisional closure and perhaps annihilated some of the poem's potential for me. That's not to say that I haven't closed poems, thought they were done, then come back three or four months later to find that they needed deep revision. Then I start over completely.

So the poem organically grows line by line until it's done. A line or two might be a great day a la Yeats.

You bet. But what's more interesting to me is that preverbal shadow. Ironically, how tangible it is!

In the title poem of your recent book, you write "Seconds and smoke / Into what shape will our shapelessness flow." That seems to me a real important line for the entire book. Time as a shaper. How our shapeliness finds form is the recurring interrogation of the voices.

In *The Seconds*, I was trying to use every possible connotation of that word—time, damaged goods, the seconds in dueling—those devoted souls willing to step forth and assume someone else's passion. Many characters wonder, in the midst of their pain, if they are not stand-ins for the troubled gods, those firsts who fail to appear.

Do you believe that?

I believe that my characters are troubled by that possibility. But another focus within the book is wonder itself—wonder as awe and wonder as question. A few lines from an aria by Hasse are alluded to several times in the book: "The sun is pale / the heavens, troubled / I tremble before my own heart." That third line was so haunting to me: the self and body division, the self and self-division, the sense of the line as it refers to time, to chronology—the self stirring before the body does. And finally, the wonder of that finite stirring, the wonder of that wondering.

Gillian Conoley was born in 1955 in Taylor, Texas. The author of four books of poetry, Some Gangster Pain, Tall Stranger, Beckon, *and most recently,* Lovers in the Used World, *Conoley is a writer engaged with exploring where formal conventions, traditional structures, and language itself break down—leaving a reader with a poetry resolutely opposed to easy categorizing. A graduate of the M.F.A. program at the University of Massachusetts, Conoley's work as poet, editor of the independent literary journal* Volt, *and creative writing teacher have put her in the position of observing contemporary American writing from a variety of perspectives. The recipient of numerous awards, Conoley currently teaches at Sonoma State University in California.*

GILLIAN CONOLEY

Gillian and I spoke just outside of San Francisco during summer 1998.

Do you consider Emily Dickinson as the beginning of the Modernist period?

Yes. I think that everything about her work, but specifically her relationship to language, makes her Modernist. Her poetry is a poetry of great uncertainty and doubt, which manifests itself on every level of the poems, not just in the content or the thematic qualities or the form. And then there is the way she uses language and syntax. There are so many different associative qualities that she's working on within each individual word in any given poem. She's not going to give you only two possible readings. Her syntax is such that there's a pretty wide degree of variance in how you can experience the poems as a reader. And it's not just some linguistic game, it's a quest for knowledge and truth. She's doing it in the most skeptical, conscious way that someone could seek those things.

So, Dickinson's philosophical and epistemological orientation was more contemporary than that of the nineteenth century?

Yes, but also in terms of form. The rhymes were so unusual. Higginson says she has a "spasmodic gait" in one of his letters to her. She takes what would be the music of the standard poem of the era, or the standard hymn, and writes against it, so the music is broken down yet still hauntingly present.

Like Eliot's notion of "ghost meter." Were you as attracted to later reworkings of this skepticism by modern writers such as Eliot, H.D., and Stevens?

No, not as much. She seems to be writing toward a place where language can go no further. She seems to want to reach that place in almost every poem. There's a real lack of a sense of authority. The poems seem to be exploratory in the truest sense of being exploratory, that she really doesn't know where she's going to go with the poems. She's completely open to where the activity of the poem is going to take her. With Eliot, there's this huge sense of position. Eliot writes from a very large sense of authority and of knowledge. With Dickinson you have someone who is writing outside of that authority. She doesn't feel as though she's in command in that way. Eliot also has all that "world weariness," whereas Dickinson is much more inquisitive, more exploratory. One gets the sense of a vast, procreant, though particular consciousness examining itself as it examines the world. She's certainly not thinking about all of tradition bearing down on her.

What about some of the other Modernists? Moore? Williams or Stevens?

I think that Williams is closest of the Modernists to Emily Dickinson, probably because even though, on one hand, there is this incredible clarity with him and a transparency with his language; on the other hand, there's also this sense of the word as an object—something that the Objectivist poets really latched onto. Language as a material. With Williams there's this "made thing," this carpenter sense to the poem. I also think that his authorial stance is closer to

Dickinson. It has something to do with humility and awe. Williams' role as an obstetrician—the main thing he did was deliver babies all the time!—gave him an understanding of birth, of newness and emergence and innocence. Brenda Hillman and Patricia Dienstfrey are editing what I'm sure will be a great book called *The Grand Permission: Motherhood and the New Poetics.* They asked a group of poets who are mothers to write about birth and poetics. I wrote a lot about Williams in my essay for that book.

Williams frequently ties together the birthing and creative process, probably most famously in poem "I" of Spring and All. He also does it in many of his prose works, including The Great American Novel. *What about Modernist women poets?*

I first read Marianne Moore sort of through Elizabeth Bishop, and I think that many poets of my generation might have come to her that way, backwards. I prefer Bishop. She seems very influenced by Williams' desire to see something and render it in a way that makes it palpable and present and able to be seen, felt. Contact. That whole sense of representation is interesting. Now, in our time, representation is the whole problem. We've been given so many copies and seen so many reproductions. Gertrude Stein says in one of her lectures that a painter can't paint a representation and have it be valuable to a culture because we've seen the thing and then seen it reproduced. We've not only seen it in reality, it has been reproduced so many times that it doesn't have any worth anymore. To me, one of the really interesting questions about poetry in our age is how a poet can bring reality onto the page in a way that's viable or valuable or of any worth because of the vast technological barrage of imagery and copies that we receive and expect. There has to be that relationship between reality and art, reality and the imagination, where they connect. So, of course, that's become one of the main differences between the two, between Modernism and Postmodernism. During Modernism, the anxiety wasn't as extreme as now. Or, perhaps, the anxiety has become so commonplace it has a very different effect: it's as though our wildest dreams have been realized; they exist and best of all, you can go buy them!

In Kandinsky's Concerning the Spiritual in Art, *he considers the inability of the mimetic to capture the spiritual. He claims that representational art is only a shabby mimesis; hence, the need for abstraction. It seems that, in some ways, the need to get not just the spiritual but any reality into art, onto the page, really makes the poet explore that relationship between language and the world. You said that you felt Dickinson pushed language in such a manner. Who are some other poets who do that? How?*

Paul Celan. With him, you have a post-Holocaust situation where language and the world have been completely torn apart. He's not going to write to try to bring them together. The poems are almost prayerlike in how he will take a word apart and hyphenate it. He creates these silent, reverent spaces within the word that are simultaneously full of grief and full of wonder. The poems are spiritual, but they are not religious. It seems to me that each poem of his goes toward the void, which is a kind of genesis for him, an almost rebirth, except there is no resurrection. It merely seeks that place. With Dickinson, there's the obsession with death and in the "Master letters" the whole notion of who she's writing to. And "circumference," what she means by that term. It's almost a spatial inquiry, a writing to the void.

Lowell, Berryman, Ginsberg, Plath, Sexton?

I love Berryman and I love Plath. I don't really like Sexton; for me, she can't compare to Plath. Sexton's confessionalism—it borders on a sensationalism that is better left to the tabloids. I think that Plath is brilliant, though. I don't sense her working with language in that way, where she's consciously trying to go to a place where language won't go. She seems to be more of a poet who's recording, witnessing, traveling areas of the psyche. It seems that she charted dying, the act of reaching one's death as far as one could go, and that was her real gift. Her sense of metaphor was brilliant.

That distinction between recording and exploring seems an important one. Exactly how does language become exploratory? Could you be specific?

Language has many interesting properties. One would be that it can name something, pin down experience, even communicate well at times. And I do think that it does that. I don't think that it's just this nonreferential "material" we use. But it also fails quite frequently and perhaps then we realize that it has its own life, this procreant force, highly associative, and very linked to human consciousness. Hegel says that language is the house of being. A lot of people when they talk about language use paint as an analogy, like Jackson Pollock and the way he worked with the materiality of paint; well, we could talk about the "Language" poets and how they work with the materiality of language. But it's really not a very good analogy because paint is just this gooey stuff. It's a brilliant medium, and it does have its own system of texture and communication through color and texture, of course. But language is more than that.

I think that Stein illustrates that. Think of her Picasso portrait.

> Some were certainly following and were certain that the one they were then following was one working and was one bringing out of himself then something. Some were certainly following and were certain that the one they were then following was one bringing out of himself then something that was coming to be a heavy thing, a solid thing and a complete thing.

Those, to me, seem less successful than her book Tender Buttons *where she uses all the associative qualities of language to render reality rather than merely trying to make language work like paint.*

Right. Because language is so tied to human consciousness—it's the material that we use to think—poets really need to try to work with that, really try to recognize it. That's what Dickinson and Celan and Stein do. Berryman's language is incredible, and I take back what I said. He is working with exploration. For me, though, there's a difference between a poet who's consciously mining and exploring that field and a poet who uses language really well but for whom it's essentially a communicative device and solely that. The reason that language interests me so much is when it's used explorationally, the poet is investigating consciousness and perception. That's what's so amazing about *Tender Buttons* by Stein. There's so much sensual pleasure in her writing. It's not some ponderous, intellectual, cerebral thing but an act of luscious pleasure that can only come from using words that way, from giving them such free rein.

And especially in the sounds. It's an experiment in evocation. The words, their connotations, and their sounds evoke some sense or reality that couldn't be got at any other way.

When she violates syntax and expectation, the words are made new.

Yes, it is more a representation of human consciousness than a recording of it.

One poem in Beckon *that I think explores language in the manner you're speaking of is "On Dorothea Lange." It interrogates the question of appropriation: appropriation of an image, of a scene, of vision. In some ways it's a coda for the whole book; you have a photograph of hers on the cover. Can you talk about what you're wrestling with in this poem?*

The "used" quality of the image fascinates me—another sort of Postmodernist stance, that things come to us from outside, they're not sprouted out of your own head or imagination, they come toward you. Dorothea Lange used to go in a rental car, very nicely dressed, with her entourage of people, taking photographs of people in poverty. She had a lot of political problems with that herself, but she wasn't going to pretend that she was someone else. I think that is what all artists do. We use images that are around us and we essentially take. Dorothea Lange seemed to be fascinated by this. So did James Agee.

Is there a distinction between how one assimilates or takes images from one's "normal thoroughfares in the world" and a willful seeking of them—getting in a car and going to find those poor people. Or, say, going to Central America or the South Bronx or Africa and writing poems that come out of those experiences?

The last line of the poem is "Only what's there, there." I was thinking about when Gertrude Stein said, "There's no there, there, in Oakland." I was making a play on that. I think that what the poem is ultimately about is the whole impossibility of actually seeing something. I think that's what Williams was writing about. He was trying to have us see something. He did. I think that now that's a really difficult process to navigate. There's so much to cut through. But that's what a poet has to do. It's a very complicated terrain.

In that poem you use excerpts from an exhibit; in other poems you use a more prosaic presentation. You have a diverse sense of the poetic line. What governs your decisions in regards to lineation?

I think that what's been happening in *Beckon* and especially in my new book, *Lovers in the Used World*, is that I'm starting to see the page as a real pictorial space, not just some blank page with left and right side margins. What's happening is that I'm thinking about the space on the page as silence. In my new book, I arrange the poem with lines and spaces in between. Like this:

The World

Some are born
some are born

  selfhood marches

  across the surface an owl lifts on bony wings

Whose brain
whose brain
    furnaced

the eyelash the sparrow the cat the Marguerite
the Floridas, the Mediterraneans,

o lawful bread
o wondrous portal

Here come our enlarged and nefarious senses

(a couple arguing old world
malarky under the honeyed streaks on-site

prestidigitous platelets of cloud floating past)

Here's a form
we need to fill in

  and hold lanterns and double space into

the password for
               how we found
               time to do it

time grainy and full time mowing down

Some are born
some are born

silence throwing itself asunder spectre joyous

        Some are born
        who can use this

                        use
                        use this

They're not elisions; it's not as though something has been deleted in terms of the content of the line. I'm starting to think of the page as three-dimensional.

A field of action as per Olson?

Olson is the first person that you might think of as breaking the boundaries. Mallarmé in "A Throw of the Dice." That poem really feels three dimensional to me. The reader enters a space where you can feel in front, above, and behind you. He uses things like stars in the sky represented by how he places things on the page. It's not concrete poetry. I'm not talking about that. Using the whole page as a kind of theatre; that's what I think he's doing. At one point, he has Hamlet's feather on his cap suddenly sort of drift through the poem. To me, that's one of the great poems of our time. He wrote that poem at the height of his popularity, comparable to, say, Eliot's lofty, powerful position during the Modernist period. That's how Mallarmé was in France, and at his height, he wrote that poem, that very experimental poem. I love that idea. He had everything to lose. It was never published as it was supposed to be printed. UC Berkeley printed a translation that's close. The dimensions of the page he wanted it printed on were something like 11" by 14".

What you seem to be speaking about with Mallarmé and your poems is a movement away from the line as the integral and, perhaps, definitive aspect of the poem to the poem as arrangement of language on a page, a sharp distinction.

It still seems like working the line to me. It does. But there's more of a sense of silence as a presence, not just a piece of punctuation but a force. A silence that would be as strong as the words.

A force to make language go beyond itself?

The person who I think does the most interesting work with space is Barbara Guest. I had an interesting experience publishing one of her poems in *Volt*. Our production editor, Kim Grant, who is meticulous and wonderful, accidently sent Guest proofs that were totally screwed up. Her poems make tremendous use of spacing, and laying them out for press can be difficult. So anyway, she was really nice about it, but it opened the door for her to rethink the poem, and she made all of these changes! I was typing them in myself, and I saw that the differences between the first version and the version she sent back to me were huge. It made for a completely different music. I heard something completely different: in laying out the poem I had something close to an aural hallucination, as strange as that may sound. Guest has a painter's imagination in terms of spatial relations, much more so than some painters do. She seems to really be working with space and the line in a gestural way, and yet there's also a high sense of musical composition. And then there's what the language is activating. John Cage also experiments with those elements. I like his lectures more than the poems. It's as though he scores music as language.

How would you respond to those who look at the work of Cage or Guest or yourself and say, "Those are poems? I don't get it?" For whom is the poem written?

I find myself very attracted to poetry that has a lot of white space. Part of this attraction is that I find that sort of work restful. Not to have a page covered with words is somehow more inviting. I want to go into that world. Many poets have experimented with space. Sure, Olson is important. And Mallarmé. And also Apollinaire. I think that the sense of the line is changing and bending. It has to.

Whitman's line was experimental, and people reacted, said, "These are poems?" And some poems are just plain difficult. I'm glad that they're there, along with poems that are more accessible. Jack Spicer, for instance. Some of his poems are incredibly lucid. Others are very difficult. I guess I think that the notion that a poet is either accessible or difficult is just a bad idea, simple and idiotic. It leads to balkanization, the notion that people write this way or people write that way and we should "like" one over the other. I think such divisions are illusory. I know that there are people who are very adamant about where they stand on such things, but it seems to me that, especially now, you've got a much more open world in contemporary poetry. For example, when I read poems today in what might be called "conservative" journals, I can see the influence of Language poets all over the place. People are writing even there with a sense of language as a more complicated entity. I think that reading poetry is a reading skill that one acquires. One has to learn to read, to read all kinds of work, and to read as variously as possible. I love the story about Toni Morrison being on the *Oprah Winfrey* show, and Oprah asked her, "What do you say to people who say they have to read your work over and over to understand it?" And Morrison replied, "It's called reading, honey."

Your work exhibits a strong tension between the narrative and the lyrical. The poems utilize both, and I also see a resistance to conceding that the "I" of the poem has an authority. What is the relationship between the narrative and the lyrical?

I'm very interested in narrative, but not in any beginning, middle, end, Aristotelian sort of way. There are many poets who think that narrative is *passé* and dead end and should never be used in poetry.

Perhaps even opposed to what poetry is.

That kind of thinking is also frequently tied to a political view that linearity and narrative are tied to something dangerous, something tyrannical. I guess I think that the tyranny of thinking that narrative is a tyranny is tyrannical. I just use it intuitively. The stories that interest me are not ones where you can say, "Oh, this is the meaning! I've got it! A-ha!" I prefer narratives that are more like fairy tales, where you can't say exactly what it means, but in the story, there's an enchantment of the mind. I don't want to use stories that have one particular meaning because they seem false to me. As a poet, I don't feel comfortable giving the "whole thing" that way. I don't believe "the whole thing" exists. It assumes a kind of certainty: "Here's the whole story and now you, reader, may at last perceive it." That feels very dishonest to me. It feels dishonest to the sense of authority that a writer should take. Narratives that are interesting to me are stories that try to reach some essential human mystery, stories that don't necessarily carry meaning but carry the sense that meaning can be cast through them. Think of koans and fairy tales and stuff that isn't A=B in so simple a manner. I also have a mistrust of the "I" as a specific self on the page.

So who is the "I" of your poetry?

Oh, I have no idea. André Breton's *Nadja*! The central character is Nadja, and you never see her. If you go in a café, she's just left, and her scarf will be there on the table. Or there will be this snippet of conversation in which she's mentioned. Or someone has just seen her. She's everywhere but not there.

Sounds like an important precursor to Pynchon's V.

Yes. When I read that novel, I felt a very strong connection to that sense of free-floating identity.

So how does the mother, the teacher, the poet, the editor, the person who you physically are—how does that intersect with the page?

I think that there's a very mysterious process because people's lives do enter their work in very interesting ways. Anybody who knows a poet personally and knows his or her work intimately is going to make connections and see how each of those things is present and how each operates imagistically or on a language level. There's also wonderful poetry—such as Frank O'Hara's poetry—where the poetry is this personality. I don't think that there's anybody who's done that, used the "I" in such a wonderful, charming sort of way, and made a person in the poem whom you want to meet and know.

Personism.

Yes. He's an example of someone for whom we feel comfortable saying that the life is very close to the poetry, and there's this free-flowing dynamic there. However, it also seems to be a problem for most contemporary poets. "I" and identity connect back to the question of how can one be an authentic self in this culture and how—if that's even possible—can one bring that to the page? Derrida's idea that identity doesn't exist and that it's a societal construct is an important concept for poets, whether or not one accepts that or not. I know people who firmly believe that, and I think that it's true in some ways, but you're still responsible for your actions. It's a complicated issue. I don't know if I understand Eliot's theory of impersonality, but I like to think about that in connection with Derrida's theories about identity as construct. You have to get rid of personality—and I'm assuming that you can equate identity and personality—in order to write good poetry. In Gertrude Stein's essay, "Why There Are So Few Masterpieces," she discusses how we need to get rid of identity and time because they work against the creation of a masterpiece. It almost seems as though in order for there to be an authentic self in our culture, you have to shave yourself down to a place of "no identity." Start from scratch. Maybe that's authentic. Maybe recognize the variance and multifariousness of what we think of as identity. All I know is that I can no longer trust in a static sense of self. It's a very troublesome issue. I have a hard time reading poetry where the speaker seems very sure of who he or she is. That seems simplistic or dishonest to me. Creative personas are less problematic, like in Berryman's theatre of the self with Mr. Bones and Henry and the interlocutor.

You read probably hundreds, thousands of poems for Volt. *My sense of the journal is that it prints a range of work, which seems healthy. It avoids partisanship. What do you strive for with the journal? What do you look for as an editor? And lastly, what do you see as the role of a literary journal like* Volt *in the larger literary scene when such journals can only hope for, at most, a subscription rate of a thousand or so?*

I have always loved literary magazines and the whole history of literary magazines. The great Modernist magazines like *Blast* and *Furioso*, the ones that were really short-lived and were really just acts of love by one or two devoted people.

Frequently women.

Yes, that's true. Their vitality and importance, however short-lived a magazine might have been, are inspiring. I think that there are some great journals right now. *New American Writing* is wonderful. *American Letters* and *Commentary. Fence. jubilat. Verse.* There's a whole bunch of good ones. The magazines as objects, the book as an object, the making of the journal. I feel all of that is important. *Volt* started in 1992, and my husband and I paid for the first issue by ourselves. For the second issue we got a grant. By the time of the third issue, I'd gotten the teaching job at Sonoma State, and so now they have agreed to give me release time to edit it, and they pay for the production of the magazine. So, it's become institutionalized, which is, in one way, good, but my husband and I still "own" the magazine. We have a nonprofit corporation. The university is just sort of helping to fund it, and we're very, very grateful that they're doing that. But the independence is important. The independent journal is very important to keep alive. We have many very great journals that have been maintained for twenty or twenty-five years—I think one of the oldest ones is the *North American Review*, which was founded in the late nineteenth century. My point is that it's the "quick start-up ones," the ones that serve a purpose for a little while and then die out: those are the ones that are most vibrant and important and most interesting. *Volt* has good distribution, I think, primarily, because of its looks—it's striking. It's in bookstores around the country, but I still think of it as this small press effort. And there's a great American tradition of that sort of publication. I don't want it to become too institutionalized, staid, a long-term journal that exists mainly because of university tenure systems. I think that there are too many journals like that. It will die, or I'll kill it. I don't want to do it forever. I just like doing it.

As for editing, I edit very quickly. I put all of the submissions in an armoire, and I take them out and read them quickly. I try not to have too many biases. I try to trust my instincts. Sure, *Volt* probably leans toward the experimental for lack of a better word, but I put in narrative poems just to mix things up and to give value to different sorts of poetry. I'm opposed to a partisan poetics. But I don't think that this keeps a magazine from having a very distinct vision or presence. Magazines really do have an effect on what gets written. If poets believe that there are places in which their work can appear, it keeps them writing. If we were writing in Eliot's era, when there weren't as many magazines around, then we would have to submit to his incredible force. Power over what was published and what was not. That's a very different situation. I think that the journals are important to prevent that, useful to the health of poetry. I don't think that people write poems thinking, "Oh, I can publish this here." That's not how it works. But you do want the work to be read.

In the last decade, many naysayers have announced the demise and irrelevance of poetry. Here at the beginning of a new century, what place do you see poetry having in our culture?

I think that it will have the same place that it's always had. I have a friend who works in inter-active, multi-media, the dot.com world, and he went to CBS and Hollywood, and apparently, they're quite uptight because the median age of television viewers has risen to fifty. That's frightening for advertisers and the whole television industry because fifty-year-olds don't buy that much stuff; they've got everything. And so these media people are in a panic. So what's everyone doing? Are they all in front of computers? Maybe. But what this means is that the culture is changing, and the power that television has had over the culture, well, it's going to go someplace else. I don't know if it will go to poetry, and there are people who can live perfectly well without poetry. That's fine. There are others, though, who can't live without it. Those people will always be around.

Poetry has a cultural value and a cultural effect, even if it's not read. I think that it's a noble thing to do. The writing of poetry is a noble act. But not just poetry, making anything with the intention of true discovery. A noble act of creation with some sort of cultural, societal effect. Think about it. For once, someone is sitting down and making something with the idea that it isn't just to be used.

PHOTO BY DON J. USNER

Robert Hass was born in 1941 in San Francisco, California. In 1971, he earned his Ph.D. from Stanford University. He is one of the most recognized and celebrated poets in America. The author of four books of poetry, Field Guide, Praise, Human Wishes, *and* Sun Under Wood, *Hass has also written an award-winning book of criticism,* Twentieth Century Pleasures *and collaborated with Nobel Laureate Czeslaw Milosz in translating Milosz's work from Polish. Further, he has translated a substantial body of haiku from the Japanese, edited* The Best American Poetry *for 2001, and, perhaps most notably, served as Poet Laureate of the United States from 1995-1997. Difficult to categorize, Hass combines an exceptional intelligence with an informal ease to create poetry that is memorable and challenging.*

Robert Hass

Greg Dunne and I spoke with Hass in Spokane, Washington, during fall 1991.

John Berger says that political awareness is one responsibility of the contemporary writer of fiction. What are your views on the responsibilities of the contemporary American poet? Do they differ from those of a writer of fiction or a poet writing in another country?

No, I don't think they would differ. I think that the natural thing to say is "of course writers have political responsibility," and then there are all the examples of great writers who have been nonpolitical. So I think that the writer's first political responsibility is to the writing. It's the Robert Duncan thing: "Responsibility is keeping the ability to respond." The first place you have to respond is in your work, and I can think of a lot of writers like that. Milosz actually has a very funny poem about when he was a young man in Paris going to see Paul Valery read. Valery got up and read his golden sumptuous decasyllabic verses to this audience of countesses; meanwhile the Depression was going on and the rise of fascism. In his poem, Milosz is musing that now, after all that time, all those people, there they are still, Valery's verses.

Do you think there's a measure of decadence in contemporary
American poetry? So much of it seems oriented toward the self.

I don't think that's a sign of decadence in American poetry. I think
decadence in art happens when, as Pound says, "the line thickens."
I think that when a style, when people get bored with a great style,
and start tarting it up to make it more interesting, to put life back
into the corpse, that's decadence in writing. And an example in
general would be Postmodernist architecture. Everyone attacked
Modernist architecture for its sterility, and there was this great
Postmodern eclecticism that instantly turned into junk and cliché
because it had no central formal muscle; it wasn't committed to a
strong clear act of the imagination; it was "let's take the thing and
put gee-gaws on it." So that's decadence, when there's nothing left
but decoration to add.

Let's get back to the personal thing. It's complicated, but I think
it's rather clear that what emerged in the post-war generation out
of a return to Romanticism or a sort of Romantic reswallowing of
Modernism—I don't know quite how to say it—was that there was
this retreat from largeness of voice and vision in American writing.
It was a strategic retreat, Romantic in character, back to the authority
of one's own experience. That is, starting with Lowell, what one
said was "I'm not Hart Crane; I can't make the epic poem, I can
only talk out of my experience." It comes naturally out of the
empirical side of Romanticism; it comes out of what's pragmatic in
the American character. It comes out of a sense of historical defeat
by the sheer magnitude of events, the "out of controlness." I also
think it comes out of class changes, and I think this is the most
subtle and profound cause: In the first half of this century, an
educated upper-middle class' information sources were still
dominated by print media, which gave print enormous authority
in the world. At that time the number of people who had access to
it was smaller; I think only about ten or twenty percent of Americans
went to college in those years. But something happened between
say 1930 and 1960 that started with Roosevelt's fireside chats,
movies, Mickey Mouse, TV—cartoons happened to occur the same

year as Roosevelt's first radio talk. The mass media democratized news access because you didn't have to read; it became aural, and print and the class that produced it lost a certain kind of authority that they had had before.

I think part of our feeling of powerlessness and irrelevancy before a world that seems glitzed-out by things like Michael Jackson's nose job is the loss of a spokesman authority that Milosz has naturally. He has a clear, deeply admirable sense of the role of the intellectual as the fighter for and maker of a culture. He doesn't have any doubt that he's at the center of the ongoing life of his culture, but I think that American writers have partly lost that sense and have been partly attracted all along to the Romantic standing by the side of the road. I mean Whitman did a great trick of it by saying that I'm central and I stand at the side—"I lean and loaf at my ease." I think there are limitations to that. I feel them in my own work and want to figure out how to break out of them; that is, there is a largeness of imagination in some other kinds of writing, Neruda for example. I think of the Polish poet Adam Zagajewski who has a version of it. Because they never got locked into that lyrical autobiographical mode that I think of as descendant from Wordsworth and the empirical side of Romanticism. But that has its appeal. The great force of that personal voice is that it means to speak truly about an individual existence.

I remember reading that Goethe once said to a friend "that until the poet completely appropriates the world, he utters just subjective sentences." I think that may be the root of the problem.

Well, I don't think that's the root of the problem because the question is how one appropriates the world and what "the world" means. There are great poets . . . did Paul Celan appropriate the world? He came to feel that there was an absolute problem knowing what the words meant, and he used them brokenly, knowing what his own feelings were, knowing the difference between what he was feeling and what he was thinking. His poetry is almost entirely about not being able to tell any of these things, after the

"Todesfugue" and the famous post-war poems. He is a great poet, as is Vallejo in the *Trilce* poems, those difficult tortured poems written in prison that are about his own sexual hunger and guilt and epistemological short-circuiting. They don't appropriate the world. They remake the language that might appropriate an internal experience of it. I think Neruda is a great poet but there's a lot of bullshit in Neruda. So I'm not absolutely sure that that's true. To appropriate—that's the sort of "great poet thing"; yet there are a lot of great poets whose main work is to induce skepticism about those kinds of language and those kinds of claims.

GD: Or even what the word "appropriating" means.

I think what Goethe meant by it was taking a large public role. It would be interesting to know when in his life he said that. He began as a pre-Romantic and then defined and outlived Romanticism. It would be interesting to see the German to compare it to the same word Marx used for appropriation—to see if it echoed something, and I would guess that this quote came later, during the *Faust* period, and it was meant as a critique of the subjective side of his early poetry and getting out of the "I fall upon the thorns of life, I bleed." All of that. Critique of that kind of subjectivity makes a lot of sense to me. I think of what Dostoevsky said about Turgenev: "The only way Turgenev can describe a hanging is by pointing to the tear in his eye." With great contempt. I think that makes sense, that critique of subjectivity in writing, appropriation in that sense, insisting on a certain sobriety before the object.

GD: It seems that in some of your earliest work there is that kind of balancing between the need to speak subjectively and the need to let the world speak. For instance, in the first poem in Field Guide, *"On the Coast at Sausalito," the speaker seems to be quite literally on the coast between those two needs. The poem opens with the speaker saying, "I won't say much for the sea / except that it was, almost / the color of sour milk." And later, when he holds that "atavistic fish" in his hands and thinks of its death and*

its being eaten, he resists the temptation to moralize upon it.
Rather than moralize upon it, he lets the world speak, in a way,
by simply perceiving it:

> But it's strange to kill
> for the sudden feel of life.
> The danger is
> to moralize
> that strangeness.
> Holding the spiny monster in my hands
> his bulging purple eyes
> were eyes and the sun was
> almost tangent to the planet
> on our uneasy coast.
> Creature and creature,
> we stared down centuries.

I think my mind works by common contraries. In one way, this: a power to let the world speak through you. And in the other way: the specific human power of appropriation is generalization or at least consists of the ability to say "justice is . . ." or "this ought to be . . . ." That's a power that shouldn't be underrated. I think when I was writing *Field Guide*, that letting the world speak through you was more or less my ideal, and in a way, I realize what it came out of was the sort of Hemingway-male-American writing tradition of "I'll describe the thing; you guess what I'm feeling and thinking," which sort of derives from Imagism. So, in *Praise* I tried a little bit to say what I thought because that's also an appropriation, and there's so little intellectual risk in our poetry because most of those kinds of formulations are banal, but that doesn't mean you should get a lobotomy in order to not look like a dope.

I was curious about the two-part poem "Santa Lucia." I think
desire is a pivotal part of the poem, and it's a pivotal part of
many of your poems, but a desire in conflict. In Human Wishes
you present a very sensual world, but there seems to be a need to
work toward, as you wrote referencing Veblen, the "end of
conspicuous waste." I wonder if this was the conflict you wanted

to elicit specifically in this poem or if the piece is directly the result
of some celebratory view of the sensual?

In my imagination there is a voice, there is a side of my nature that very much wants to name, appropriate, and celebrate the physical world or the sensuous world, and I was imagining the world as if it were a woman's voice sort of saying, "I don't know if I want to be appropriated." And so since my great propositions about this were Art and Love, what I imagined was a kind of metaphor of a guy coming on to a woman, with all of his ardor—"I want to give you presents, etc."—and the woman, the world, says, "Well, maybe, maybe not." And then I read Berger's *Ways of Seeing,* in which he talks about oil paintings as a form of ownership, and erotic desire as male ownership and I went "click," and then the voice of the woman became somebody who had read Berger or at least who was doing art history or something like that, so she's thinking about art history and possession.

Yes, I see what you're saying, especially in the lines:

Art & Love. He camps outside my door,
innocent, carnivorous. As if desire
were actually a flute, as if the little song
transcend, transcend could get you anywhere.
He brings me wine; he believes in the arts
and uses them for beauty. He brings me postcards
of the hillsides by Cézanne desire has left
alone, empty farms in August and the vague
tall chestnut trees at jas de Bouffan, fetal
sandstone rifted with mica from the beach.
He brings his body, wolfish, frail,
all brown for summer like croissant crusts
at La Seine in the Marina, the bellies
of pelicans I watched among white dunes
under Pico Blanco on the Big Sur coast.
It sickens me, this glut and desperation.

The story about Santa Lucia is also relevant; there are a bunch of different stories—December 21st, St. Lucy's Day, is the shortest day of the year, so it's the most tenuous aspect of the feminine; it's the virgin girl as a brief glimmer in the middle of the dark. All the old stories about St. Lucy and the martyrologies—there are a million different legends—are basically variants on the story in which she is supposed to marry a non-Christian Roman, and she's caught between her Christian faith and her parents' political wishes for her to marry some powerful guy, so she plucks out her eyes and serves them on a plate to the guy who's supposed to be her husband. And there is, down in the mission Santa Ynez near Santa Barbara— I just refer to it in the poem—a painting done by a California Indian of an Indian girl in this barbaric looking painting, partly Indian and partly imitation of the cruelty of Spanish painting in the eighteenth century, blood streaming down her face, holding out these eyes on a plate.

So out of that set of associations, this voice comes on. I mean, it started as a critique of my worldly glad-handing. And now it's become a different sort of voice. You know I've done a third one; I think I'm just going to accrete Santa Lucia poems over my life because I keep hearing them. I have another about half-finished; I hear a few more lines of it every once in a while. This woman speaks to me and I write it down.

I was also curious about your enumeration of the sensual and the wonderful description—all the fantastic culinary descriptions and how you look on that aspect of our being—the sensual aspect in the face of the loss. You wrote about it in the Milosz essay: the sensuality of now versus the loss that will be and the loss that is history. In your work it seems to be coming to a very personal level, which is interesting.

I don't know what to say about it. It's one of the great mysteries to me. I think in *Praise* I use that epigraph which is great; one of the kids, one of Kulya's friends, the boy who dies at the end of *The Brothers Karamazov*, and Alyosha are going to the funeral, and they're walking back to the wake, and the kid says to him, "Isn't it funny, Karamazov? All this sadness and then pancakes."

So much of life is like that. So, I don't know what to say about it. It's certainly one of my themes. What interests me about Milosz is that it drove him into a kind of philosophic theological dualism that took me a great while to understand; it's such an unAmerican way of thinking. There's part of him—you know that last poem he read from *The Separate Notebooks*:

> Pure beauty, benediction: you are all I gathered
> From a life that was bitter and confused,
> In which I learned about evil, my own and not my own.
> Wonder kept seizing me, and I recall only wonder,
> Risings of the sun over endless green, a universe
> Of grasses, and flowers opening to the first light,
> Blue outline of the mountain and a hosanna shout.
> I asked, how many times, is this the truth of the earth?
> How can laments and curses be turned into hymns?
> What makes you need to pretend, when you know better?
> But the lips praised on their own, on their own the feet ran;
> The heart beat strongly; and the tongue proclaimed its adoration.

So that's the conflict in him, and, in a way, his version of it is this guilt that he feels because he feels every time you praise nature you praise death, you praise suffering; that it's kind of a collusion with the enemy to go around saying "Isn't the fall beautiful?" "Isn't the sunrise beautiful?" Because it's the same thing that produces cancer, malformed babies, the horror of the food chain, pain, suffering— not human moral-political evil, just the way things are. And yet we go around saying it. I don't know what to say about it.

Do you agree with him?

It's hard to argue against. I mean, if you want to talk about decadence, it would be a shielding against this knowledge or flight from it; it seems impossible to cut off beauty from suffering. I remember talking with Bill Stafford about his and Robinson Jeffers' work, and he said about Jeffers' darkness, "Sure, but not all the time."

Bill had a kind of idea that "this poem is about this" and "this poem is about this." I mean when you're in a good mood, you write about good-mood things; when you're in a bad mood, you write about bad things. That doesn't seem satisfactory to me. And yet I don't have a religious thought about this conflict; I would like to, some day: either to have a Buddhist view and say "is" and somehow accept it all and then let it all go in a loving gesture, and then I could write the poem of that like a bolt of lightning; or, on the other hand—and I waver between these two poles—to be like him (Milosz) and say, "Yes, I reject this world. I love this world and I reject it in the name of its survival. I don't accept this fucking place and its rules. I think that it also exists somewhere else transposed, and at some level the human religious imagination is right, and this isn't our home because it's too cruel and senseless."

I don't quite say either thing to myself; I sort of hover between the two, between being a monist and dualist with respect to suffering and beauty, how you take them in—love and horror. So where I am in relation to it, I don't know. I've been writing lately about my childhood, which feels to me like coming to the dance after it's over; everybody's written about their childhoods; everybody's sick of the subject, and I'm finally writing about it, but the things that are interesting about it to me and haunt me—some of it is in the poem I read last night—are the agonized feelings I have about what feels to be the waste and the unhappiness of my parents' lives, about how unredeemed they were and are, and I feel until I figure out those emotions in myself, I can't get to the general. This is that thing about individual experience versus appropriation of the world: I can't talk about it in a general way until I untie the knots or at least know the knots in my own nature.

Do you think this might have been the problem with Hart Crane and his attempt at creating the myth—appropriating the world—because he never solved those initial, personal conflicts?

Yes, but what's the problem? If Hart Crane has a problem, there should be more problems. *The Bridge* is a great poem. Crane isn't my idea of having a problem, even though out of personal agonies of other kinds he killed himself. But I don't think the problem is in the attempt or that it fails actually—as it fails at a certain level because, as an act of an imagination, it may not be in touch enough with the actual America. There's a poet, Ann Winters, who's written a piece in which she wants to argue that *The Bridge* is misunderstood, that it is essentially a tragic poem, that it is not an epic. It's not a failure at all if you read it carefully. She has this whole rap about how Winters and Tate in their early criticism sold the world on the idea that it was a transcendentalist, Whitmanic poem that failed and that's been the party line ever since. She says if you really read "The Proem" and "The Tunnel" and "Indiana," the undercurrent is fundamentally tragic and not American optimistic, and that the poem is in no sense a failure, although there may be places where the language is excessive. I haven't gone back and studied *The Bridge*, which I love, to think that out for myself, but it's interesting.

> *GD: I've always been struck by what I see in your work as an exploration of desire, wants, and needs. There seems to be a questioning as to how far we can go with our appetites before they turn against us in an almost carnivorous way, eating us alive, as with Ugolini, in the translation you read last night, who might be said to have been eaten alive in Dante's hell by his own desire for power. I know that in Japanese poetry, desire is central. And perhaps this is understandable if one considers the Buddhist belief that all suffering comes from desire. Still, after a thousand years of poetry, they continue exploring it as Yosano Akiko did in the thirties, writing those beautifully erotic poems praising desire.*

Yes, I remember hearing about her, but I've never read her.

> *GD: In one poem, for example, the speaker attempts to call a*

*monk away from his meditation practice and to fulfill his search
for "the way" by fulfilling his sexual desires. These poems were
shocking then and remain shocking today. So, when I encountered
your exploration of appetites in conflict, I wondered how you
envision desire?*

Through what lens do I see it? Yes. Well, one way to talk about it is
the difference between need and desire. Desire in one way initiates
lyric poetry. Sappho in the Western tradition. In Japan, Komachi.
This would assume that when lyric poetry, or some would say all
poetry, gets invented, it is initiated out of an erotic longing so intense
it becomes ontological in its sources. So that longing exists in poetry
and, of course, in life. The other thing to say is that in both cases—
Sappho and Komachi—it also has something to do with the leisure
class, that kind of erotic feeling, which I suppose gets back to the
decadence issue in a certain way.

There's something more admirable about dealing with need than
longing. But, in fact, we live in a culture in which our central
condition is in a way longing, not need. Even though we don't
often get our needs met and chase symbolic objects of longing
instead of meeting our real needs. So there's a whole moral side to
this issue. Somebody said in an essay, that in the seventies I put
desire on the agenda of American poetry. It wasn't a perception of
mine, but if it was so, and a group of us found ourselves writing
about this subject at the same time, it may be that we were
particularly the children of this condition. There are two parts to
this. On the one hand, in my case in writing *Praise*, it was an effort
to step away from just this personal voice by talking about ideas: "I
think, so this is an issue." So that was a way of trying to appropriate
the world.

On the other hand, by stepping back and naming—what Rilke
called, quoting Valery, the "noble idea of absence"—you took one
step toward decadence, a further abstraction from real appetite and
need. I think of the Gary Snyder poem about being incredibly thirsty
and running down, plunging his face into the water and drinking
and seeing a trout looking at him. That's to know your animal nature

and it doesn't have to do with Rilke, absence, desire. And what Gary has done in a way is strip his life down to one in which he's trying to get his car started a lot. Make sure that his solar batteries are working. He's trying to make a life in which he stays in touch with need. But it's possible to argue that longing is the great riddle and engine of human life.

GD: *Yes, he says, "True affluence is needing nothing."*

But one can say at the same time that he's been married four times and he has addressed an impulse that's made that happen, which is one of the things that puts him profoundly in touch with the rest of human beings, as opposed to that amazing self-reliance which sets him apart. I could make the argument that for him it's made a constructive life; he's made himself a moral exemplar, but it hasn't completely separated him. He's downplayed the parts of his life that put him in touch. If that makes any sense.

It seems in Human Wishes *that the thread of consciousness in the poem, on occasions, presences certain things into the poem. For instance, in "Spring Drawing" where the voice speaks of a woman's breast and the woman comes into the poem. Could you discuss this in terms of the functioning of the poetic mind and maybe in terms of the form of the poems?*

Complicated. Say a little more about what you mean about the presencing.

There seems to be, in the poems, in the mind behind the poetic voice, a thought, a disjointed thought, something peripherally connected to any linearity within the poem, and from that disjointed thought there springs a concrete, objective force that mimics or manifests the thought—as in the case of the woman in "Spring Drawing," as if desire can bring something to life.

That's very interesting. I was aware, but I've never described to myself that thing that clearly. But I did feel like one of the things that was interesting to me about the poems was the quality of unexpectedness in their development that was yet followable. I actually started those "Spring Drawing" poems as I was reading Michael Palmer's *Notes from Echo Lake*. It's "Language" poetry, or at the edge of it, at the Mallarmésque edge of Language poetry, and it's beautiful writing, and it was very appealing to me. I was feeling somewhat resistant to the kind of beauty and the mysteriousness you get from discontinuousness, so I found myself thinking, "I wonder if I could do this," and I found I couldn't quite do it. Or maybe that's just a way of saying that "it doesn't interest me to do it." I'm much more interested in the way the mind, my mind, or "a" mind, tracks one thing to the next. I was slightly aware of these things springing out of their proposition. It's interesting to me that the first poem was . . . . It begins something like:

> A man thinks lilacs against white houses, having seen them in the farm county south of Tacoma in April, and can't find his way to a sentence, a brushstroke carrying the energy of brush and stroke
>
> —as if he were stranded on the aureole of the memory of a woman's breast,
>
> and she after the drive from the airport and a chat with her mother and a shower, which is ritual cleansing and a passage through water to mark transition,
>
> had walked up the mountain on a summer evening.

When I was doing that, in just the way you described, I imagined the "she" being generated by the metaphor, and when I showed it to some friends, they all immediately thought it was a poem about a "he" and a "she," that it was a sort of relationship poem, but the woman just fictionally showed up for me in the poem. So I had to do a lot of rewriting to try to get it so a reader would feel what I was feeling, which is that these are sort of parallel inventions and that it's not a poem about a guy and a girl, and I say it at the end; I think I added the line: "The hes and shes of the comedy may or may not get together" just by way of saying, "I'm not talking; this is not a covert complicated way of writing a love poem."

You mentioned the "Language" poets. I've been exposed to some of their work—Susan Howe and others—and I find much of their work very difficult to read. Do you consider Palmer's work similar or just borderline?

Well, he's written two terrific books—*Notes Toward Echo Lake* and *First Figure*. He's associated with the Language poets and he appears in their anthologies, but he dissociates himself from what he takes to be their central aesthetic proposition, which is that they want to create, they want to abolish subjectivity by making sure the poems can't be explicated. They want to somehow decenter consciousness; that is, their ambition is to finally throttle Romanticism to death. Hence a poem in which there's no "I," no subjective center. Palmer perceives his poems as proceeding from a subjective center and being paraphrasable ultimately. But sometimes it's hard to tell the difference between one of his poems and one of somebody else's who's not trying to make that connection. There's a playful surreal side to him; he's oblique and difficult, sort of Wallace Stevens and Ashbery made more difficult, but the writing's so beautiful, intelligent and playful, that you're interested anyway.

Going back to the subject of decadence in art—I recently read an article—and there are obviously numerous pieces on the subject— by Mary Karr, "Against Decoration," which talks about New Formalism. I was wondering if you might share your attitudes toward this movement.

New Formalism was a bunch of younger poets feeling like the hegemony of free verse was getting boring. And that's part of it, but because of the people who gave it a name like that, they also tended to want to write about contemporary American subjects in a plain language with a skeptical kind of wise guy tone, so there was also that sort of X.J. Kennedy allergicness to the American sublime—the attitude of it. That attitude is in the writers I can think of, whose work I don't know very well: Paul Lake, Dana Gioia, Timothy Steele, Brad Leithouser, Mary Jo Salter, who mostly get associated with the idea of New Formalism. I think it was sort of a Reagan era starch, a desire to get away from the "raggedy-ass sixties." It was to some extent also anti-Romantic. I like formal verse. I'm not very interested in the clever side of their writing. It seems very limited.

I wanted to ask, in the context of your comments on form, about the section in Human Wishes *of prose poems. What does that form hold for you? Is it an exploration?*

It was when I was doing it. The prose poem for me, the appeal of it, is twofold. One is the proposition of formal unity in a paragraph. Just the proposition of it: the paragraph as a form. It's connected to print. The other is the various propositions implied in the rhythms of prose, abstracted. You know, the suspense of sentence like in a Le Carre novel or something like that. "Prague is not, like most of the dark European cities, even though, she thought, as she walked down the street, some of them . . . ." There are a whole bunch of different connections, direct sentence, short sentence, looping sentence, and so on. So that seemed delicious to me. There's also a certain kind of objectivity and sobriety to the proposition of the prose poem if it's not the manic Surrealist, "Wow, look how much wild stuff I can pack in here," quality. It was a way for me to get some of the rhythms of expository prose and some of the matter that belongs to expository prose into my work. Narrative. It was just interesting to experiment with. I think when I began, my idea was to use it as if I were taking photographs. Use it as a kind of documentary thing: I saw this young woman and man in a museum passing a baby back and forth. I wasn't interested in getting into the rhythm of verse the texture of that thing; I was interested in describing it. And the most natural way to do it was in prose. Then within that, as with anything, you can find great formal things to play with. Contrast. Two parts/three parts. Different rhythms. And so on. I had written a lot of them. I had originally thought of publishing two books—we talked about doing them at the same time—one of prose poems, one of verse. But in fact I didn't like enough of the prose poems. For example,

Museum

On the morning of the Käthe Kollwitz exhibit, a young man and woman come into the museum restaurant. She is carrying a baby; he carries the air-freight edition of the Sunday *New York Times*. She sits in a high-backed wicker chair, cradling the infant in her arms. He fills a tray with fresh fruit, rolls, and coffee in white cups and brings it to the table. His hair is tousled, her eyes are puffy. They look like they were thrown down into sleep and then yanked out of it like divers coming up for air. He holds the baby. She drinks coffee, scans the front page, butters a roll and eats it in their little corner in the sun. After a while, she holds the baby. He reads the *Book Review* and eats some fruit. Then he holds the baby while she finds the section of the paper she wants and eats fruit and smokes. They've hardly exchanged a look. Meanwhile, I have fallen in love with this equitable arrangement, and with the baby who cooperates by sleeping. All around them are faces Käthe Kollwitz carved in wood of people with no talent or capacity for suffering who are suffering the numbest kinds of pain: hunger, helpless terror. But this young couple is reading the Sunday paper in the sun, the baby is sleeping, the green has begun to emerge from the rind of the cantaloupe, and everything seems possible.

The longer poem you read last night—"My Mother's Nipples"—
is in both prose and verse, and you experiment with that in some
of your other works. What's the main attraction of that for you?

Well, singing and talking. I had already been doing it when I discovered the way Milosz did it. I don't know if you know these poems but they're so amazing to me. "From the Rising of the Sun" and more, later, in *The Separate Notebooks*, where besides fooling with different verse forms, he fools with the different rhythms of prose, like sort of free verse poems, and then much more formal poems—this section is written in a de Maupassaunt short story language (quotes Milosz): "He found on dusty shelves, the pages of the family chronicle . . . ." And back into "I didn't choose California," then a sort of long—this is, in Polish, very near a formal elegy—poem about three of his friends who were killed in the camp and then prose commentary and sort of a natural musing notebook language on having written the poem. It just lets so much happen.

Do you think it's a difficult book? I read a review that said it "brings together all those voices that simultaneously exist within the poet," and that seems an accurate description and also a recurring aspect of his work.

Once you get to know the voices and get some grounding in the philosophical orientation, then it's not difficult. He thinks of himself as a very accessible writer and he's very contemptuous of Modernism. He's always telling me that I should be more direct, that I'm too subtle, that it's vanity, etc.

GD: You both went to Catholic schools, didn't you? Do you think you can articulate how that has affected your work?

Yeah, oh sure: the religious imagination, imagery, the language of prayer. It's interesting. He and Seamus Heaney and I had dinner one night, and we were reminiscing. Milosz in Lithuania in the twenties, and Seamus and I in Belfast and San Rafael, California— or he lived just outside in the suburb and I lived outside—we all knew the same prayers. Milosz asked me what my first favorite poem was. I recited a prayer to Mary: "Hail mother of mercy, our life, our sweetness and our hope," and Seamus recited the next line: "To thee do we cry, poor banished children of Eve," and so on. There's all the jokey American Catholic stuff about sex and confession, but there's also this rich cosmology there.

You mentioned one of the Basho anecdotes where Basho says something like, "The trouble with most poetry is that it's either subjective or objective," and the disciple said, "You mean too subjective or too objective?" and Basho said, "No," and it made me think of a writing project in which I have great interest, tracing the genealogy of the Romantic voice in contemporary poetry—a consideration of the role of the authoritative in poetics. I wonder if you could comment briefly on your take on the relationship between early nineteenth century British Romanticism and contemporary American poetry.

First of all, your project sounds very interesting. And very ambitious. Nobody's yet made the account of the connection very well between Romanticism and Modernism and whatever is going on now. All the labels for it are not useful. Partly because nobody's described the territory very accurately. But it's clear that what it is, part of what it was, is a reemergence of Romanticism out of impatience with the Modernist solution of impersonality. It just brought back in, fragmented by the Modernists, all the questions about subjectivity/objectivity of voice in the Romantic tradition. To me the Romantic tradition is fragmented by having the twin ancestry of Nerval and Wordsworth, and—Keats is a kind of halfway house between those two which makes me think about something we were discussing earlier concerning the "Ode to Autumn." What's interesting to me is that it's sort of the first Symbolist poem. It's the moment when Romanticism got rid of tendentiousness. One way I see a lot of the formal problems involving the Romantic poem is that they had a new idea of knowledge and therefore a new idea of what poetry was, but they still had the eighteenth century model of how to end a poem—which is with a statement of some kind, a summing up, as if rationality or common sense finally was somehow ascendant at the end of the poem. Keats wrestling with that "Do I wake or do I sleep" and by putting "Beauty/Truth" in quotation marks, and then finally in "Autumn" he figures out how to let the image do the speaking.

PHOTO BY MEG ESCUDÉ

Brenda Hillman was born in 1951 in Tucson, Arizona. A graduate of the Iowa Writers' Workshop, she has been associated both with the most experimental work coming out of the San Francisco Bay area and a more traditional lyric strain in American literature; her poetry defies easy classification. Although she is profoundly interested in Gnosticism, she is also a poet very much involved with the mundanity of contemporary life; that is, her work does not shirk an attachment to the material world in its plummeting of gnosis. Her methods for uncovering the "secret knowledge"— mystical apprehension of the godhead—are as varied as the subject matter and formal shapes of her poetry. Hypnosis, radical textual experiments, even an attempt to render the transformative processes of alchemy in a textual representation on the page have all been elements of her practice. Brenda Hillman's six books of poetry—including Bright Existence, Death Tractates, Loose Sugar, *and, most recently,* Cascadia—*constitute an important exploration of poetics and the spirit, an exploration compelled by aesthetic, political, and spiritual obsessions. She has received many awards for her poetry, including National Endowment for the Arts and Guggenheim fellowships.*

BRENDA HILLMAN

Brenda and I talked in Kensington, California, during summer 1998.

In your poem "Magdalene," there's a line, "So few women in the text," and it seems to me that this is a statement of tremendous implication. How does this absence shape a woman poet's initiation to poetry?

It's impossible to know the extent of it. The text referred to is, of course, the text in general and the Bible in particular. I ignored the absences of women for a long time in my reading, though the first three poets I loved as a young girl were women—Edna St. Vincent Millay, Dickinson, and Plath—if you don't count the authors of the *Psalms*. But when I read Plath as a teenager, I barely noticed she was female—this was just after the appearance of *Ariel*. When I read her work later, I did notice, and that put me on a precipice looking over the other side. The Modernists I had started with were Eliot and Stevens; then I read the rest of the Modernist canon, the Symbolists, the Surrealists, and studied poetic traditions and movements in a systematic way. In my heart I felt deeply divided between the crazy ones who observe how their senses leave them and the ones who want to make sense. So I was thinking more about image, style, the imagination's various ways rather than matters of gender, and when I noticed how few women there were,

I felt missionary zeal about speaking to that absence. Whatever forces had seemed to stop women—the forces of history and economic circumstance and the body—had been changing for a while—this was in the early eighties. In the Bay Area at that time, it became impossible to ignore women in poetry.

So for a while you had ignored the absences. Can you describe the effect of being immersed in so many male writers? Or, to put it another way, if poetics are gendered, as many think they are, how does it affect one's poetics to be immersed in such a masculine broth?

Your awareness shifts. I'm not sure whether anything about writing can be only gender-specific. Surely there are experiences only women can have, and some that only men can have. Many of the stylistic devices that are said to characterize the writing by women poets in the last two decades—the use of the fragment, polysyntactic structures, non sequitur—are of course standard Modernist practices. You can trace nearly all technique to previous technique if you get down to it—one thing might come from Mallarmé, or from H.D., or from Stein. But it seems that a lot of exploratory writing in the last few decades by women has come out of a feeling of new freedom, that there is a different air to breathe, and this is probably different for each writer. When I was working on *Death Tractates*, I was aware of making a new form of feminized pastoral in territory that hadn't been worked before, but I certainly heard the origins of it in what I had studied, and I guess my "masculine broth" had always been a mix. Besides the Modernists, I remember being obsessed with Baudelaire in my freshman year of college, then André Breton. My friend Luke Menand and I sat around reading Jim Tate's poetry after Surrealism class. If you have a decent education in poetry as an undergraduate, you feel like you're crunching through autumn woods that are very populated, very full of spirits, and you can hear every twig snap. All young writers feel that everything has been done by the great dead guys, and some of the women of my generation experienced this odd double effect—perhaps it's the opposite of what Bloom calls the "anxiety of influence"—one of my friends called it her "excuse me, I'm coming through." One of my teachers in grad school—Sandy McPherson—taught a course in women's poetry. I read Bishop and Stein and H.D. for the first time. Some of us were also reading Donald Allen's anthology, stuff that wasn't really on everyone's list, like Wieners and Duncan and Ashbery. When I moved to the Bay Area there was a lively community of women poets; my first friend, Patricia Dienstfrey, was helping found Kelsey Street Press to publish experimental poetry by women. That small press and *How(ever)* played important roles in my thinking about form and process and women's writing. I guess the answer that I do think about being a woman poet in a time that has been important historically for women's writing, but for me and for most of the writers I know, gender is only a part of it. Often I go back to this early exposure to Millay, Dickinson and Plath.

Millay and Dickinson are very different poets. Correct me if I'm wrong here, but it seems as though your attraction to Dickinson has endured longer than your attraction to Millay. Why is that? What fascinates you about Dickinson and brings you back to her work?

Well, Dickinson is before her time, and Millay is after her time. She's a traditional nineteenth century Romanticist. I read Millay when I was nine or ten because my dad gave me the book. Her kind of lyricism seemed to me a place of freedom, the musical mode of a single soul pleading. It was magical yearning for the fullness of sound.

Early Yeats does that for me.

Yeah, same sort of dynamic. Dickinson is the mysterious otherness that included everything. She invented or brought into the light rare things that had existed always in the spirit but hadn't been voiced. Things one doesn't know one has inside are brought forth, and she did so many things—the fragmented form, the flexible reflexivity of the phrase, consciousness as the main issue, there's nobody there and everybody, the text looking at itself—a sort of pre-Post modernism. She gets at the absolute radical center of the universe where it doesn't exist.

Which poems are your favorites? In which do you see this dynamic most vividly in?

"My Life had stood—a Loaded Gun," "After great pain, a formal feeling comes," of course. "There's a certain Slant of light," "Pain has an element of blank"—generally the great *pain* ones! I did a little edition of Dickinson for Shambhala, and the selection I made is in some ways a cross section of poems about the types and degrees of spiritual difficulty. It sort of seems like the incremental examination of the conditions of the mind is all most poets are good for, and Dickinson's genius lies in her language of agony and enduring what it means. The ones that are most about the impossibility of knowing how to exist. The titlelessness of her work is connected to her concept of heaven, and having a heaven that exists both as an absolute and not at all, she gives us this vacancy "above." She looks up into the beyond and sees a faceless eternity that isn't reflecting the self back to her. But of course, she couldn't do it all; poets after her had to continue this work.

Do you think that the pain Dickinson articulates is connected to the concept of gendered poetics? The poet who's usually paired with Emily is granddaddy Walt, and his poetry—although not without its moments of intense grief and suffering—is generally more optimistic, ebullient, exuberant. Does gender play a role in that?

I don't know. There is something right about pairing Emily and Walt, and I know people who are actual couples whose personalities or world-roles get archetyped and established. It may not be about gender difference because I know same sex couples who are paired in people's minds that way: one as the intensely inward and spiritual and the other as outgoing and earthy and so on. "Emily-and-Walt" is so odd because both poets are ecstatics, but their ecstasies take dichotomous forms. Here's one whose anxiety imploded; here's one whose anxiety exploded. This goes back to the question of gendered poetics. Fragments and polyphonies—perhaps you can see the great gathering of power in Dickinson's hesitations and pauses, or perhaps you see matters of gender more in subject matter than in any stylistic matter for these two writers. They both incorporate masculine and feminine, and this becomes a form of dialectical vision in Emily's references to the female speaker as a boy or a man, as well as Queen of Calvary and in Walt's bisexual love poems. Their split identities come out of working within a canon of their own time that would lock her out and only haltingly accept him.

This question of gendering is frequently undertaken as part of a political reading of a given poet's work. How do you think that poetry and politics intersect?

What do you mean by political? What aspect of political poetry interests you most?

I guess what I'm thinking about is when poetry attempts to engage specific issues that we usually associate with the public writ large, commentary on race, war, gender issues, economics, social justice. I realize that identity is frequently wrapped up with such discussions, but I also think that we can make some distinction between, say, the lyrical impulse of Millay and the poetry of witness of Forché.

That's a good question, and there are several ways into it. Often the language subverts intention, and when poets take it as a specific challenge to do as you describe, to try for a kind of poetry that addresses social issues, such as the kind that focuses on the present environmental crisis, and so forth, the poem has its own idea of what it wants to do and it cannot exist without its own ethics. In *Loose Sugar*, I meant to write a book on the imaginary substance of

time, using experimental forms, and I or it had to take into account
the senselessness of the Gulf War and gasoline love while I was
writing it. Having thought about matter as entrapment for the
Gnostics, I was thinking about the will of the body and sex and the
beginning of time as a freeing thing, and suddenly, a really idiotic
war happened, which put my students' bodies at risk. It began to
seem that my inquiry sometimes had to be bound up with political
and social issues. The kind of commentary you refer to—making
political statements—is very hard to do in poetry without falling
into terrible cliché or smugness. What seemed most drastic about
the eighties was how scary Reaganomics was, or were, and the figures
of Reagan and Bush. Those jokes about Reagan turning off his
hearing aid in meetings, that sort of thing. *The Contra deal*—my
god. The eighties, in one way, had been a batch of hideous ironies.
I wrote about it in a little poem called "No Problem," which is a
rather heavy-handed item. Thinking about forms of identity and
how nationalism was invented to wreck male bodies made me sick.
Thinking about gasoline made me think about mixtures of things
from under the earth, which made me think of alchemy, which was
also what my interest in Gnosticism had led me to, and the Gulf
War led to thinking about nationalism and my childhood experience
of Postcolonialism in Brasil, loss of language and remaking the
mother tongue, and it all wound up together! I found that the
political interests could not be separated from the rest of it when
writing that book.

That gives us insight into Loose Sugar. *Some people have
identified the act of writing poetry in our age as a political act—
because it goes so in the face of economic, social and various political
agendas. Do you agree with such a sentiment? Or, to get at the
question a different way, are the personal and political always
intertwined?*

The political and the personal are mostly intertwined, if you believe
in the personal. Some people's hopes for making writing more
political comes from the guilt about the uselessness of art among

people who are trying to write poetry in this country, especially young poets who are under pressure to do something useful with their M.F.A.s and who feel guilty for sitting around writing poetry because they were told it is a sort of useless thing to do. And in a way, all art is useless. But original language engages us in moral difficulties. It makes us hear words past the cliché; it takes apart the world and relanguages it in the process. My poems are difficult and full of weird devices. They aren't going to be too useful to enact social change. I read at a couple of Gulf War protests and thought about the limitations of polemics.

Is there any way to avoid compromising one's aesthetic while writing such poetry? Subtlety and political poetry don't seem to go together too well.

Much political poetry is terribly polemical. Yeats might be a good example of someone who achieved grandeur and beauty without always being subtle, but I find "A terrible beauty is born" a true and powerful statement about revolution. Irony is almost never subtle, and in political poetry it is nearly always a second rate tool. I'm obsessed by several things right now as a writer besides the main thing of "how does language embody reality and how can I get there?" One of them is syntax: the relationship between the phrase or the sentence and the line, how something comes to represent in broken or fragmentary writing. I had been reading a lot of writing by thinkers such as Irigaray and Cixous, and I began thinking about this more in *Loose Sugar*, the unsettledness of primary thought in a first language as the key to a sort of spatial imagining. My mom's first language was Portuguese, and we lived in Brasil for a few years when I was a child. I felt her language leaving her body as a perceived absence or silence, especially as I also had a caretaker who spoke only in Portuguese. Later in memory, I heard this as a deranged syntax that also reflected the child's confusion over the spirit-states and the mess of the fifties in Brasil.

Syntactical ruptures that are subversive.

That reflect the fucked-upness of a socioeconomic time. The only way writers can protest is through language.

> *Giving up on—and this connects back to Ma Dickinson and Pa Whitman—the false lineages, these false continuities, and realizing what a mess it all is.*

To see how broken something is, to reflect that accurately, can be a political act. And an act of survival—getting through the day. How to get out of the deadness with deep enough feeling to survive with pleasure. I sometimes think sentences have to be screwed up in exactly the same way as we've screwed up the weather. So the multivalence of the sentence can reflect the vanishing ozone layer. Right now I'm working on poems about the way dirt breaks as we break inside—dirt, dioxin, and desire.

Another obsession?

Meaning, or so-called meaning. Meaning and how it gets here, in a completely mysterious universe, and the search for its language. What to do about meaning, meaning as the by-product of the general buzz, like ah-ha, the surprise chamber that is the arbitrariness of signs but that produces depth soundings anyway. This is very tied up with questions about whether and how each word refers to its thing, and its sign-force-system activity. I'm not sure whether I can ever disconnect the quest for meaning or reference from metaphysical issues in my own poetry, or that I want to stop a search for it—but that is, oddly, not an essentialist quest but an existentialist one. Meaning not as something that gets through but something that I will never understand but that *is,* no matter what, reverberating in the labyrinth of each word so that knowing it gives power in each of the tiniest motions. When we go down into the mystery of the word, what starts there? What is an experience within and outside of a line of poetry that presents it? That's what I want to know. There's a disequilibrium between the consciousness of a poet and "it" that torments us. The whole question has a lot to do with the interest in odd syntaxes. Just as it's interesting to think about the soul in the afterlife, the geographical position of it, it's interesting to consider whether meaning is embodied in syntax. It's certain that meaning does not come through language as light comes "through" a window.

Obsession?

It's tied up with that, but more particular—the kind of magic and suffering of each moment of human consciousness in the search. I'm sort of thinking of the three layers of human existence here, for the Gnostics, the body or material, the pneuma or spirit and the psyche/soul. Individual approaches to the problems of fear and suffering and inexplicable joy interest me very much. And the question of what an experience is can never be an aesthetic or philosophical question only. I teach at many writers' conferences, and people bring poems that are moving, heart-wrenching depictions of lives, and sometimes there's only a little good writing, so I say, your job is to let that experience meet its excellent and memorable language, to respect and love words so you honor them by using them with magic and consciousness. People think they're stuck in their plot, in what happened to them. What happens to you is beyond your plot, your own narrative or nature, so your poem is an object that transcends its singular use, it strips the ego out of you. What happens to you is the moment of the poem, of the seam/ seem between your noticing and building; it is not necessarily in your autobiographical data, but it is much more deeply the soul of experience in language. What speaks when we speak, or cries when we cry? An individual consciousness has its own inscape, to use Hopkins' term, and it resonates with other energy that is absolute, even if God is metaphor. In poetry, we take the best of what we know from individual experience, deepening it with the collective consciousness, and mostly we think of that as the soul. I guess the soul's my favorite metaphor because the other term of it will never be known, the thing on the other side of the equal sign. That's why the mystery traditions are interesting—they were looking for it.

Let me play devil's advocate for a moment. If poetry is so valuable

*in exploring this realm of God and soul, then it seems to me that
accessibility would be paramount. If the message is so important,
one would want to get it out there. In the twentieth century,
though, many American poets have chosen the other route—of
difficulty.*

I question the term "accessible." A poet's job is to put forth the best
of the movements of her or his consciousness, by which I mean,
the shapeliest dreams. Sometimes—or often—dreams are not
straightforward or continuous. When the travelers consult the oracle
in classical literatures, there is much indirection. A lot of meditative
poetry is abstract and doesn't tell stories or is hallucinatory and has
inaccessible imagery. Much that is great poetry might speak to fewer
people rather than many. Lots of students ask, "How hard are we
supposed to work on understanding this stuff?" But really it's nearly
impossible for Americans to fight through sentimental impulses to
feel the awe of most amazing poetry. In the visual arts, people are
willing to experience a large degree of abstraction—with Kandinsky,
with Rothko, with Pollack. Less so with poetry. Challenging and
abstract language may be necessary for the human spirit, but people
may not get to our most difficult writing—it takes more time to
read, for one thing, so teachers would rather teach crappy poetry
than great work. In a way I don't blame them, because you have to
go slowly, to make a case for challenging work.

*Judgments along the lines of "best" or "poor"—"good" or "crappy"
—aren't exactly* de rigueur *of academic criticism these days. Many
take umbrage at such distinctions. Why are you so confident in
asserting such distinctions? What does a great poem have that a
crappy poem does not?*

Let's take the opposite of Dickinson's saying about the top of her
head coming off, let's think of the between-the-legs feeling going
inside. Whatever makes you want to have that energy and feel it
erotically within and with another listener. When I discover
something that's magical in language, my impulse is to put it in my

journal so I can blend with it while writing it, admiring it all the while. The mergey feeling, when you are sexually in love and want to rub yourself with it. Of course it's good to make really strong distinctions between what excellent or amazing writing is and what not-excellent or terrible writing is. I'm very demanding on my own work and often write dozens of drafts by hand. Superlatives are another issue—I'm loathe to say "best" or "most" or "greatest" because poetry is not like a chevron of geese with one little goose out front.

You're articulating the feeling that overcomes you when you encounter greatness in poetry, but can you talk more distinctly about the attributes of the work?

There are lots of poems we come to love because we are told they're great poems and we get educated into seeing how the little machine works, and that brings forth a feeling in us. It takes years to understand a poem you love. I still turn to poetry the way I turned to it when I was a child, because it does something for me nothing else can; it assuages the loneliness or terror of being alive in a language that can't be put in any other way. Sometimes it works with flame and sometimes with water. "After great pain, a formal feeling comes." The line can only be like that. What is a formal feeling? Such intense poetry makes me feel an energy that is common to all minds, and a beauty that will save us, I believe, absolutely, but only for moments at a time. So when I read through magazines or new books that come to us—we get sometimes ten new books a week at our house—mostly I'm looking for a moment of vision and originality of language. Some surprise that has to do with authenticity of the soul having invented something in original diction or metaphor, that has a set of shifts that take us from philosophical or even metaphysical concepts or abstractions into the stuff, the physical solid matter, or the quotidian, and back again really fast. That's the kind of thing I like. The magic poems that are beautiful—phrase oriented, that experience the textures of language and make love in the smallest phrase. The imagination that finds embodiment in many ways, through weird syntax, through metaphor, through conflation of idea and image. A way of refreshing things so that they're not familiar. The style doesn't have to resemble mine. For example, I like Stein and Bishop probably equally.

Your exploration of alchemy and Gnosticism connects to poetry as being able to usher in the spiritual and otherness that is larger than we are. The mystical-visionary tradition as articulated in poetry is compelling. Do you think that poetry has a connection to the spiritual that the other arts do not?

No. I think all arts have connection to the spiritual. But I don't know what it's like to be another kind of artist; it's like asking me to become a porcupine. Maybe it is more fun. I love watching pop musicians on music videos, and dancers, but if you asked me whether I'd rather be one, I would say no, not just because my love affair with poetry is pretty satisfying but because it interests me slightly more that poems are the best version of our most common thing, which is ordinary language. If, when we went into the 7-11 for Trident, we hummed or danced to the cashier instead of saying "thanks," things might be different. I experience poetry as the coolest form of muttering to the cashier or to yourself in the 7-11. But that also makes it tough on poetry because we use the commonest tool for it.

That's an important distinction. Poetry uses language, which has so much connection to all our other interactions. A more intense usage but the same medium. The other arts are distinct. For instance, music's nonreferentiality puts it in a completely different category.

It certainly is. But then there's the whole thing I was talking about earlier—how reference works, and the degrees of referentiality, and theories of this—the work of Hejinian, for example, that owes a lot to Gertrude Stein's various musics, and other Language poetry. What would it be like to have your main form of expression be wordless? What is it like to be a dancer, to put it out there and to have no residue? That's a pure thing, the mystical tree. Yet it seems so lucky to have poetry as an important task. It's one thing that interested me about Gnosticism—the fact that meaning and experience and language are coterminous in the place of knowing; Gnostics were all involved with secret passwords to get you to the next level, that kind of thing. I use trance work and hypnosis a lot for composition. Much of what's in *Bright Existence* and *Death Tractate*s came out of hypnosis; then I shaped the meditations into poems. I'm not that keen on languageless meditation, to be honest. I like meditations that hold the word as a talisman. I hate the thought that whatever is the mystical ultimate doesn't have language in it. I want the afterlife to be a Berkeley café with a sort of slow composition of poetry, lovers dismantling pieces of slightly stale bagel while trying to say difficult, true things to each other while the kid in the corner listens to the Pixies in a headset.

Would you describe yourself as a dualist?

I don't know any more. I used to think, "Yes, for sure I'm a dualist," but now I'm of two minds about whether I'm a dualist or not. We used to take poetry books to war protest sit-ins; when they arrested us at the ROTC building, I was reading—like, O.K. better to assume it's useless and improve your mind while they haul your ass out of there. Living in Berkeley, you get a lot of "it's all one." Well, I'm sort of "we're all several," but it's the same several every time I reflect on it, so, actually, I think I'm not a dualist after all, I think I may be an animist because I talk to rocks and stuff. But while you're talking about it, you talk about the talking about it.

Isn't that quality reflected in the formal aspects of your recent poetry? You've mentioned the syntax and such, but the use of the page seems equally relevant. The use of subtexts and pretexts, so to speak, as a sort of running commentary that is connected to but not part of the poems.

The little commentaries between pages are just little blips in consciousness like the cracks in the universe at the start of time. There's the extra stuff at the bottom of "blue codices." The extra elements on the page came from the idea of letting the margins relax. I got interested in alchemy in the early nineties; alchemists were trying very hard, you know, to make one thing out of another. I was thinking about Jung's writing about depression. The alchemists seem to me quintessentially hopeful. Marginalia would come forward on my page, the little penciled scratches, in a kind of hopeful way. I had been dealing with a pervasive depression that seemed sort of redemptive, where it's all hopeless but interesting, many shades of blackness. I am visited by that often, then it passes. Voices impinge from outside. In drafting *Death Tractates,* I had scooped the derangements into the verse, made the little exceptions into parts of the poem. But with the poems in *Loose Sugar,* I decided to put them there by themselves, just let them linger. Marginalia at the bottom that won't be reused. Little comments or images. This idea of having the ash at the bottom of the page came from considering the alchemist's furnace. It falls out and stays there and the phoenix rises from it.

Like in your recent poem "A Geology."

Yeah, though those are somewhat different. I thought of those corner words as "signal words," a kind of assignment of what to use on each page. Rather than as ash or leavings, I thought of them as wordseeds, like sticking your seed packet for melons on a little stake in the dirt: here's what I started with. I was trying to work them in and thus give the rather wild poem a sense of internalized necessity or fate. I'm interested in using the whole page as a different way of inventing. I got this by reusing a lot of spatial soup stock from Mallarmé. Also from my reading group—we were reading work by the Oulipo group in France; I had always been interested in secret measuring devices, secret ways of counting, etc. I became interested in working with constraint and measure even as whatever is free about free verse continues to be engaging. Constraint as freedom and freedom within constraint. Setting little goals—not traditional metrics or rhyme, but little secret formal assignments to see if I could achieve them while the soul worked on its group wildness.

And could you apply these notions to the formal dimensions of the poem?

In different ways, and certainly not in a way that would restrict the activity of the poem, if it turned out that the interesting path was another way. Like, you can get started with thinking about numbers of lines. The twelve-line poem had been of interest. The business of having secret assignments connects with the alchemical poems in *Loose Sugar*, and in the title sequence at the end—there would be this little phrase at the top of the page that would kick off the poem. Then I drew a line after that phrase—a sort of mirror that doesn't necessarily happen in real life. The words that you get before you get the title are like the things that happen in a room before you enter; they are part of the form, part of the shape, if only we could hear more purely. I discovered in *Death Tractates* that what is most interesting about inner forms of abstract meditation is straining to hear the conversation that is going on whether you're in it or not. You're always in a fragile relationship to a fragmentary conversation.

In Loose Sugar, *we find* Chevron Tankers, *Star Trek, the discovery of sexuality, Woolworth's, as well as many disparate presences. I find that fascinating because I don't think that there are many contemporary poets who are willing to gather in so many different aspects of the world. Is this assimilation reflective of your attitude toward poetics at this point in American literary history?*

My poetics, this mixing of levels and tones and subjects, reflect a messy soul looking at a messy, amazing world. So poetry makes shapes of the mess. There's a line in "Thicket Group": "You have changed the assignment to Swirl." I don't know about literary history; the world needs many different types of poetry. I began to think we have to write poetry we need to read more than poetry that we need to write. Anyway, I started putting that stuff in my poetry in the early eighties. How could you not put *Star Trek* and . . .

The Pixies

I love the Pixies. I like that kind of music very much. I was away from music for a little and suddenly kids were drumming in my basement and I was raising a couple of punk rock kids. I like that sort of music. I like television very much also if I don't need to be looking at it. I have to say I haven't liked movies too much, but a little while ago, I started liking them better. I'm very happy about that.

What movie turned the tide?

I think it might have been *Woman in the Dunes*. It was a tough time in my life and it became one of my top movies. I think maybe my favorite movies have sand in them. But I'm not quite used to movies; I'm still getting used them. It is hard just to stare straight ahead and attend to their dominating power. I used to be terrified of them. You were stuck in the dark with everyone even if you wanted to leave. I prefer almost all television to movies, especially any sort of sports or game show. Culture makes it into poems no matter what— supermarkets, music, going to the library, TV, driving, rats in garbage cans.

> *How do you balance this interest in culture with your attraction to a more spiritually-driven poetry? Eliot's* Waste Land *versus* Four Quartets *might be an interesting lens through which to look at this question.*

I think it's all mixed in together. Eliot is surely a great artist, though I go through periods of being sick of him. If only he had heard *Blonde on Blonde*. For Modernists, I actually prefer Stevens and

Williams at the moment, though Eliot was my first love. He actually didn't go forward in *Four Quartets*, he went sideways. *The Waste Land* was the great derangement, the great rearrangement. Lowell and many poets came out of the inner lining of the coat of that poem, what Eliot didn't want to tell us about the anguish of his individual life but somehow included it anyway. I'm more interested in the fragmented-falling-apart-generalized-speakingness of that poem. He's the one who showed us about all kinds of culture entering poetry—often seems to have to do with irony, with the ironic distance one needs in order to see a thing. Of course, we can have many flavors of ironists—I think of Rae Armantrout taking a close ironic look at southern California in her succinct poems. It's obvious to note that we don't have to balance spiritual interests with culture because they're all tangled up together.

Is it difficult to be hopeful about the significance of your work or about poetry in general?

Well, it's easy to be confident about the need for poetry in the culture, and I love the activity of struggling to write it, though mostly it comes from a difficulty of expression, from wrestling with the dread of nature and mind-boggling difficulties of being alive. I'm glad to be a poet in this time. On the other hand, it is hard not to feel crushed by how little your average person cares about it, and, of course, I'm grateful to have an audience and glad when people write letters out of the blue. Some people have a very specific set of readers but it's different with my work, and the audience is continually refreshing itself. There's this magazine in the Bay Area called *Rooms* that began as a collective, editorless text some years ago; the founders of it had the idea of asking about fifty of us who were interested in innovative work and experiment to start sending fifty copies of one of our pieces in progress. They would bind it and mail it back out to us. There's no editor; there are several collators who bind it and mail it back to us. People send all kinds of poems in, Xeroxed on all kinds of paper, with illustrations. It's a beautiful thing.

How does a project like this connect to your assertions about "the best" work?

Well, I don't think magazines can possibly present only the best work. Some of it is uneven or is in draft form, and some is excellent writing. I sent one poem which I had written fifty times in pencil because I felt phobic about typing it.

You're mentioning this as a reason for hope, this nonacademic sort of venture that's connected to getting poetry out there.

Getting poetry introduced in the culture. Sometimes exploratory poetry is associated with academic life and sometimes not. "Language" poetry has been heavily associated with theory and conferences, which isn't always a bad thing. It has meant that some of that work is presented only in narrow areas. I'm glad that much of what is adventurous in contemporary poetry is becoming less ghettoized now. *Rooms* may be also a very limited format, but it is the kind of publishing any group of people could do—to get their work disseminated. It's a sort of anticompetition mechanism. Trying to exchange texts with a greater ease. So that's one way to do it. I think the good old Xerox machine is the best, getting your work into the hands of friends. Not just books and magazines, individual poems. I think those of us who teach need to teach cross-reading, to read across aesthetic boundaries, so that what is exciting isn't just a narrow sense of avant-garde or experimental writing, but crosses and remixes the categories. Students can get a good idea of what's being done in the art at any one time. It's very discouraging that so much good writing becomes balkanized because of territoriality and specialized claims. I taught a course at Iowa in which I used the poetry of fourteen women writers—among them Guest, McHugh, Glück, Susan Howe, Olds, lots of others. Not everyone liked everything, of course. I think things are changing because of a greater acceptance of variety and I feel pretty committed to this as a teacher.

A desire to enlarge the canon, enlarge the texts?

So that there's a range of what's possible, and that's a cause for hopefulness.

Edward Hirsch was born in Chicago in 1950. He was educated at Grinnell College and the University of Pennsylvania, where he earned his doctorate. Hirsch has taught at several colleges and universities and presently teaches in the creative writing program at The University of Houston. A poet of diverse talents—utilizing narrative, lyrical, and dramatic elements—his books of poetry include For the Sleepwalkers, Wild Gratitude, The Night Parade, Earthly Measures, *and, most recently,* On Love. *His most recent book is* How to Read a Poem and Fall in Love with Poetry. *He has won many awards, including a Guggenheim Fellowship, the National Book Critics Circle Award, and a MacArthur Fellowship.*

EDWARD HIRSCH

Edward and I spoke in Sewanee, Tennessee, during summer 1998.

Many poets and critics attribute the beginning of American poetry in the twentieth century to Ezra Pound. Is this your understanding of American literary history or do you see someone else as the origin?

I suppose that in a historical way a great deal goes back to Pound and the other Imagists. It was Pound, after all, who urged American poets to use the language of common speech with precision, to create new rhythms, to enjoy an absolute freedom of subject matter. Pound recognized that Yeats was the greatest poet writing in English at the time and that Eliot had "modernized himself on his own." Pound also opened up American poetry with a wide range of voices in *Personae*. I'm grateful to him for bringing the Provençal poets into English and for the marvelous translations of *Cathay*, his best book. But I dislike the person he became, and for me it was never *The Pound Era*, to employ the title of Hugh Kenner's brilliant critical work. It was the Wallace Stevens and Hart Crane era, the William Carlos Williams and Marianne Moore era, the Edwin Arlington Robinson and Robert Frost era.

Describe your attraction to Stevens.

Romantic poetry was somewhat derided in my education, perhaps because of Eliot's prescriptions against it. The first poets I fell in love with were the Metaphysical poets. I loved (and still love) the way that intellect and feeling come together in the work of John Donne, Andrew Marvell, and others. I love the wild ingenuity of their best conceits. George Herbert was also a poet who was important to me. So, my initial reading in high school and college was not passionately attached to the Romantic poets. Later, when I read Stevens and then Crane, I began to see the foregrounding of imagination as one of the great projects in poetry. I loved the grandeur of the poetic line in Stevens, and I intuited that the blank verse line connected Stevens to something important, to the great poetic lineage of Romantic poetry—to Wordsworth, Coleridge, and Keats. I didn't have a language for it at the time, but I was discovering the sublime in poetry.

> *I understand your attraction to some aspects of Stevens' work; however, Stevens' epistemological inquiries—in spite of their magnificence and beauty—have always left me feeling that he is someone uncomfortable with the physical world; I don't feel that in your work.*

Well, both Stevens and Moore are poets I admire, but they can be very cool. Stevens has his deep passions, but mostly they are suppressed and have to come steaming to the surface from a long way down. One of the things I saw as my task was to add the heat to whatever I learned from his work. I felt and still feel much closer—in terms of the passions of poetry—to Keats and to Shelley, who give such high priority to emotion. Intensity is all.

My reading of the modern poets was that they offered me wondrously different things, and my task would be to supply some of the things they didn't offer. I felt I had a place at the table. I thought, "What if you took some of that discursive intelligence in Stevens and gave it tremendous warmth and heat? What would happen if a Stevensian poetry was written with the same kind of passion and intensity as, say, others might associate with a poet like

James Wright?" I wanted to keep the intelligence without losing the emotional effect. I learned from Stevens a certain way of thinking in poetry. In terms of emotional temperature, I always felt closer to Hart Crane.

In terms of the passion that I think you're talking about, Crane is probably the polar opposite of Stevens.

I like the way the language moves ahead of the thought in Crane. Crane is especially important to me now, and it's interesting that when I encounter many young poets, they don't know how to read a poet like Hart Crane. He's too baroque, too rich for them. When I first fell in love with Crane, what it meant wasn't so important. It was how it sounded that mattered. I heard the great oracular notes of poetry. I heard the prophetic cadences. I still hear them.

I could make almost no sense of "Atlantis" the first time I read it.

Neither could I, but I felt that glorious upward striving. I felt the urge toward something large and grand and transcendental. I didn't know what it was, but I heard it in the sound of the words. I felt that Crane was lifting me toward something.

You've written very fondly of Robert Frost's work. How does he fit into this picture?

Frost is one of the American poets who has meant the most to me. I love the dark side of Frost. I first discovered the darker Frost when I read Randall Jarrell's two essays on Frost in *Poetry and the Age,* "The Other Frost" and "To the Laodiceans." Those pieces were thrilling to me. I'd only really thought of Frost as the poet of walks and talks in the woods. I didn't cotton to the image Frost cultivated as a Yankee farmer. I didn't yet know about the deeper Frost that Lionel Trilling had called a "terrifying" poet. Because of Jarrell, I began to discover the terrifying, the unremitting, side of Frost. I fell in love with the poem "Desert Places," which is still a poem I love very much. Those dark poems of Frost's gave me a way to think about a language that could articulate the extremes of human feeling.

The two poets who best articulated despair for me—better than I could have it articulated myself—were Hopkins and Frost. When I read Hopkins' late, so-called "terrible sonnets," and when I read "Desert Places," I felt they had articulated an anguish that I, too, had felt, but didn't know how to touch or write about. I began to think about how the formal cadences of poetry could be shaped to those feelings. The poet was a maker who had taken unwieldy feelings and shaped them into something that was, hopefully, enduring.

When we think of Modernism, we might think of the dissolution of metrical poetry in order to accommodate the new modern sensibility and its fragmentation, anxiety, and such. What you seem to be speaking to is the ability of the "old ways" to accommodate these changes in sensibility.

I wouldn't say so much the "old ways" as the "oldest ways," the ways of archaic poetry, of Orphic poetry. I am thinking of a poetry that rises from speech toward song, that builds to a rhythm of incantation. The devices are just a way of working the magic in poetry. Look: Frost was a great modern poet and he wrote mostly iambic pentameter. Stevens wrote wonderfully as a blank verse poet and as a free verse poet. I don't think I would want to sacrifice either of those methods. I think that the dichotomy between so-called formal poetry and free verse is a large mistake in American poetry. Many great poets have used the full resources of the language to articulate the world. Pound is a good example, I think. We wouldn't want to lose the early Imagist free verse poems; nor would we want to throw out the strict meters and rhymes of Mauberly; nor would we want to "sacrifice" some of the incantatory cadences of *The Cantos*.

The story that we tell ourselves that Modernism is the breaking loose into free verse and away from traditional verse is much too simplistic. There's Marianne Moore writing both a syllabic poetry and a free-verse poetry, remaking syllabics to an American idiom. There's William Carlos Williams inventing a new triadic line for American poetry. At the same time, we have Stevens and Crane writing eloquent American poems using the blank verse line. We also have the collage of *The Waste Land*, which does use the devices of iambic pentameter and rhyming to extraordinary effect only to rupture them. The devices of poetry are wide ranging. There are many ways to the promised land.

It's true that we've had—since Milton began to loosen poetry from the bondage of rhyme—an increasing strain of a certain kind of freedom in the versification of poetry. We wouldn't want to lose that. Free verse has been an essential American mode since Whitman, but it's not the only American mode. The stories that we tell ourselves about the history of American poetry are greatly reduced for some poets' polemical ends. When we examine the reality of the different types of poetry that our great poets have written, then we discover that it is quite various and often ties us to the "oldest" traditions in poetry much more than one might think.

That makes sense. When you think about the poets of mid-century—Lowell, Berryman, Sexton, and Plath—they, too, write in many modes.

There's a similar dynamic connected to the so-called Confessionalism of the poets of the Middle Generation. Not many people have thought about the fact that, for instance, the poets of the Middle Generation were masters of the dramatic monologue. Berryman, Lowell, Schwartz, Jarrell, Bishop: all wrote wonderful dramatic monologues. The story of American poetry moving from the forties and fifties and the mode of high artifice to the more confessional one of the late fifties and sixties, written supposedly from a more authentic self, that story is simply not borne out by the nature of the work. For example, I think you have to read *The Mills of the Kavanaughs* as one of the important books in Lowell's development in which he adopts a whole series of fictive voices, voices that were not his own. Those voices help teach him how to take on the voice of a supposed person, "Robert Lowell" in *Life Studies*. My sense of it is that the range of American poetry continues to outstrip the narratives that we create about the historical development of that poetry.

> *So many manifestoes and polemics revolve around those narratives.*

A greatly flawed essay in this regard that's had much too much of an effect is Olson's essay on projective verse. It's part genius, part mumbo jumbo, and it has been badly misused. Olson divides radically between "open" and "closed" poetry. That's a story that poets and critics have gone on telling each other ever since—that there's a closed or academic poetry and an open or nonacademic poetry. This doesn't fit the facts at all. It doesn't fit the facts of Romantic poetry; it doesn't fit the facts of Modernism, and it doesn't fit the facts of what poets have done since the fifties. Yet we go on in a sort of exhausted way, reiterating these old conflicts. Wars are renewed over these tired polemics. Friendships are made and destroyed around this absolutely artificial designation. The notion of an avant-garde in the academy holds absolutely no water at all. I refuse to think in those terms. Consider those sonnets of dark love by García Lorca, which are wonderful, openly homoerotic poems that he wrote before he died. Are we to understand those homoerotic sonnets as traditional or avant-garde? Or take one of the great last poems by César Vallejo, "Black Stone Lying on a White Stone." Are we to think of that as a traditional poem and not an avant-garde poem because it's a sonnet? Or are we to think it's an avant-garde poem because of the startling things that Vallejo does with verb tense and language? Vallejo creates a wild disturbance within the prescribed form. To me, the terms of description that we often use, these categories, are fairly useless, and yet we keep on repeating them. They're unhealthy for American poetry, or what I could call American poetries, something which is rich, vital, and diverse. I don't approve of any restriction that would limit American poetries, especially when it involves throwing out other aesthetics.

One terrific example in this regard: the female lyricists of the twenties. If you look at most literary histories, you'll read about Eliot and Pound and Moore and Williams and Stevens, but you won't hear much about Louise Bogan or Edna St. Vincent Millay or Eleanor Wylie. These poets didn't write free verse; they didn't get with the Poundian program. They continued to write sonnets, and they were widely popular and widely read, but they, in effect, have been written out of literary history. What they were doing is very striking to me; they were remaking the love poem, and they were rethinking it from a female perspective, where the female speaker is not the beloved but the ravenous lover. They engender the sonnet in radically different ways than the sonnet had been previously engendered. If you look at most of our literary histories, you won't find them treated in any detail because the primary narrative that we tell is about Ezra Pound and the success of free verse. The Poundian strain was crucial, but it shouldn't be used to exclude everything else that was written.

> *Of course, what you're speaking to isn't just part of the narrative about modernity. Today we have "Language" poets, "New Formalists," and so on.*

In 1926 Marina Tsvetaeva said in her essay "The Poet on the Critic" that "Poetic schools (a sign of the age!) are a vulgarization of poetry." I think the divisions—neo-Narrative, neo-Formalist, etc.—are not helpful. Our country is so fragmented that these "schools" help give people identities and help them find a way in the world, but to me they are divisive. The loneliness of poets (remember that Richard Howard called his splendidly wide-ranging critical book, *Alone with America*) is a sociological phenomenon. I don't like ways of dividing the pie that exclude people, and I think that the ethos of American poetry should be an inclusive one. It should be open to all kinds of poetry. It's as if poetry is a piano and most poets only know how to play the same two notes. Most of the resources of poetry are lost because of this two-note ethic.

*Your work certainly avoids such reduction. The poetry is very
wide-ranging.*

Thank you for saying so. I've gotten so much from so many different
types of poetry that I've wanted to respond in kind, to give
something back. In many ways, I feel as if the poet is a vehicle, a
vehicle of responses to different feelings and voices and people and
characters. Keats' idea of negative capability has been very important
to me. I take seriously the notion that the poet gives up a personal
identity and is saturated by something else. Whitman is wonderfully
helpful in this regard because he moves up and down the ladder of
being so fluently. I remember the passage:

> Through me many long dumb voices,
> Voices of the interminable generations of prisoners and slaves,
> Voices of the diseas'd and despairing and of thieves and dwarfs,
> Voices of cycles of preparation and accretion,
> And of the threads that connect the stars, and of wombs and of
>   the father-stuff,
> And of the rights of them the others are down upon,
> Of the deform'd, trivial, flat, foolish, despised,
> Fog in the air, beetles rolling balls of dung.

Whitman understands that the poet is a vehicle to everything
alive. The world is permeable. The voices of the enslaved and the
voices of beetles and the voices of thieves and dwarves and the
voices of birds are as important to him as the dominant voices of
history, the voices of the victors. His Orphic calling is a way of
speaking back to power.

It seems to me that as a poet I want to be as open and receptive
to the world as possible, to see the world alive in all its parts.
Whitman loved archaic poetry and he loved ballads and he loved
folk songs and opera and he didn't see any conflict between making
poetry new and returning poetry to the origins of all poetry. He is
a great model for us as American poets because he is so inclusive,
because he fuses traditions, because he takes poetry forward into

the future even as he returns it to its archaic roots. Whitman understood that chants and charms and spells and incantations all have various functions in the world.

In On Love *you have many poems that aren't quite dramatic monologues and aren't quite persona poems. How do you understand the voices in those poems as functioning?*

I think that the notions of dramatic monologue and the notions of persona are too narrow and confining as people usually think of them. This is true even of poets receptive to their use. Of course, there are some poets who are opposed to this sort of poem on principle because they are under the mistaken notion that they only want to speak in their own so-called "authentic" voice. In writing programs, students are frequently given the assignment of writing persona poems, where you take on the voice of another. To me, that doesn't have anything like the kind of emotional authority and weight that I think you feel when you believe you are the vehicle of another voice, where another voice seems to be speaking through you. Where it's both your own voice and another voice speaking at the same time. I believe that in these twenty-five poems with different speakers (from Diderot to Colette) there is also a lone questing speaker, a lover seeking and desiring the absent beloved. There's a dialectic in the poems between separation and fusion, between autonomy and blur, between the lover and the beloved. The voices of the speakers in the poems are ways to think about love. Each one represents some aspect of love. The speaker is at the same time Marina Tsvetaeva or Guillaume Apollinaire or Tristan Tzara and also me. I don't think they are exactly dramatic monologues because I don't think you are meant to believe that the previous historical voices are really speaking. I think you see the poet peeking through the mask, speaking through the voice. It's a little like a drag show where you put on different voices and costumes and they allow you to get at certain feelings and emotions. At the same time, each one tries to be as true as possible to the voice that the poet is inhabiting. The poem tries to get as close as possible to the facts of, say, Tsvetaeva's life. It tries to bring us as close as possible to her poetry, her great rapturous feelings in poetry. I don't know if we have a language for what it means to be both yourself and another in a poem. To see yourself as the vehicle for some other voice that is also your own.

All twenty-five voices together, then, would offer some kind of encyclopedic portrait of modern love. In this regard, for example, it was important for me to have a radically political thinker, such as Bertolt Brecht, in the series. It was important to represent a wildly Dionysian ethic, such as you get in D. H. Lawrence. It was important to try to articulate an incredibly witty lesbian ethic, as in Gertrude Stein. A mythical perspective, as in D. H. Lawrence. A powerfully homoerotic one with the dastardly clever Oscar Wilde. You have a strong feminist argument with the Margaret Fuller poem. A figure who's terrifically important to me in this regard is Emerson because he is such a deep devourer. Emerson believed in the transformational power of love. He was so receptive, so open to all kinds of voices and powers.

I should mention that experimentation of this sort is not, in the body of your work, a new thing.

Yes, this has always been part of my work. I value it. There have been people who have been comfortable with one aspect of my work and uncomfortable with another dimension of it. Both parts of it have always been crucial and integrated. At least they were meant to be integrated. For instance, in my first book, *For the Sleepwalkers*, it was important for me to have waitresses and factory workers and shopkeepers and sweatshop workers and people that I hadn't seen appear in poetry often enough. I wanted to be the vehicle of those voices. I also wanted to be true to my experience of falling in love with art itself. I didn't see any split or difficulty moving between being a waitress in Stonefalls, Arkansas, in one poem and being Paul Klee in another. It was exciting. Baudelaire speaks to this when he says that "the poet enjoys the incomparable privilege that he can, at will, be either himself or another. Like those wandering spirits that seek a body, he enters, when he likes, into the person of any man. For him alone all is vacant . . . ."

In these two distinctions, you're speaking to different voices than you're working with or from. But I can also think of several poems that are personal in a different way, for instance, the elegy "Fast Break" or the sexual epiphany of "The Skokie Theater."

I always felt that the "voice" poems were deceptively personal. I think speaking through another voice is useful and passionate if it allows you to say things you might not otherwise get at. The virtue of this other kind of poem—where the dramatic speaker is clearly someone other than yourself—is that it allows you to get at material that you couldn't otherwise get at. It liberates you. But do you remember that Emily Dickinson said that the speaker in her poems was a supposed speaker, a supposed person? The supposed person was "me" in other poems. But I always thought that there was as much heat in the poems spoken through voices as in those poems. It's true that, especially in the move from *For the Sleepwalkers* to *Wild Gratitude*, there is a change. In the later book I started to use a voice more often that was much closer to my own. I started to mine my own experience more directly. Instead of, say, speaking from the point of view of a poet that's meant a great deal to me, such as John Clare, I wrote "about" John Clare from my own perspective.

I tried in a poem called "Three Journeys" to bring together two diverse elements in my work because I felt they were getting a little schizophrenic—there were the poems that were elegiac and personal, like the memorial poem for my dear and beloved friend Dennis Turner, or the poem about a girlfriend and our first erotic encounter in "The Skokie Theater"—and these other cultural and literary interests. I wanted to unite them, as I felt they were united in me. So in the poem "Three Journeys," a speaker, some version of myself, follows a bag lady through the streets of Detroit and then associates her with John Clare. The poem parallels two journeys—

the journey of John Clare when he escaped from a mental hospital and walked home across England and the journey of a homeless woman as she walked around the streets of Detroit. In the process of writing the poem, I began to feel that in some terrible way I was using the homeless woman in order to say something about the suffering of John Clare, and I began to make that also my subject, to give the homeless woman and John Clare exactly equal weight. One's sympathy needed to go out to them. One needed to approach each of them with one's full range of human response. That was the discovery. The third journey was my own. After that, I realized that it was always crucial to me to bring as much as possible to whomever one is writing about. I don't want to split off the world between those who are literary and those who are not.

Since *Wild Gratitude*, I've written many extremely personal poems, poems that are revealing and try to turn the knife against the self. There are also a lot of family poems in *The Night Parade*, and I tried to place those poems in a larger social and historical context. I wanted them to reverberate outward. I suppose I'd like my poetry to be equally personal and impersonal. There is something intimate and literary in the poems about artists; there is something objective and implacable in the family poems. Joseph Brodsky has a wonderful piece about Cavafy where he describes the two main modes of Cavafy's poetry: one, where he writes poems about fleeting, homoerotic encounters of, say, forty years ago, and two, poems about various minor historical figures, some of whom he has made up, some of whom really existed. Brodsky says that the remarkable thing about Cavafy is that there is something cold and impersonal in the rapturous love poems, and something intimate and personal in the poems about minor historical figures. They have a kind of counter weight. Cavafy is a splendid model in this regard.

In For the Sleepwalkers, *you have a short poem called "Little Political Poem" after Nazim Hikmet. It begins,*

Tonight I saw so many windows

blazing alone, almost blazing together
under a single sky, under so many
different skies all weaving together

through so many different countries . . . .

*This poem's "politics" are so much more subtle and ambiguous than,
perhaps, the political poetry of other writers. And yet it certainly
has a didactic element. What is your understanding of the
relationship between poetry and politics?*

The poet wants justice. And the poet wants art. In poetry we can't
have one without the other. I love Nazim Hikmet, the great Turkish
poet. My poem borrows and adapts one of his images. I picture a
single window blazing alone—an emblem of solitary
consciousness—and imagine it somehow blazing in communion
with all the other singular windows. It's a daydream of unity, a
poem about identity and difference, about the underlying
connection, or near connection, between people. So close together,
so far apart. I love the passionate open-heartedness of Hikmet's
work, but his communist loyalties seem terribly simplistic at this
late date. We can understand how he came to them after all; he
spent all those horrible years in jail.

His poem about the life of the pencil.

That's "Since I Was Thrown Inside," a wonderful poem. So are
"Some Advice to Those Who Will Spend Time in Prison" and
"On Living." He's a heartbreaking Whitmanian poet. I associate
him in my mind with Miguel Hernandez, the splendid poet who
ripened to full maturity during the Spanish Civil War. But Hikmet's
politics also seem naïve. He still believed in communism at a time
when it was, perhaps, still possible to believe in it. But we all know
now that he was mistaken in his faith in communism. He moved
to Russia when he was released from Turkish prison and never
renounced communism. His communism, like Neruda's, seems
terribly misguided to me. I love the sense of brotherhood in Hikmet,

and I love that same sense of brotherhood in Neruda, but I also think they should have brought a little more skepticism to political realities. I have a democratic ethos, but I'm skeptical when it comes to didactic political programs. We don't have a great political poetry in America, perhaps because American poetry is so ahistorical. We have a poor sense of history as Americans, and so we have had to look to other traditions that do have more integrated political poetries. Is it possible to have a poetry that is humanly involved, politically engaged, politically skeptical, and quests for justice?

What of Eastern European poets, particularly the Polish?

I love Polish poetry. I also love much Hungarian and Czech poetry. I hear tonalities in that poetry I don't hear in American poetry. When you read Zbigniew Herbert and Czeslaw Milosz and Wislawa Szymborska, you begin to feel that political engagement in American poetry is often naïve. These are poets who have truly reckoned with what it means to live in the twentieth century. It seems to me that if there is any task or goal for the relationship between poetry and politics, then it's for poetry to be engaged with what it means to live in this century. I'm thinking of a poetry that doesn't turn away from the suffering, the historical calamities, of our century. I'm struck by the fact that the great Polish poets are, in my opinion, historical poets who wanted to become metaphysical ones. They don't want to be mere "witnesses." They don't write the poetry of political "engagement" *per se.* Yet they can't ignore a little thing like the destruction and the occupation of their country. They're really interested in getting at the truth behind the facts. They are skeptical of all "isms." They want to investigate the nature of reality. I see a dialectic in Polish poetry between history and metaphysics, between living inside of time and outside of time. These poets are simultaneously pulled in two directions—toward the historical world and toward the transcendental one. They're compelled to register the fluctuations of change; they're interested in the stability of truth.

The dialectic that you're speaking of made me think of Milosz's series of poems "The World," written during a period of historical extremity yet focused on something beyond that horror.

Exactly. "The World" is a perverse poem. Milosz got a lot of criticism for it at the time because other poets couldn't understand how he could write about such things while the world was being destroyed. That was the point. I love the Hungarian poet, Miklós Radnóti, who came to such a terrible end. In the thirties Radnóti published a book called *In the Footsteps of Orpheus*. It consists of his translations of European poetry—from Horace and Ovid to Goethe and Heine to Apollinaire. What was Radnóti doing translating this poetry while the Germans were getting ready to march into Hungary? I think he was trying to keep alive an idea of Europe at a time when Europe was becoming a site of barbarism. He was asserting the ideal of Europe as a place of civility, and he was doing so against an encroaching darkness. Sometimes translating poetry can be a brave and humane act.

It seems to me that some of the interest in the work of poets and writers like Radnóti who were, literally, martyred for the word, comes out of an homage to the extremity from which these writers wrote. Writers in America won't experience anything on a similar scale . . .

Let's hope not.

. . . so they lament the lack of "depth" in their own work and try to assuage this anxiety by praising poets who have died for the word.

We have to watch that. I remember Milosz saying, "You American poets would envy the hunchback his hump." We don't want to go so far as, say, George Steiner has gone and say that poetry flourishes under totalitarianism. I think for example of all those poets—and potential poets—who died at the hands of the Germans. I remember a debate between George Steiner and Joseph Brodsky on television. Steiner said that totalitarianism is good for poetry because poets have to find ways to circumvent it, and they rise to the occasion. But Brodsky would have none of it. He said that freedom is the most beautiful thing of all. We shouldn't forget the beauty of freedom. And we don't have to envy the hunchback his hump. There's plenty of suffering around us. We live in this century, too.

In your work of the last several years, I've seen a turn toward pursuit of the ineffable; how do you understand the relationship between poetry and religiosity, poetry and the spiritual?

The sacred is a great subject in poetry. For poetry. I am deeply interested in what you might call unauthorized testimony. It's true that in my work there has been an increasing interest in the divine, in poetry as a quest for the divine. I always loved Metaphysical poetry, but as a young poet the ineffable didn't seem like my subject. I saw spiritual matters as crucial to poetry, but I didn't see the quest for transcendence as part of my own poetic project. That changed when I began to write the poems that became *Earthly Measures*. The figures in *Earthly Measures* become vehicles of an argument about transcendence. I think that *Earthly Measures*, as a book, is that argument about transcendence—-whether this world is enough or whether we need some other world. There's a tremendous longing for some other world operating in the poems. There's also a critique of that longing. I think of the book as a kind of pilgrimage, a search for the divine. At the very end of that book it turns away from the other world toward this one. The philosophical and religious thinker who has meant a great deal to me is Simone Weil. She thinks so hard about transcendence and the quest for it. She links the quest for transcendence to the suffering of people around her. There's a tremendous social consciousness and sympathy running through her work. I was moved to poetry by two particular elements in her life and work. One is the year she worked in a factory. The other is her three mystical contacts with Christianity.

She was driven to her knees.

A thrilling experience. She had such a deep spiritual hunger. It was matched only by her formidable intellect. I wanted to see if I could dramatize those three experiences in a poem. Simone Weil's mystical contacts are the far end—one end point—of *Earthly Measures*. The thing that troubles me most about Weil is her hatred of the body, her turning away from earthly concerns. I don't critique that element of her in my book of poems, but I critique it insofar as it is present in myself. I love Weil's notion that unmixed attention is prayer. In the last poem of *Earthly Measures*, "Earthly Light," the Dutch painters of the seventeenth century are held up as a model of an art that turns not to the other world, but to this one.

> Because this world, too,
> needs our unmixed attention,
> because it is not heaven
>
> but earth that needs us, because
> it is only earth—limited, sensuous
> earth that is so fleeting, so real.

The argument in my other books has much more to do with affirmation and despair. Each book raises the question of whether or not it is still possible to affirm in spite of all the evidence. I love the statement of Roethke's that "despite the dark and drek, the muck and mire of these poems, I want to be one of the happy poets." *In Wild Gratitude* I make it pretty clear that I, too, want to be one of the joyous poets, I want to affirm. But I don't want to do it naively, by turning away from the sufferings of the world. The argument about affirmation and despair continues to run through *The Night Parade*. I see these books as journeys, as undergoings, as my own dark nights of the soul. The question of affirmation and despair takes on a religious dimension in *Earthly Measures*. The end of "Earthly Light" turns to earthly love, to eros. It led me to the poems of *On Love*.

Here we are at the end of the twentieth century; do you think that the affirmation you were pursuing is possible? Are you a "happy poet?"

Well, praise and lamentation are two of the deepest impulses in lyric poetry. The earliest poems we have—the Egyptian Pyramid texts, the ancient Hebrew poems, or the earliest Greek poems—all include poems of lamentation and poems of praise. To me, the two elements go hand in hand. I wouldn't want a poetry of praise that doesn't take up the counter truth of lamentation, and I wouldn't want a poetry of lamentation that doesn't remember the gifts, to praise. Rilke says something like this in the *Duino Elegies*—praise walks in the land of lamentation.

Simone Weil's "gravity" and "grace."

That's a glorious way of putting it: the descent of gravity, the ascent of grace. Both things live in us. I find the impulse to praise in the earliest poems, in the great archaic poems of people everywhere, in Christopher Smart and Walt Whitman and Gerard Manley Hopkins. It's one of the deepest and strongest impulses in poetry. I'd love to be a poet of praise. So, too, the poetry of grief and lamentation is one of the deepest and most longstanding elements in poetry. The elegy is one of our necessary forms as we try to come to terms with the fact that people around us die, that we, too, will die. We need the ritual occasion, ritual making of the elegy. That dimension of poetry is fundamental. I would very much like to see myself as part of both traditions. To me, the two greatest impulses in poetry are elegy and praise. I would love to write a poetry that brings those two impulses together.

Christopher Howell was born in Portland, Oregon, in 1945. The author of seven books of poetry, including Sweet Afton, The Crime of Luck, Sea Change, *and* Memory and Heaven, *Christopher Howell has been praised by writers ranging from James Tate to William Tremblay. That range of praise speaks to the variety of quality work Howell has produced—as well as the uniqueness of his vision. Lyrical and narrative threads, sharp declaration and musing meditation, clear imagery and surreal atmosphere, incisive monologues and dreamy visions: Howell's poetry draws on a variety of traditions and practices. Editor of the literary journal* Willow Springs *and the successful, independent Lynx House Press, he lives in Spokane, Washington, where he teaches in the M.F.A. program at Eastern Washington University.*

CHRISTOPHER HOWELL

Nicholas Twemlow and I spoke with Christopher in Emporia, Kansas, during spring 1995.

For the last seven years, you've been the editor for the Bluestem Poetry Prize, and in the course of that service, you've probably read thousands of manuscripts.

I believe when we began, in our first several years, we had 350-400 manuscripts and then it shot up to 600. And it's been climbing slowly for the last three years; we're up to about 680.

Can you say anything about the poetry that you see in these manuscripts? Do you see the poetry becoming more homogenized, more of a certain type? Formally? Thematically? Are most of the poems lyrics or narrative? What common motifs do you see in these manuscripts?

I do see the poems as predominately narrative; I guess that's the current mode of preference. And the poetry that doesn't stretch itself toward a story tends to stretch itself toward discourse, toward the presentation of ideas as a kind of justification for itself. That is, the poetry which seeks to become fully realized in the emotional response of the reader is in the minority, just judging by the books and manuscripts I read. It seems to me that there's a sort of herding instinct in the arts, and it's probably always been true. People imitate what they conceive to be successful, and not always what they respond to most directly or passionately. So, I suppose you could say there is some cynicism filtering into the compositional process, but this is even more true, for me, in the published work I read. I see less experiment, or what looks to me like legitimate experiment, than I'd really like to see.

Something you said about narrative poetry interests me. I also think of narrative poems in terms of two types. First, the narrative poem that is event-driven—a poem that wants to tell what happened. And second, narrative poems that just go through the motions of telling a story in order to reach some ideological point at the end. Is that the same distinction you're talking about?

The end isn't always ideological. Sometimes it might be more properly described as aesthetic. I see a lot of people puzzling over how they apply a kind of aesthetic mask to the poems, something which will disguise their confusion about what should go into them. Again, I'm not just speaking of Bluestem submissions here, many of which are very strong; my conclusion about a lot of poems now, no matter how well written, is that they aren't about anything. And what I mean by that is not that they don't have subjects, but that they don't have results.

What about the formal aspects of the poetry? Does the "herding effect" also lead to sloppiness?

I don't see a lot of strong formal consideration in these poems. Period. I see people worrying on line-endings. Of course, that's in the current mode to just, you know, open the line, the line that's not end-stopped, that is basically predicated on the sentence. I could probably go back through fifty percent of the manuscripts that we get at Bluestem and reconfigure most of the poems as prose and you'd never, reading them over, realize there was ever any kind of poetic intention. So all of that intention, if you like, that project, is not really in the language, but in the simplest aspect of the poem's structure, the line-end. Which seems kind of cosmetic. I would like to go the other way; I would like to be able to look at poems that no matter what the configuration you put them in, they would still have some kind of drive, a kind of compression and intensity in the language itself that would finally work. Maybe it wouldn't work equally well in every structure, but it would work in some way to begin to call forth a response that the reader could not hold back. I don't have that kind of response to a lot of what I read. You've heard this criticism before, and there are many different ways of saying it. You could say, for instance, that many of the poems that are supposedly part of our cultural conversation today do not seem to have been necessary poems. Again, no matter how clarified their technical elements, a lot of what passes for important work is simply poetry written on a certain subject or because of a certain excuse; the writer is not driven to write by this cloud of interior mysteriousness that finally must be penetrated by language. When we speak of this mystery, we're speaking about the complexity of the individual, but it's the world, too. Political poems—all kinds of poems with some kind of public focus—are related to the complexity of the individual, also, or they aren't poems; they're just political.

> *NT: Something I've experienced in workshops is a sort of silencing of poetry: seeing it on the page and occasionally reading it aloud, but for the most part, studying the poem on the page. I think there is something different in our response to the textures of the poem when it is a physical process. What are your responses physically to poems that strike you?*

Well, there's the old Dickinson line about the top of one's head coming off. I think when a poem works like I want a poem to work, it essentially creates a disruption in the time continuum. I no longer care that time is passing.

NT: Can you describe this disruption?

I'm probably not second by second aware of that response. I can become aware of it while I'm reading without shorting out the response if the poem is good enough. Sometimes, if my response does short out, it's because I've discovered that the poem is a trick and not a poem. But usually, if it's a real thing, there's nothing reading it can do to screw it up. I like the feeling that a sort of invisible freight train pushing me through life has suddenly backed off, and there is the world of one's self. I use self in the sense of the totality of the self, the conscious and the unconscious together, a clear view of oneself as a whole being. Not a fragmented consciousness shoved around and connected to all kinds of lineal contrasts. That's what a good poem does for me. And it does it better than, say, a good work of art or music, although those things do something like that; it's just that language seems to have my emotional number.

Can you think of an example of a poem that you go back to for this experience?

"To the Muse," the James Wright poem. It gets me every time. In spite of the fact that I've had it memorized for thirty years. Some others by contemporaries would be Michael Heffernan's "Lacrimae Rerum," Albert Goldbarth's "The Story of Dorsett," Heather McHugh's "Third Person Neuter," Michael Van Walleghen's "The Spoiled Child," Bill Tremblay's "Song for Jeanie," James Grabill's "Suddenly Tonight I Am Listening," William Ryan's "Devolution and The Rigorous Language of Science," Robert Hass's "Meditation at Lagunitas," "Song of Myself," Dickinson's "There's a certain slant of light . . ." and many, many others.

I realize this is something that's difficult to talk about, but is there some feeling that you get as a reader that tells you a writer has penetrated into the mysterious? Is there something in the language? Are there specifics that, after the fact, you can pick out as contributing elements that have made a poem and fueled the intensity of the experience? Or does such an experience ultimately remain something amorphous, something you can't talk about?

I think there are a number of ways of talking about it, but that, in effect, they comprise a complex of their own, similar to the poem itself. Because there's no diagrammatic or Aristotelian means that describes it to me. And I think that's wholly proper. The good poem ultimately defies that kind of translation or explanation. I would say the poem that would do this would have to have words that resonate. Maybe not all of them, but enough of them that resonate, not just on the surface, but back through all of the various implied meanings to the mystery of why there should be such a word: all the way back into its own silence. And there should be enough of these that, I guess, your own wonder is continually renewed as you read through. And it's not even just exactly the words themselves, but sometimes the gestures in the poems. I think of that line in "To The Muse" where Wright says, "Still, it lets you / Walk about on tiptoe if you don't / Jiggle the needle. / It might stab your heart, you see."

That "you see"; I don't know how to explain why that performs what I've been describing as a resonance, that gesture coming off an explanation into an appeal for agreement which is in itself rhetorical. Of course you see. But you also see, or feel, let's say, that the emotional weight of the simple utterance "you see" is so great, it is as though the reader spoke those words, spoke them to a child. And that poem, or any poem that is going to work the way I'm suggesting, has to work as though the reader composes it while reading it. Has to. So, in a way, it's your (the reader's) experience. Not experience written about, but experience itself, the experience of knowing.

The intensity that you're talking about connects to Poe's belief that the lyrical impulse is central to poetry, how the long poem is just a string of lyrics with "filler" in between—we can't be elevated out of time for fifty cantos.

Well, I think we can, if the cantos are in some way distinguishable, knowable, from the whole. Pound's *Cantos* acknowledge this by being progressive and interrelated without being interdependent. Pound knew that one long poem, without some kind of structural breathing, is finally going to faint. And that wasn't what he wanted.

The rag-bag of many things, including the moment of lyrical intensity. So, in some ways, there's really a whole different set of criteria that one would bring to bear on the long poem. Can you think of any recent long poems in the last five, six years, that have interested you and perhaps say why?

I liked Brendan Galvin's *Wampanoag Traveler*, though it isn't absolutely continuous, has little breaks and subtitles and so forth. And I liked portions of Mark Strand's *Dark Harbor*, though it sometimes seemed held together more by shape than anything else. I thought Primus St. John's *Dreamer* was terrific, but like the Galvin book, it has a sure historical context to help it along. Then there's Nathan Whiting's *Buffalo Poem*.

The Postmodernist long poem? We had a Bluestem submission last year from a guy named Brian Johnson; it was a finalist: one long monologue with elements of both Ashbery and the Spanish Surrealists. Very interesting, but I do not know who, besides Bluestem or Lynx House, would publish it: the commercial presses would, I think, find it insufficiently dry, for something supposedly experimental. The university presses, mostly, would find it too experimental. The more active small presses (like Sun & Moon) would find it insufficiently ideological, aesthetically.

Have you read Peter Dale Scott's Coming to Jakarta?

No, I've not read that. While we're on the subject of long poems though, I should mention Bill Tremblay's book, which he's turned into a novel. I've really never believed that. I saw it in manuscript when it was a two-hundred page poem called "The June Rise," which was the title it has appeared with, as a novel. I think it has just marvelous properties. And part of its strength, again, is that it provides some way-stations where perspective is offered, both backward and forward. I think the endless poem is a lot harder to get hold of: one that has no subtitles, no sections, no natural breaking points. Not that such can't be written or hasn't been written. I'm just not sure our rapid-fire culture is equipped to process that kind of experience, unless we are talking about Dante, where we have a whole moral and celestial schematic in place and we have definite narrative lines and we have a whole mythological structure for reference. I mentioned the book by Brian Johnson; I liked it, but it was a very uncommon piece. In general, I would think the Postmodernist long poem is likely to concern what postmodern life seems to be for the majority of people: difficult, but not unusual; unhappy, but not desperate. Or the Postmodernist long poem might be something so purely theoretical it offers no emotional access.

The Maximus *poems.*

Yeah, the *Maximus* poems are really attempts at elucidating Olson's compositional theories. I think that's the proper way to read them, and, in fact, having read them again not long ago, it seems to me the only way you can read them. Except in terms of their ideology, they're pretty opaque anyway.

That's very distant from the emotional, almost religious intensity you were talking about a few minutes ago. A much colder interaction with the text.

Yes. That's not to say that persons who accept Olson's theories, who try to work them out, don't occasionally, or maybe even often, write perfectly luminous, mysterious, spiritual poems (though I am not aware of any "long" ones), and mean them that way. But Olson himself did not seem to do so.

Many of the manuscripts that you receive surely come from creative writing graduates. Do you think that the creative writing program as an institution somehow feeds into what these poems are lacking in terms of intensity, craft, and mystery?

Well, they're very crafty. And I think many of these poets are quite young, the people who submit to this contest.

Do you buy the notion of the "McPoem?"

We used to talk about the "Iowa poem." Which is another version of that.

What's the "Iowa" poem?

The "Iowa poem" was a 37-line smoothy, which, at the end, lit up a cigar. It didn't have any real reason for being, but it had no flaws. It had a perfect surface. And, lest some latter-day Iowites take me amiss, it was Iowa Workshop people who came up with this term. They saw it themselves. They understood that, yeah, in a way, if you concentrate only on technique, then maybe you finally get poems that are all technique. And there is lots of that. But some of these people will grow up. They'll have experiences that are undeniable and utterly mysterious, and penetrating these, knowing them fully, will require some kind of language they do not have and that will have to be discovered. I'm not terribly worried about, say, the impact of the creative writing program on the culture. It is sometimes annoying that there is so much impact on the literary economy in the short run. In terms of grants, awards, publications. There's a lot of ready-mix stardom. That really isn't my concern anyway. My concern, as a writer, is my own work. As an editor, my concern is finding authentic and interesting work, which I'm always able to find. So, I don't have any real disparaging remarks about the writing programs other than this notion of the M.F.A. as a career-track degree: university teaching as a career-track is misleading for students. Not because the jobs aren't there, although there aren't that many, but because the jobs that are there, the kinds of jobs that they'll be doing, are really a lot more demanding and intrusive than the jobs they would have been asked to do twenty years ago.

You don't just get a creative writing position and then they leave you alone and let you write poems and teach classes. Now, the new creative writing teacher must consider that he/she must, in order to feel a success, "get on" in the academic world. So, you really have to belong to any number of organizations and care about them and participate in their conferences and run for office, etc., just like scholarly colleagues. Now—ask anyone who has come out of an M.F.A. program in the last ten years—you have to write essays and publish them prominently; preferably you should have a book of them so that your critical colleagues can see that you're a serious intellectual. And there's a great deal of emphasis on the press that publishes both your creative and critical work. It used to be a tenet, among writers at least, that books were to be approached on their own terms. I see that fading in the glare of the Reaganization of all economies in the last decade. Now people are encouraged to read the impress and the acknowledgments page and make judgments about a book's content before reading it; and the judgments really can't be about its quality but are instead about its negotiability in the marketplace of promotions, jobs, grants, and reading fees. I don't think this is the way to live; it makes doing original work difficult.

Which connects back to your earlier comments about the "herding" process.

Yes, and so it bothers me a little that so many people are in a way being prepared to enter a professional context that is in decline. Maybe that's too strong; but at the very least, college teaching, for the vast majority of writers, is a meaner and more difficult occupation than it was a generation ago, while for a tiny minority it's an unbelievable gravy train requiring practically no actual work. And the creative writing programs I don't think are saying that. What they're saying is the job market is really tough and if you're going to catch up with it, by God, you'd better get up to speed! My impulse is to slow everybody down. Slow it down. Find something essential. Hold on to that. Listen to your own breathing a little bit more. So, I depart, not categorically, but stiputively, from some of what's happening in the creative writing programs. And I don't want to point fingers or blame anybody. These people who put these programs together are urgently concerned for their students. They want them to get jobs. So they're pushing them and pushing themselves. But one should remember: failure to get a job, or a sufficiently prestigious job, in the academy is not a meaningful comment upon someone's talent, character, or anything else. And on the other side, a lot of truly crappy writers teach at prestigious institutions. It is best to think of writing as the career, and teaching—banking, baking, candlestick making—as a job. And it is best to measure success as a writer in terms of one's own sense of excitement and growth in the writing, not in terms of publications (though important for other reasons), prizes, and teaching positions. As a creative writing student in the seventies, I was told and shown these things. The competitive atmosphere in the country now is such that many writers who teach have forgotten that "career" need not be materially defined. But before I forget to say it: I still love teaching and I care about my students, but university teaching is not my career.

What Modernist writers do you find yourself returning to, rereading, trying to get a better hold of? Which ones do you like?

That's a good question. I've turned most frequently in the last five years to writers who have been skipped over. I think of Roethke coming in at the end of the high Modernist period, for instance, and nobody quite knowing whether or not he ought to be crowned or what. Was he a Modern? Certainly he was nuts enough. I like to spend time with him, because he seems to me a transitional figure of a kind. I like Weldon Kees who had a kind of a renegade sensibility. I think he understood the Moderns that came before him and incorporated much of their toughness. But there was something about them—maybe their upper class *hauteur*—that he really distrusted and I like his distrust; it's part of what makes him original. I read Robinson Jeffers, who was ideologically opposed to a lot of the Modernist project, but who's clearly a Modernist in his applications, in the pattern of decision that he imposed on the writing itself. I don't really go back to Stevens that much or to Eliot. And those were sort of the big band-wagon guys when I was in my twenties, studying literature and writing. Marianne Moore and H.D. I still read and enjoy. I've always had a preference, though, for Pound. Part of that, I guess, because he, again, is sort of a loon, and you realize that you don't have to take everything he says literally, because he certainly didn't. And he was just disconnected enough, and egomaniacal enough, to say and do some things that were pretty much impossible for everyone else. And as a technician, as let's say a person who is seeking to discover form, or the potentials of form, I don't think we've fully understood him, yet. So I still read and reread *The Cantos*. I like to read them aloud, even though the Greek defies me half the time.

And the ideograms?

Some of those I actually know. I usually don't admit, publicly, my affection for Pound because the political shit has gotten on him to a point where you can only discuss him now with an asterisk. It's incorrect to admire him. I read Whitman frequently. I've always read Emily Dickinson.

> *You mentioned a distance from Eliot and Stevens and your attraction to Pound, and with Pound, whatever the emotion may be—anger, disgust, frustration—he doesn't mask it. The emotion is something that he vents. Whereas, in Stevens, "the mind of winter" is often the prevalent one. How do you feel about someone like Williams, where that distance between self, poetry, and the world isn't there, where the poem is more transparent? Do you read him much?*

I don't read him very much, although of course I did read him exhaustively in graduate school. He doesn't seem to me as rich potentially. He's very interesting. He's kind of comforting, too, in the sense that he speaks in such a familiar and accessible voice. Even in *Paterson*, which is, intellectually, very complex, the language itself, word by word, is right there, rather intimate; it's your language. So you feel invited in, even if it's a very strange room once you get in. But, in the end, I find Williams an American poet in more ways than one. Or, let's say, "the poet of America" in more ways than one. I think that his language wants to imply objectivity, and the particular way he does that implies a kind of affection for the material world, which is fine, except that in America the material leads to the technological and industrial and beyond . . . to Thorstein Veblen's vision, now passé, and then on to Wal-Mart. It's not quite worship, and it's not as obvious as it is in Sandburg, but it is there. And the way in which so-called material values are evolving in the postindustrial world is so disturbing to me that I stand back from Williams I guess.

So you don't feel he penetrates the mysterious either?

I don't find it as powerful an impulse in him. He is happy to interact with the surfaces pretty much. Once in a while he gives you a sense of the depth of the moment, which I like very much. That poem about the housewife, for instance, the moment when the bottom just drops out of one of those lines, is very nice. The feeling of a person having a kind of emotional response and not diverting it, letting it happen "as I bow and pass by smiling." You find moments like that in Williams, and I like those moments, but, as I said, I don't spend as much time with him as with others. I read Lowell, Robert Lowell, another person who crawls in at the fag end of Modernism. He was in line to take over the crown and throne from Frost; and that in itself is interesting, because I think Lowell himself believed that, too. So, his belief may be responsible for some of the high tone in his early work. And then when he hits the sixties, his tone changes a good deal, I think because he recognized the very idea of a literary giant was an empty benefice and very controlling; believing in it was like believing in a patriarchal deity who is temperamental, arbitrary, and asleep most of the time.

Is there a particular work you would point to?

Notebook is the one that really looked to me like a change. If you compare it to *Lord Weary's Castle*, you can hardly believe it's the same guy.

> *One of Pound's achievements is hammering home the importance of literature in different tongues. The Romance traditions, Oriental poetry, the Provençal poetry. In many ways, with* Cathay *he really stimulated the interest of many poets in Chinese and Japanese literature. What literature in translation do you find yourself going to? What do you think some of the great contributions of translation have been to American poetry in this century?*

Well, to begin, Bly did American writing a terrific favor by becoming obsessed with Latin American poets. I think he may have overstated the case for translation as against what he saw as smugness, a kind of insularity in American literature in the fifties. Nevertheless, no one else has put the case for translation any more effectively than he did, overstatement or not.

> *The contemporary poet-critic Sam Hamill is certainly a champion of translated work.*

He is, isn't he? Well, poets Bly introduced, through his books and his *Fifties, Sixties,* and *Seventies,* what have become known as the Latin-American Surrealists—although that never seemed to quite fit—those are poets I still read quite frequently. There is a noticeable difference from one translation to the next, but that really doesn't diminish my appreciation; in fact, looking at these texts, it's always clear that there's a different cultural sensibility in operation here from the one that I am automatically accustomed to, which is a kind of refreshment. I read Tranströmer, and he's someone I became interested in because of Bly's translations. I don't know Robert's actual familiarity with the Spanish—I don't know how those translations are done—but I do know that he has an excellent command of the Scandinavian languages, truly excellent. So I trust those absolutely. I had a great time reading Tranströmer, and once again with his work, you can see a unique cultural perspective layered into the language, and even a bad translation probably couldn't get it out. So, one of the values of translation, surely, is that it reminds us our language is a mode, some kind of organic mirror, which can show us otherwise virtually invisible patterns of cultural exchange and value. And there are hundreds and hundreds, thousands, of these throughout the world, all those world views and teleological longings embedded in sounds and marks! It is really important to recognize that your own native speech, as well as thought, is only one among all these other embodiments of consciousness.

To get back to your question, I think American poetry has changed enormously since the fifties, and the availability of poetry in translation has had, and continues to have, a large role in that change. It used to be said, rightly, about something always being lost in translation. Frost quipped that what was lost in translation was the poetry. But I'm not convinced about that, finally. It's a sort of psychological travelog that you take when reading a poem that's adequately translated out of the Persian, the Swedish, the Spanish. It's opened up American writers' sense of form. In the early fifties many people were really reaching back into the English tradition for definitions or templates of a poem. Well, the English is just one tradition. All those fifties and sixties translations of Lorca and Neruda and Vallejo and Trakl finally forced the question: why should writers learn only from their direct cultural and linguistic antecedents?

And as for Cathay?

The book was mismarked somewhat by the hue and cry, the howl of linguists, who proclaimed immediately that Pound was an imposter, that he was basically making these things up. *Cathay* did not, at first, get wide distribution or serious study because of that. And you don't really get anything else Chinese until Arthur Waley comes along and then Rexroth. Waley did that Knopf book, which I think was picked up by a book club and went into thousands of American homes; my uncle, an engineer, had one. And those are excellent translations.

What other international poetry do you read?

I like to read poems in Italian just for the sound. And, although my Spanish is absolutely rudimentary, I like to read Spanish poems. I particularly like Vicente Aleixandre. I like a lot of Vallejo, although Eshleman's translation does not move me as much as some others. I did a little work in Chinese, more than fifteen years ago. I worked for five years to translate a little group of poems that I liked and that seemed to me simple enough that I could get them. I finally produced a manuscript of twenty-some pages that is probably horribly flawed, and I don't even know if I can call the poems translations. But I put a certain value on the activity itself, even if I don't really know the language very well, because it nails your attention to the words, to all the shadings of nuance. Even the words that you don't know, in some ways your struggle to know them heightens your—whatever the inquisitive organ is, whether it's the ear or the eye or something imbedded in the term sensibility.

So it's not just the reading of translations that's good to do: translation itself can be a kind of healing dance. Kinnell says that you shouldn't do it too much because it becomes seductive in itself, and you start getting all of the pleasure of writing poems without having to do all of the work. That you shouldn't allow yourself too much of that. But I always had to work so hard doing these things that it was never a problem for me. Someone is going to publish that little book of Chinese poems, I think. I've held onto it for years.

Translation is one of the five legitimate types of criticism according to Pound.

I think that's right, if you consider criticism a heartfelt and genuine investigation rather than, let's say, an attempt to demonstrate, and thereby possess, the ultimate interpretation of something. I have also played around with translations from Swedish and Italian.

Is it something that you recommend to your students?

What I do with the undergraduates is provide them with a text in a foreign language and tell them they have to produce a translation, but that they can't look at any dictionaries, that they have to intuit, to respond to this strange pattern of sound and morphology. And, oddly enough, it has something like the same effect that doing an actual translation has. It releases them a little bit from, let's say, the tyranny of intention. I mean, they are usually so driven by intention in their work that they can scarcely attend to what they are actually writing. Intention overshadows the work; this exercise helps bring them back to the page itself, to the sounds, the shapes of the words, the ink. Graduate students I usually encourage to try to do some translations, no matter how many days it takes them, no matter how hard it is. I just think it's good for the soul.

And certainly invigorating in terms of working with syntax and the possibilities of a sentence. A related question: in the last thirty years, we've seen more and more poetry translated from Eastern European languages, poetry that has come out of contexts of suffering and oppression, "poetry of witness." What is your take on the American interest in and celebration of work out of these contexts? Do you think it stems from guilt?

Actually, I don't think there has been a whole lot of celebration of their work; I think we tend rather to celebrate the individuals.

Do you think there's a hierarchy of "who has endured the most" that guides some of the interest in this work?

There is that, and I think Americans are sensible of their degree of blessing with respect to everyday life; the fact that in many, many societies around the world, people have known and/or continue to experience profound and widespread oppression. In this country, while there are oppressions of various kinds and of various groups, the majority of people are more or less left alone—I'm speaking of *direct* oppressive intervention; we have *plenty* of indirect intervention. And, in the past twenty-five years, we've come to realize that that's unique. It's just not the way life is everywhere. So, the treatment of Eastern European writers may be partially guilt-driven, but I don't see a strong, definite response to the *work itself* as political. Many writers and teachers have an innate distrust of political writing if the subtext of the word "political" is leftist. One of the good reasons for this distrust is that in a lot of so-called political writing, the politics overpower the writing, and you can see that very quickly. One of the bad reasons is that we just don't know how to respond to suffering, and our naïve approach to some of this work you're talking about reveals this.

We believe—let's say America generally believes—in the magnificence of our "system," and if other people haven't achieved a perfect system, what can we do about it? I mean, should I be expected to sell my car and give the money to some Cambodian? That kind of thing. If you really take the political message and you say that poems by Jiménez should be read literally, then it's like taking the words of Christ literally. You have to *do* something. In America we don't want to do anything. Or we want to keep doing what we've been doing. So, I think there's a certain amount of intentional ignorance in this response. We can look at our recent political history and see that, politically, Americans are willing themselves into unconsciousness. You don't elect Ronald Reagan as President of the United States if you're really on top of the game. People wanted to forget the game.

Presently we live in a somewhat politically tumultuous time in this country. How do you understand the poet's role in our country;

for example, if he or she thinks something is reprehensible like the
cutting of financial support to various social or environmental
programs, what is his or her response? What is the relationship
between poetry and the political sphere?

Well, I think that we have internalized Aristotle in our Western
societies. We understand our lives in terms of categories, and we
can see that the maintenance of good order as we define it is in
some ways reliant upon maintaining these distinctions, these
categories. So you have "work" and "poetry" and "church" and "sex"
and various other pigeonholes. And there's "politics," too. I don't
think people who like poetry are entirely immune to this, although
they are more likely to be aware of their alienation and lack of
integration than lots of other people—people who don't read poetry,
don't write, and don't care about it—would be. But, in terms of
response, I don't think the poet responds *because* he/she is a poet,
and I don't think anyone is bound to respond in any particular way...
I mean, just because you're a poet does not mean you have to write
poems about social and political issues that involve or attract you.
But I do think that the integrated person acts in accordance with
his or her concern. If funding is being withdrawn from a program
you consider essential, you go to meetings or write letters or do
canvassing *or* write poems or all of those things. And if you're
outraged about Bosnia or Newt Gingrich or the Trilateral
Commission, you express that clearly and you try to be effective.
What you don't do, if you care and if you want your life to stay
whole, is nothing.

Such categorizing is very distant from the dynamic you were
talking about earlier, the fact that, when you're reading a great
poem, you're confronted by the bare "self."

That's right. It is distant, and it accounts for the position of poetry
in American society. Poetry doesn't reinforce those categories; it
breaks them down, and people don't want them broken down,
because when they are broken down, finally, you have to integrate

your life. And when you do that, then there are all kinds of things you have to give up and change. Political poetry when insistent and accurate and timely almost always calls for more than just a "Yeah, right on." I remember during the Vietnam War, particularly, that it was understood—and not just in the realm of literature— that many of these distinctions were either blurred or broken down, so that people attending a reading against the war would come up afterward and burn their draft card—people who didn't ordinarily read poetry, let's say, but who understood that some response was called for beyond silent agreement. The context for that kind of response is quite dispersed or maybe it's there but is just diaphanous right now. I don't know. Carolyn Forché says that writing poems is itself an inherently political activity. I've heard that for years, and I don't buy it. It seems self-congratulatory to me, and it suggests that if you write a poem about some issue, then you've done your bit, stuck your neck out sufficiently. I don't mean to put Carolyn down— she's stuck her neck out plenty, and she had her reasons for using that line—but I couldn't use it; I'd be embarrassed.

You had a seminar here recently about literature and the Vietnam War at which several writers talked about the war and their work. I can think of a number of contemporary writers— Bruce Weigl, John Balaban, and Yusef Komunyakaa—who are veterans and write poetry with a political bent. Does their work somehow bridge the categorical divisions you were talking about earlier? How do you think that war shaped a writer's consciousness?

Oh man. I can only try to respond. The experience of Vietnam or of the military during the Vietnam War was way beyond disillusioning to a generation that had grown up on John Wayne movies, that had, really, just grown up to believe that the description of America and the world which America had evolved in order to protect its economic interests was literal. I mean, that's no secret, right? That description was destroyed by the experience of the war and by the experience of the military itself, which was in no way benign, mostly unconscious, full of banality, cruelty, stupidity, and waste. Arrogance, on and on. So the people who went through that experience, whether they were of a literary turn of mind or not, were really—let's say—"liberated from their programming" in ways a lot of other people weren't. You simply could not believe in that billboard poster of the happy man, wife, child and Plymouth. You couldn't believe in *Father Knows Best* or *Leave It To Beaver* or *Ozzie and Harriet*. None of that was even an issue for these writers who survived the war. So what's an issue? Primal stuff: power, sex, madness, justice, the truth. Those things, and you can see it in Komunyakaa's work clearly. He doesn't care about anything else, so that's what he writes about. And he writes very well and so even if he wrote about trivial stuff, his skill would be recognizable. But I really think it's the emphasis that's brought him the notoriety he deserves. It comes out of the war, and a lot of other writers were shaped by it, too. John Balaban is one of them, Weigl another. W.D. Ehrhart. There's a writer out in Arizona, his name is Lee Vandermar, who's a Vietnam vet and as good a poet as I know, but who won't publish.

Why?

I hesitate to say too much in speaking for him, but it seems to me because to publish is to in some way participate in this suspect system, by asking for or accepting its acknowledgment. And maybe, from his point of view, the system is more than suspect, maybe destructive. More than that, maybe evil. The war shaped his thinking, which shaped this point of view, which is extreme, perhaps because his experience was extreme. But he still writes poems, hasn't given up on language as a means to knowledge. And maybe some day the world will see those poems. I hope so.

NT: What about the impact of such competition and reward upon the writer? For me, looking toward enrolling in an M.F.A. program, I feel that I'm competing with other writers with whom I may share many things and with whom I would prefer to sit down and talk. Poets competing for grants and award monies—

this creates a strange environment. Aside from not really looking at the heart of the work, it creates competition that could be destructive.

To take one particular tack with the question—you could say, well, in terms of the technical proficiency of the different poets, there's always going to be some more or less legitimate comparison. But it's also true, going another way, that good poets don't compare— as good poems, like friends, don't compare. Also, going another way, such comparisons are time-bound. The implication of a response of, say, an M.F.A. selection committee, may be that "this person is a good poet and this person is not." Whereas in fact, if the same committee could assess the work of these two writers over twenty years, it might not be able to make a qualitative differentiation. And if pushed, I think most people on selection committees would agree: we haven't created any kind of mechanism, any means by which it's possible to assess potential, or even to read through the narrow, culture-bound criteria by which we judge a person's work at any particular stage. When denying someone admission to a program, selection committees say that "this is a practical decision and we hope it doesn't discourage you." But their response is attached to this academic edifice, which is a bureau, a public bureau, and is bound to be reductive in most of its concerted actions. However the poet's work is received by anyone anywhere has little to do with the poet alone in his/her room in the middle of the night with a sense of what must be written. One of the things I love about the Bluestem competition is that it affirms this lonely vigilance: all those people out there struggling to give birth to something. That's different, and that is the important thing, the poet's privacy, the poet's "secret" as James Wright called it. And this sanctity in which the writing takes place is more important than anything that may ever be said about somebody's poems.

So, okay, it connects to what we were talking about earlier in that we have this materialistic society insisting that only surfaces exist and that they are all one is bound to. Aside from, of course, certain well-known truths that just so happen to support this view.

Competition, in the sense that you're talking about it, is both a product of and initiator of the society that goes to war for its own best interests. Or let's say a *system* that goes to war for its own best interests. I don't think that American society *per se* really went to war in Vietnam, and that's probably why there was so much squawk about it, and why, finally, we ran out of there with our enormous, mechanized tail in a knot.

There's a political question that emerges from what I've just said: what is the real American society? Is it the power structure that kind of keeps everything moving in a single direction, or is it the accumulated minds and souls of the participants? That seems to be a good area for the poet, in delineating that difference, and I think it can be made very explicitly political. People who come here as refugees from other political systems, maybe, aren't as valuable to us in that way, in discerning the extent to which we are managed, controlled, and manipulated by this complex of interests that are not ours, that are not the people's.

At the end of his well-known poem, "The New Poem," Charles Wright says "It will not attend our sorrows. / It will not console our children. / It will not be able to help us." If poetry is as ineffectual as Wright describes, what, exactly, does "the new poem" do?

It lights a cigar. Well, in the context of the poem I see where those lines go. If we were to take it as a statement, I don't agree with any part of it. I think that poems, even the "New Poem" (and who knows what he means by that?) does console. A good poem is a joy forever, something like that. If Wright's lines are meant to refer to Post-structuralist theory-driven work, then I can't be so categorical in my disagreement.

What do you think about the influence of theory on contemporary writing?

I think that aspect of the Postmodernist project is just about played out, frankly. As it's been applied in poetry, it seems to me a kind of logical cynicism in response to the old vision of the battered but unbowed individual, alone in the universe, that was one of Modernism's central myths, and I think it's fairly impoverished. In terms of theory itself, actually, forget the literary applications, how many times can you assert that the actual subject of a sentence is the sentence itself? Or how many times can you assert that, because of the forces and pressures and social constructions and hidden manipulations bearing upon any given writer in any given time, you cannot ascribe to any writer authorship of anything? And of what value is it, finally, to say such a thing when you are in no way compelled to say it, when you can choose the other direction and arrive at a more useful and integrative view? Since we can only say so much about the origins of language and the individual's control of it, what we're left with is what we have, this text that somebody wrote and we must respect. Why cut off your own head? I think we're ready for a change in the philosophical weather. I know I am, anyway. Again, speaking as someone who has read hundreds of manuscripts over the last few years, a lot of writers manage to suggest—not that they wish to, but they manage anyway—that they are bored. I think that they're bored with this point of view— not the assumption that all meaning is allusive, but that it doesn't exist because it's allusive. Which is a step theory has encouraged writers to take.

Because there is no objective repository of meaning does not mean there is no subjective repository of meaning. There's no particular hierarchy between the subjective and the objective. Why shouldn't that be an occasion for joy rather than an occasion for despair or cynicism? I think that the next movement will be a movement to connect us back to the unconscious or to connect our literature again more strongly to the wellsprings of meaning.

George Steiner uses a phrase to characterize Deconstructionists.
To paraphrase, he calls them satyrs at play before the temple of

*logos. In many ways, you're calling for a poetry that is religious
and aimed at unearthing mysteries of being. The question that
comes to mind is how can we emphasize the importance of such
work to a culture that would rather watch* Monday Night
Football? *I guess what I'm trying to say is that I wonder if, at a
practical level, we're not fooling ourselves about there being any
hope that such work could ever reach many people.*

I don't see how we have any real choice, frankly. I mean, what we're
doing, or, as I see it, what our literary culture as a whole is doing, is
not taking us anywhere. So, I don't see that we can worry about the
practicality, or the saleability, of new modes and ideas. In fact, I
don't know how poems are going to fare against Network shopping,
but I feel this kind of resonant, transcendent work must be written
and that we'll be better off when more people are writing it than
are presently. Many people are writing what they're writing because
they think that's what will get them published. I think that if they
followed their real impulses, our literature's movement toward "the
mysterious" would be very obvious.

I feel I encounter a lot of despair in my interactions with people.
There's a big deficit of hope, and the centered and passionate writer's
response to such a condition, usually, is to try to penetrate it, and
when you do that, I think you're into the zone of the deep image. If
more people were being honest—I don't mean to say that, it sounds
like I'm putting a lot of people down; I don't mean that—I think if
more people left the tracks, followed their passion and curiosity,
we'd have a more interesting literary culture, and maybe one that
had more impact on the society at large. You can't try to
accommodate yourself to the devil and expect to end up doing the
right thing. I remember reading an essay by someone who shall
remain nameless in, maybe, *APR* [*American Poetry Review*] years
ago, which was castigating some poet for using too many images
and refusing to explore the frontiers of narrative and statement. At
that time, I thought of language as essentially metaphor, and poetry
as a kind of mill that creates language by means of metaphor. What
does it mean when you have people in national publications saying

metaphor is bad, and what we should really be doing is making flat statements? And it sounded to me like an accommodation to a society that's aping its own economic system, procreating as many mirrors for that as possible. Saying, "It's all material, don't pretend that it isn't. It's all surface." So if the things you write address and emphasize and employ principally these surfaces, they're much more easily commodified and they'll sell. People will understand them, too. But I think people can get profound pleasure and value out of things they don't necessarily understand with the front part of the brain, and I'm for a poetry that gives us psychic and spiritual room to move and become.

Claudia Keelan was born in 1959 in Anaheim, California. The author of three books of poetry, Keelan's poetics speak to her desire to rediscover an ethical imperative for the art. From her earliest collection, Refinery *(winner of the Cleveland State Poetry Prize) to* The Secularist *to her most recent collection,* Utopic, *Keelan's poetry is concerned with justice amid the damaging dynamics of a frequently hurtful culture. To put it another way, Keelan's poems posit a necessary change in perspective from the rigorous hierarchies and categories of a violent world and seek to articulate and embrace the provisional and indeterminate to show that in such indeterminacy there is capacity for compassion. A graduate of the University of Iowa Writers' Workshop, Keelan directs the M.F.A. program at the University of Nevada Las Vegas.*

CLAUDIA KEELAN

This interview with Claudia was conducted during the summers of 1996 and 2001.

Many of the women writers with whom I've spoken have articulated a problematic relationship with their early study of poetry; that is, they were immersed in a male canon and had to actively—and sometimes exhaustingly—seek women poets with whom they could form connections. Was this your experience of "coming to poetry?"

No, I can't say it was. In fact, part of my delight in my process of "coming to" was finding access to the world and language of my own father who I love very much. My "problem" came later and it has more to do with stances in poetry and with questions of mode, of composition, which are only strictly related to gender in its etymological origin. My original reasons for writing poetry were rooted in the primary need to find my self, to find the expression for the girl I was. I studied music in college and eventually gave it up for poetry, which was more directly personal and led me to the versions of the self I sought. This stance was one derived from the hangover of Wordsworth and that arm of British Romanticism which privileged the authority of the autonomous "I" rather than the dispersed self of Coleridge's "Dejection Ode" or the poet of negative capability described by Keats. These attitudes regarding the nature of the self are not in themselves either male or female. Look at William Carlos Williams' *Kora in Hell* and *Spring and All*. Those are feminist texts, as the late Troubador poems are feminist poems (and some of those poems were anonymously written by women). The lady cannot be reached. Further, to define Her would be a limitation. I've forged connections with those poets and composers, painters, philosophers, saints, mystics, ordinary people (St. Francis, Keats, Melville, Stein, Williams, Creeley, Notley, Susan Howe, Charles Ives, Simone Weil, an Amish baker I knew in Murray, KY, my husband, Donald Revell), whose methods of composition refuse to limit any part of what we call Being.

> *What about the poets you see as less open, as exclusionary—who would you classify as such and why?*

I don't want to draw lines in the sand. Since, in my poetics, both poet and poem are involved in a perpetual becoming, I have no access to the exclusionary.

> *Fair enough. But doesn't the teaching of poetry and poetry writing usually privilege the lineage you first mentioned, at the core of which is the autonomous "I." How did you, in your reading or through instruction you received, get around that lineage—or, to borrow your word, "stance"?*

Does the teaching of poetry revolve around that? Perhaps it does at this current moment in classrooms in America, but I went to Iowa, where I'm teaching this year, and then and now the argument revolved around issues of, well, style. Issues of mode, of syntax, considerations of ambiguity, its use and misuse, etc. Poetry itself, great poetry, never empowers a singular perspective.

I wanted to write, to teach, a living poetry. Time gave me the most instruction. It showed me how one is many, how desire for autonomy is a purgatory one could avoid if one were simply faithful to the temporal. I found companions in my reading. Thoreau's "Walking." Keats, who told me the poet must be Nobody. Williams, who retraces the living lineage of Beauty in his essays and especially in *Spring and All* and *Paterson*. The courage of Gertrude Stein taught me, in time, in a syntax dedicated to the processes of time in time, ("Composition as Explanation" changed me forever). And the Ashbery of *Three Poems* and *Flow Chart*—remember? "The cult of moi being essentially a dead thing . . . ." And others. "The Sermon on the Mount" is also a pretty snappy number.

> *And yet, one of the central dynamics of your second collection,*
> The Secularist, *is to get beyond "the teacher . . ."?*

Yes, but the last lines of the book read: "In the end, I couldn't love / the others nor the balloons / someone dared among the wreaths / but turned back toward /the God's dead son / his mute suffering / word of my word, flesh of my—" And in *Utopic*, in "Tool" there's the admission: "The one I wanted to teach / proved to be my teacher: / Christ's sermon on the mount, / Buddha, with the lamb on his shoulder, / love at heart . . . ." That poem goes on to say hey, don't follow me, follow ideas, the good ones, the whole ones, the ones that don't exclude.

> *I see. And yet to get to these conclusions, you had to read through*
> *a number of different writers, movements, "stances."*

Yes, yet it's more accurate to say I had to write through a number of writers, movements, and trade or redefine stances. Susan Howe calls herself a redactor, someone who revises a book simply reading. I feel kinship with that idea because it calls on notions of responsibility and, I believe, of history. "Tradition is now," Creeley says—thus my reading and writing must not subordinate the present historical moment to the past.

> *I'd like to ask you about a few poets. Whitman and Dickinson are*
> *usually held up as the grandpa and grandma of American poetry;*
> *what compels you about their poetry?*

Temperamentally, I'm drawn more to Whitman. His ambition is endless! He seeks reciprocity shamelessly; he takes us through the whole gamut—me to you, male to female, God and Gods, self and nation, culture and the atom—all the while refusing to reduce any single element. He's generous and overblown—look at his lines! It takes an enormous amount of breath to read them, an enormous heart beating to have written them. "Song of Myself" and "Crossing Brooklyn Ferry" and the desperately tender "Out of the Cradle Endless Rocking"—I almost can't stand to read his poems because of what they ask me to give—and what they give in return. Dickinson is in Luther's "lonely church of one" and she is doing honorable work there. It's strange. She writes a poem like the one about keeping the Sabbath in nature and says—I think she says— nature is her tribunal. And then there are her many poems dedicated to transport, as she calls it, which I read as a metaphysical idea— away from here, in other words. For Whitman, paradise is on earth, "look for me under your boot soles." It's interesting that those who dislike Whitman's poetry often do so for his excessive, vatic prosody. He's not interested in Art. He's after something much larger than that.

And what about Williams and Stein? How do they fit in?

Whitman and Dickinson are still nineteenth century poets, so to the extent that we're defining lineage here, I suppose you could say that they serve a grandparently role. Williams and Stein, as I said earlier, have been more directly responsible for my development as a poet. William's definition of the imagination is crucial, opposing as it does the urge towards false unities in artistic practice. I think his adage "no ideas but in things" is badly misunderstood, which is why his masterpiece *Spring and All* has always been excerpted so reductively, highlighting the "things" in the poem, e.g. the red wheelbarrow, the note he left to Flossie about the plums, the portrait of Elsie, instead of the relation of those things in time, in season. He's a great poet of synecdoche, bringing as he says in the prologue to *Kora in Hell* many broken things into a dance, "giving them thus a full being." His early work, it seems to me, opposes metaphor, the easy transfer. Even in *Paterson* the use of metaphor is generative; in other words, things are by natural law in relation, and so if the poet is desiring nature, the poem that results will be in endless relation, endless transfer. That's good news. Beauty, in his definition, is convulsive, partial, in need of rediscovery. Stein wants to show the seams, grammatically, of time, of time in a composition and the "continuous present" where we all live. She dares to say that poetry composed as "in situ" is ethically unsound, which is certainly why she loved Picasso and Matisse so much, since their paintings were also dramatically challenging status quo idealities of form in composition. In "Composition as Explanation," she argues that the "classic" is something that has already been seen and understood and so earns the dubious distinction of classicism. Others have made the same argument about Eliot's work—that the reason his work was so embraced was due to the fact that it was an extension of nineteenth century Symbolism. The critics could read it with old tools.

And what about the other Modernists?

Pound. He is, of course, the Modernist who actually defines the movement. I came to him later, and somewhat grudgingly because of teachers I had in the beginning who despised him without even knowing the extent of his thought. The *ABC of Reading* is still a very important book—I require it in beginning workshops.

I admire the ambition of *The Waste Land* very much and the humility Eliot arrives at in *Four Quartets*, but I think his notion of the objective correlative is a limiting one and, historically, another misdirection for the politics of identity. And Stevens—I was very early seduced by the gorgeous sound of his poetry, the brilliant evasive maneuvers of his imagination. He's a moving character because for all his protest, he knows that the world is real, and that's exactly what bothers him . . . the question he asks of Ramon Perez at the end of "Idea of Order at Key West," that insistence on "can you tell me why?" He wants to know why the human imagination accepts the lights and fishing boat as real, after the power of poetic imagination he's attained just by looking in the sky. That's a real dilemma, I know. Ultimately, it's not a position I share.

I'd also like to ask you about the range of works you've listed as being seminal to your poetic self: other genres, a variety of religiosities, philosophers; how have these multiple genres specifically shaped the formal aspect of your poetics? And what about other sources of inspiration besides the literary?

The formal aspect of my poetics continue to evolve, but I can tell you that I've always been interested in the shapes that justice makes, which in my experience is often an invisible form or one only gained access to via the body's reaction. You could say the invisible is the truth withheld, or the very fabric of the truth, which is the version I prefer. Finding form takes patience; it involves waiting. Creeley's ideas about duration have influenced my idea of the line, his take that experience—or the poetic subject, if you prefer—has a duration of its own, as does the poet's perception. Putting those two elements in relation to each other creates another duration, which is the time of the poem, as well as the time in the poem. Physiology has a lot to do with the shape the poem will make. Susan Howe is the first poet who, for me, records history convincingly in poetic form. Reading her, you're forced to the awareness that history itself is a trapped thing. Then you get the incredible gift of watching one woman free history into a shape she can believe again. She doesn't ask the reader to accept her activity of release as another version of history—she's a lyric poet and she is speaking for herself—she simply presents that release and it is the poem. While remaining entirely "personal," both Creeley and Howe summon, ask, or coerce the reader into an active position. The meaning inside the poem is one thing; how a reader is compelled to act, to respond, is another. That's an individual problem, which makes it a question of ethics. Simone Weil works a similar field, as does Charles Ives, though they work with philosophy and music. Reading *Gravity and Grace*

I participate in a model of action—the content and the form of those small fragments are themselves active friezes of detachment. The only way you can read them is to detach, in some sense, to give yourself up for dead. It's painful if you don't want to. She's intent on making a model of behavior that will make the world work justly, and what she does instead is summon the body of the divine. Her work is also entirely personal—she's the martyr, not you—and yet its witness takes a form that compels me to action. Charles Ives' music refuses harmony because it is after reality, and so "Yes Jesus loves me" must be—interrupted? Or demonstrated?—by boys throwing stones in the river. The generosity of these artistic practices broaden the available reality and so are participant with civil and religious communities that take their definitions from the living action of their participants.

I follow you, and what you've said makes sense, but there's a doubting Thomas in me that hesitates to believe that civil and religious communities and the pluralities they encompass really allow for justice and ethical living in the world. What I'm trying to say is, help me see a concrete, vivid example of an aesthetic object—poem or painting or piece of music—that broadened the reality of a living community and helped shape a more just world.

How does the Vietnam Memorial strike you? Or the Civil Rights Museum in Memphis? Those are forms dedicated to revision, to witness and to participation. The Vietnam Memorial is entirely about culpability, a black wall, or river, the memorial-seeker walks beside. When you look at it, you see the names of the dead and a reflection of your own face. And, in order to be sure that the living are seeing the names they seek—there are so many and very minutely engraved—they bring tracing paper and write the names on it. No, that structure, along with the Civil Rights Museum, revise the very nature of witness. No longer can the pilgrim go to the shrine—the Lincoln Memorial, the *Pieta*, Lourdes—and feel as if she has arrived and does thus achieve consolation. There is no consolation for the Vietnam War, for what we do to each other because of racial difference. And if one is a citizen, truly a citizen, one accepts responsibility for the things her laws, her country, does in her name. The Vietnam Memorial and the Civil Rights Museum articulate the living shape of true witness.

> *I understand what you're saying, but those are public monuments, shrines, museums; aren't they different—in essence—from what a poem is?*

No, a poem is not different from a shrine, a memorial, a museum. It is a PLACE (stanza means place) where the arguments of the culture take place.

> *OK. In your recent book,* Utopic, *you shape a poetry which articulates many of these same concerns, and I'd like to talk about that book in a moment. I wonder, though: doesn't poetry seem marginalized by "the culture," and doesn't that make its comments on these "arguments" somewhat inconsequential?*

I think it's "the culture" that's insignificant, illusory, not the claims of poetry. Language is evolving all the time. It would be short sighted of me, even hubristic, to put too much emphasis on my contributions to it. At the same time, I'm always gratified by the legacies of history. What is important and lasting makes its way across time. I realize this is a traditional view of the role of art. I'm comfortable with this view because I know there are always those in the present who hear and confirm what to others remains incomprehensible. I could imagine a culture more sympathetic to the proposals of poetry, but I don't have access to one. So I'm trying to live and affirm a renegade's proposal. I'm very uncomfortable with the notion of "community" that is proposed by certain poetics, and by organizations such as the AWP [Associated Writing Programs]. Sounds like consensus to me. I'll have nothing of it!

> *Tell me about* Utopic. *What made you want to write that book? There are many voices lingering behind the text—presences in*

*the text and they are important; tell me how those voices coalesced
with your voice. Emerson, M.L.K., and Simone Weil are a
disparate troop—how do you understand all of their presences?
How can you briefly describe the "utopic" vision that the book
articulates?*

Keats, King and Weil are the angels of the book, mostly, for me.
Emerson is there as a transparency—I'm sure he'd approve. King,
Keats and Weil are all utopian idealists. Their ideas are keyed to
the reciprocity between self and other, to the erasure of the distance
between self and other. King's urge towards the "beloved
community" is a civil model of Keat's concept of negative capability.
Likewise, Weil's conversion pushes her from philosopher to mystic
saint—one who is dedicated to "via negativa," the negative way.
Traditionally, the Bodhisattva embarked on such a spiritual journey
and refused entry to Nirvana, knowing that Arrival made Nirvana
moot. Same with King's concept of community. The community,
the movement towards community, must never end. Diaspora must
be insured so community is living, evolving. Keat's take was personal.
He knew he had to lose self to see objectively; he understood that
being a poet was to accept the passing, the versional, nature of both
self and time.

*Do you think that his poems articulate that vision? "Ode on a
Grecian Urn" in some ways seems to argue the opposite.*

It depends on how you read the statement the urn makes. "Ode to
a Nightingale" certainly is in conversation with the passing; in fact,
the whole structure of the odes themselves (strophe-antistrophe)
seems predicated on the same kind of dialectic I'm talking about.

But what of the quotation itself?

I think it's interesting because it is in quotes. The rest of the "story"
the urn tells is through the images on it. It sounds like an echo to
me, one that Keats may be tempted by, but one that his poetry
ultimately, and his letters explicitly, refute.

You're a teacher. Describe how this profession, from teaching in Boston to teaching in the South to teaching at UNLV to teaching at Iowa, has affected your poetry.

My life has always been nomadic. In fact, I've now lived in Las Vegas (of all places!) for, technically, 6 years, though last year I was teaching in Iowa. I suppose that my sense of place and people is very influenced by that fact. There is always the next place; there are always others. This makes me happy and when I'm happiest I experience my life and project as a classless one and the citizens of my city and the students in my classroom as the Demos who I love and am of.

A few more questions. Tell me about living in Las Vegas. I'd love to hear your take on that city.

The longer I live in Las Vegas, the less I understand it. As you know, my husband Donald Revell lives part of the week in Salt Lake City, part of the week here, so our family spends a fair amount of time shuttling between Sodom and Zion. Salt Lake does a very good job of keeping out all the "freedoms" available 24 hours in Vegas: gambling, sex, all night gun ranges, and for the kids, roller coaster rides through the New York City skyline. So all that is at the edge of our lives at all times, and when we're in Salt Lake City, the angel Moroni over every temple lets us know he's watching, which somehow fails to comfort me every time. Las Vegas is continually in the process of remaking itself, which makes, on one hand, a city where a Blackjack dealer can afford a house with a swimming pool, and on the other, a hundred year-old American city with no solid infrastructure. The schools don't open on time, though they build many each year; the dust from construction is so thick that everyone is developing respiratory problems. The U.S. government is in the process of sending the entire country's nuclear waste to be buried at Yucca Mountain, a military base 40 miles west of Las Vegas. And out my window, the desert is still there, barely, and a few herds of wild horses still roam nearby. I don't know. Perhaps one really does write one's life. Utopia means "no place" and ecstasy means "to be placed outside." There's a lot to be done here and there are no rules of order already in place. I like the present in such wilderness.

What role do you envision for the poet given our government's recent action in response to terrorist attacks on the United States— what looks to be a period of fear and violence?

Obviously, every one is off balance at the moment. Gertrude Stein was right, as usual, in "Composition as Explanation," that war demands attention to the present and so instructs an immediacy usually relegated to the margins of our free time. I'm teaching a Gender and Literature course right now based on Whitman's concept of the body electric. We'd just read "Song of Myself" when the first plane hit the trade center and the message of inclusiveness there, the insistence of self being other—it was the only word for the moment and continues to be, I believe, no matter what polarity you describe: man-woman, citizen-nation, nation-world. Any definition that does not take the Whole into consideration is an incomplete one. Radical freedom is the only whole measure—that's what I hope to teach, to reach.

Yusef Komunyakaa was born in 1947 in Bogalusa, Louisiana. He received an M.F.A. in creative writing from the University of California, Irvine, in 1980. Komunyakaa's poetry has been celebrated by many distinctions, including a Kingsley Tufts Award, the Ruth Lilly Prize, and his nomination to the American Academy of Poets. From what many view as his breakthrough book, Copacetic, *to his recently published* Talking Dirty to the Gods, *Komunyakaa's experiences in Vietnam and as an African American growing up in the South combined with a fervent attraction to jazz and blues have led to the shaping of a unique and important body of work. Other books of Komunyakaa's include* Neon Vernacular, *for which he won the Pulitzer Prize,* Dien Cai Dau, *and* Thieves of Paradise. *He is currently a professor of creative writing at Princeton University.*

YUSEF KOMUNYAKAA

Yusef and I conducted this interview in the fall of 2001.

How did you come to poetry? What poets or types of poetry first interested you?

I came to poetry by reading some of the traditional British poets in grade and high school. I wrote my first poem in high school. I wrote a poem for my graduating class. It was a hundred lines long, I think. Twenty-five quatrains. I took two collections of poems to Vietnam—Hayden Carruth's anthology, *The Voice is Great Within Us* and a second anthology, the title of which escapes me. I took my very first creative writing class in 1973 with Dr. Alex Blackburn at the University of Colorado, Colorado Springs. I've been writing poetry ever since that introduction.

I think that reading poetry is so important. It kept me abreast of a certain kind of poetic sensibility, a certain language used with concision. In retrospect, I realize that—since my father was a carpenter, I assisted him early on and his tinkering with things, how he would measure a board and search for precision—I realize that my time with him taught me something about writing as well. The ability to go back and revise; revision for me means to "re-see." I understand revision as a very important element of writing.

Can you recall specific poems from those anthologies that engaged you?

The very first poem that I memorized was actually Poe's "Annabel Lee." The second poem I memorized was a poem by James Weldon Johnson, "The Creation." In Hayden Carruth's anthology, I discovered Robert Hayden for the first time; I discovered Nemerov and other American lyric poets. But also poets who were writing a narrative poem as well.

That's a common distinction that many poets write and speak about; it's also a distinction that many writers see as collapsing. How do you see the dividing line between narrative and lyric poetry? How does your work explore those boundaries?

Of course, the narrative is story encapsulated. The lyric poem takes us back to the Greeks, a poem that would be sung, accompanied, really, with instruments. For me, there's always an argument within the context of the lyric; I'm particularly thinking of Shakespeare's 154 sonnets; there's always an argument, there's always a discursive turn—that's as important as song and story. There's probably also a kind of in-depth feeling in the lyric impulse that perhaps separates it from the more conventionally narrative poems. And yes, what's been happening in contemporary poetry—because, perhaps, of a modern sensibility—is that there is a collapse of these two distinctions; for me, that's the most interesting poem, one where the lyrical and narrative are happening at once.

You've spoken about poets from several different periods and backgrounds; it seems that many American poets in the twentieth century have felt it important to align themselves with certain groups—or as part of certain traditions. Stevensian, Poundian, and such. Choosing Williams over Eliot, and so on. What do you think about those lineages? What are the most significant "moments" in twentieth century American poetry?

For me, Williams is important for his use of the short line, the kind of vertical poems that had to do with speed, that had to do with contemporary philosophy and such. The opposite—the use of the longer line, which creates what we might call a horizontal movement and which is conducive to meditative poems—is also interesting to me. This makes me think of what Richard Hugo said—that a poem should have long and short lines, a variation between the two. In a way, I've tried to incorporate both of those impulses.

Robert Hayden has been very important to me, and I've read him closely. With Hayden, what happens is that he internalized the lyrical impulse of Keats—he started with British writing, but of course Hayden has such an American voice and his concerns are quite American, and so he transformed this impulse.

I'm also thinking of the Harlem Renaissance poets I read early on, especially the writers of the protest sonnet. There's a lyrical intensity there coupled with the narrative of everyday responsibilities. Poets such as Claude McKay and Spencer writing what might be called a very traditional poem, but at the same time there's something underneath those poems that defies the lyrical impulse.

Countee Cullen certainly also comes to mind. Hughes, too. Those are the frequently anthologized polarities of the Harlem Renaissance—Cullen the lofty lyric poet, Hughes the storytelling songster of the street. That distinction always rang false to me; both artists seem so concerned with both the music and discourse.

I think you're right. Hughes' sensibility is quite different, though. He comes from the Midwest—Joplin, Missouri. I have this idea that individuals who came from the Midwest were more individualist in their writings; I think that it has to do with time and space more than any thing else. Hughes is an experimenter, and at the same time, he's taking on the tradition of the blues.

There are other Midwest poets that I'm thinking about in connection with this, such as, of course, Eliot. Eliot internalized the speech of the Midwest. He's really, in many ways, a Southern poet, too. The river shaped him. Another poet is Kenneth Rexroth, who came from South Bend, Indiana. I'm surprised by the experimentation of his work. Someone like William Burroughs, coming out of Lawrence, Kansas. I think that he was born, though, in St. Louis, like Eliot.

Berryman, from Oklahoma. Those vast empty spaces between place and place—the elaborate stretch of time it took to travel between them.

Right.

Usually when people think about experimentation in American poetry—or American art writ large—they think about the coasts.

I think that the inventive sensibility comes out of the Midwest, the heartland where there is such expansiveness of time and space.

Music is obviously very important to your work. How do you see jazz or the blues formally and thematically impacting your poetry?

It's not necessarily the music's structure, but the temperament. In jazz, there's always that element of exploration. In a way, improvisation means exploration, the ability to start at any given place and go in a number of different directions and at the same time not have a circular structure but an appropriate arrival elsewhere. That's applicable to the poem. The poem has to have an almost discursive element. It doesn't have to be lineal; it can incorporate many different things and at the same time have music that is natural, that hasn't been necessarily played over and over until it is a too well traveled map.

In listening to you talk about music and thinking about your attraction to the heartland, I just flashed on Kansas City and Memphis as musical centers of origin.

Charlie Parker coming out of Kansas City; Miles Davis coming out of East St. Louis. And others. The blues in Memphis. Again, that vastness of time and space affecting a certain sensibility or a certain tenacious urge for change—I don't know if the artist is overtly conscious that he or she is being different. I don't think that's the situation. They are playing what they feel and see. In both cases—poetry and music.

What about other art forms?

I love many paintings. I love the image in poetry. So I'm linked to the visual image as well. I like a number of different styles. I'm quite attracted to many abstract painters, even painters like Melvin Louis, who's not really well-known but who I see as important. Jacob Lawrence has been important to me because of the rituals within the content of his work, the rituals of daily life within his art. Romare Bearden has been very important, his collages especially. Bearden had so many different styles. He imitated European art early on, and then he discovered something very American. That American aspect influenced his work from then on.

One of the great interests of many American writers in this century has been poetry in translation. Are there any particular poets from other countries who have captured your imagination?

Milosz is important. It's hard to say, though, if his work is really "translated" in a certain sense because of how closely he works in collaboration. Yevtushenko. And for different reasons, Baudelaire is important to me. That wild sensibility. Mallarmé. Some of the Surrealist poets, the chances that they took, especially Breton and his *Manifesto*. In reading that book, I realized that it was a huge dare, an attempt to put things back together after World War One. This dare had everything to do with a kind of imagistic healing.

Yes. And taking poetry with you to Vietnam suggests art's importance in political contexts. How do you understand the relationship between poetry and politics?

Adrienne Rich's book *What is Found There* is important to me. It is a book on politics and poetry. Even silence is political. We are social as well as political animals. As long as the politics are not on the surface, poetry of that sort works for me. When the politics are on the surface, driving the whole impulse of the creative piece, then I see it as problematic. A whole political symbology can be *inside* a work. I'm thinking of Picasso's *Guernica*. In fact, had his work been overtly political—and it was very political—then the painting would not have meant as much to me. But the violence and the big sweep of the painting captures a viewer.

Does poetry possess any power to affect the political sphere?

I think so. Not in ways one might usually think of, though. Interestingly enough, in times of crisis—social, political, and emotional—we tend to go to poetry for some kind of guidance.

Some might say, "Thank goodness that it doesn't have power in that sphere."

Yes. I agree. Its existence is not nourished by power.

Maybe consolation and guidance are the opposite of power.

Perhaps.

Talking Dirty to the Gods is in some ways a very different book for you, especially formally. How did you come to the four-line, four-stanza shape?

I thought that I would write a few of those. The shape tempted me for a few reasons; it seemed to have a visual symmetry that was interesting; at the same time, I wanted a poem that had more of a barren, fractured design within the contents. Inside of the poems, there were some things going on quite different from what the poem looked like. Visually, the poems seemed so controlled; once one gets inside, though, one gets inside the flux, inside the possibility. I wanted those things to collide inside of a small space.

There are more allusions in these poems than your other work.

Yes. One thing that I like about the blues is that there's a great deal of satire and innuendo. I wanted the poems to work like that, and allusion helps create that layered effect. I also wanted to have fun.

Was your composition process with those poems the same as in earlier books?

The earlier work—the way that I wrote them was that I would write everything down and then I would very systematically cut back the poem. The sixteen line poems of *Talking Dirty* would usually begin with me meditating on them at length and the poem would find its form. Very little cutting. The revision was happening somewhere beforehand. I think that it was happening inside my head even before the poem got down on paper. Many of those poems I wrote when I first came to Princeton, and I would walk to work about two miles, and I would write the poem inside of my head. The poem was being shaped that way.

Many of your earlier works are driven by a strong sense of actual external place rather than the internal, meditative space about which you're speaking. Louisiana, Vietnam, and other places, as well.

Growing up the South in the fifties as a black man makes the pathos of place internalized. For any writer or any artist, for any person, he or she internalizes a place and the elements of it become portable in that sense. We take it with us. The music of a place is part of that. I mentioned Eliot earlier. I think that that's what happened with him; in *The Waste Land*, we hear how he has internalized the many musics of St. Louis.

I internalized Bogalusa, Louisiana. I knew every little nook and cranny of that town. I wasn't afraid of the mystery of the place around me. I would walk out in the middle of nowhere in the middle of the night, and I didn't feel threatened by anything. I knew it that well. Australia, where I also lived, was so different. That landscape, though, began to dovetail with what I had already internalized. That's also what happened in Vietnam. In Vietnam, I wasn't afraid of that landscape because of where I had grown up. It's difficult for me to think about someone coming from a city like New York or L.A. and being plunked down in Vietnam. The landscape alone would be enough to frighten, all that mystery and strangeness. Growing up in Louisiana, though, where there's thick vegetation because of all of the rainfall and humidity and the fertile atmosphere, I suppose parallels Vietnam and made it less frightening for me.

I lived in Memphis for a number of years, and although some consider that to be the South, the difference between that city and "the Deep South" seems profound.

The South has been informed by Africa.

What do you mean?

I'm thinking about the individuals who initially worked the land in the South. Those Africans. In working the land, even if it wasn't your land—in fact, it's your burden in many ways—there is still a development of a love for that land. A certain respect for that land because one is giving one's fingers into the dirt, planting the seeds. Members of my family called it "the good earth." There's a certain kind of relationship with land that comes out of that; one knows the names of things. The names of the trees, animals, and the rituals, as well.

In recent years, though, people seem to move around a great deal more. Has that eroded that sense of place?

If one spends one's childhood in a certain place then it's taken inside—that's what I mean by internalizing the landscape and the landscape becomes portable. We move it around with us. It becomes a sort of psychological overlay for everything else.

Hence, Eliot should always be seen as an American rather than British poet.

Further: Eliot is a Southern poet.

What most interests you in contemporary American writing? How do you understand the relationship between the art of poetry and wider culture?

I suppose those poets who are still writing poems that reflect their experience, and I'm talking about physical experience as well as imaginative experience. I'm not as drawn to the overly experimental poets because I do think that there's a kind of experimentation going on that involves, if not planned, rehearsed erasure. It's incidental erasure. And maybe there is a reason for that; I hate to be a complete skeptic. But now, for the first time, we have a number of writers who have fascinating and urgent experiences to propel their work. I was looking at a little sign in a car window that said, "Just when I turned on the right channel, somebody changed the channel." For the first time, we have individuals who come from marginalized communities, and they are writing poems and those poems come out of experience, very distinct experiences. Many of the experimental poets—it seems as if those poems come out of everything but experience. The poems come out of certain kinds of cultivated practices that have to do with reading the right books. Consequently, we can probably program computers to write those poems based on the intake of certain details from theory books and encyclopedias and what have you.

Pound's "Only emotion endures" seems relevant here.

That kind of experimentation for the sake of experimentation is riddled with false notes. I agree with Pound. Emotion says that there is a person there.

PHOTO BY JEANNE C. FINLEY

Born in 1952 in Augusta, Maine, Dorianne Laux's route to poetry has been different than that of many other contemporary poets; a single mother who held down jobs as gas station attendant, sanitarium cook, and maid—among others—before emerging as a poet, her work is charged with a grittiness that makes it memorable and compelling. Laux's first book of poems, Wake, *was published in 1990; two subsequent volumes,* What We Carry *and, most recently,* Smoke, *have continued to explore Laux's unique capacity to conflate lyricism with narrative strategies in poems littered with the everyday—from laundromats to Led Zeppelin, her work embraces and transforms everything it contains. The recipient of National Endowment for the Arts and Guggenheim fellowships, Laux teaches in the creative writing program at the University of Oregon.*

DORIANNE LAUX

Dorianne and I conducted this interview in late summer 2001.

Many women writers have articulated a problematic relationship with their early study of poetry; that is, they were immersed in a male canon and had to actively—and sometimes exhaustingly— seek women poets with whom to forge connections. Was this your experience of "coming to poetry?"

Not exactly. The first poets I read—I was twelve—were Robert Frost, Carl Sandburg and e.e.cummings; it was what my mother was reading. She had no women poets in the house or I would have found them, though I was happy to read Frost especially. But I was interested in novels for the most part and read many by women. In my late twenties, after writing hundreds of terrible rhymed and metered poems, I began to want to know more. I took a night class at the local junior college where my teacher, Steve Kowit, introduced us to the world poets. Again, most of the poets were male, poets I fell in love with and still love: Neruda, Parra, Pavese, Paz, Vallejo, Hernandez, Machado. I paid little attention to poets other than these, even though when I go back I see the names of Milosz, Celan, Seferis, among others. I just wasn't yet interested. The U.S. section was comprised of six men. Plath and Sexton represented the two women. To tell you the truth, I don't even remember reading them, and for a while, had little interest in the U.S. poets at all. After seeing my poems, Kowit gave me an anthology of contemporary American poetry and told me to pay special attention to Olds and Forché. After reading them, I immediately went out and got copies of their books and immersed myself in the writing. I remember being absolutely ecstatic to find them and to see that there was another language that I could utilize, the language of women. I think my metaphors were instantly enlarged, charged by the reading I did. I quickly began to see the possibilities in my domestic surroundings—rags of cloud, jam jars filled with roses, laundry on the line: the banners of the household.

I moved to Berkeley with my young daughter in the early eighties, and my partner at the time, poet Ron Salisbury, introduced me to the works of Ai, Song, Clifton, Kenyon, Dove and Stone. While in Berkeley, I forged a friendship with the San Francisco poet Kim Addonizio. Soon after, I began to meet other women poets with whom I've had long and important friendships, Jane Hirshfield and Brenda Hillman among them. I met Sharon Olds for the first time when she was a guest in a class I took at the UCB Extension program taught by Alan Soldofsky. Louise Glück and Linda Gregg read together at the Berkeley Library. I met Marie Howe one summer at Breadloaf. For three consecutive summers I attended the Napa Valley Poetry Conference where I met and was taught by poets Forché, Kizer, Doubiago, Hirshfield and others. I remember Forché pointing out how few women were teachers and Doubiago commenting on how few were represented in anthologies. My consciousness of these issues was awakened more fully there, and I began reading poets like Rukeyser, Akmatova and Szymborska, Komachi and Shikibu. By the late eighties, I was at Mills College where I read, finally, Plath and Sexton, as well as Dickinson, Bishop, Levertov, Rich and more. It was a women's college so there was a lot available to me and many, most, of my teachers were women, and writers: Chana Bloch, Sheila Ballentyne, Diana O'Hehir. My art teacher was the late Jay Defeo and Diana Russell taught my Women's History class.

It's interesting to see how much things have changed since 1965. At that time, I would never have dreamed that there were women poets in our past or that there might be women poets working among us. I found out soon enough how wrong I was. So, though there were few women poets in those early years, I have since been blessed with a vibrant and enduring abundance. Pimone Triplett, a colleague at the University of Oregon, said something interesting the other day. She said that for the first time in history, women poets are influencing women poets—they have a strong lineage that can be traced into the present day. I would add that we also now have young male poets who count women among their influences, and so, soon I hope, the distinction will no longer be so necessary. We can see the scales beginning to shift into balance. It's becoming a richer world.

You mentioned in your answer "the language of women." Could you talk a little bit more about what you mean by that phrase? Your examples speak to subject matter, but I sense that it's a liberation much more important than that, perhaps having formal, even syntactical implications for poets.

There probably are, but I'm not a poetry historian. The fact that Olds had developed a unique way of working with the line and that Forché was a master of the line was not lost on me, but I didn't study it in a formal way; rather, I struggled to gain mastery through imitation. I never studied Dickinson's use of form and syntax either, though reading her allowed me a kind of freedom, much as the work of Whitman and cummings allowed an entire generation of poets a freedom to expand and explore. I think of Brenda Hillman or C.K Williams, for instance. All these poets were my models, so that my study, such as it was, was conducted almost solely by imitation of both men and women. What I think most impressed me was that because of women's voices, the landscape of poetry had been given wider range. My interior world was something I could now attach to a domestic landscape, a psychological landscape in which I lived and experienced life. My knowledge of this landscape was vast, physically, intellectually, emotionally, and I knew the language well— it was the language I spoke: I yelled directions to my daughter as I taught her to drive or spoke words of love or rage, fear, awe, distress, disgust. I understood its rhythms and loved its rhymes, its plosive power, its rhythmic surges. Come here. Stay Out. Go home. The language was not pumped up, but rather a language that resembled ordinary speech, the language of people in community, only better. Not noble or cynical or austere, but somehow, because of this more quotidian familiarity, calm in its authority, sure of itself.

Some would argue that the liberation you speak about has a definite political dimension. How do you understand the relationship between poetry and politics? What is your definition of "poetry of witness?"

Right now, as I write this, a man is walking down the middle of my street. I hear his voice first, raised in song against the few cars swishing by, strong syllables ferried by his breath into the October air. I stop writing for a moment and stand up to look out my window. I wait for him to come into view, for his body to reveal to me something about his voice. The words, if they are words, are in a language foreign to my ear. I'm fearful for a split second, that the end of the world has come and that I have been caught unaware— the TV and radio off, I haven't yet checked the headlines. Through the branches of my lilac tree I see his brown shoe emerge, the cuff of his black pants, the shirt on his back is white, and he has taken off his coat which is draped across one arm as he strolls, on a Sunday morning, maybe home from church or an AA meeting or a quick trip to the corner store to buy a pack of cigarettes. Is he singing because he's overcome with joy or deep in grief? Is he afraid and alone and so he sings? I'll never know, but I will be his witness, again and again. And to the silence he leaves behind after he turns the corner and what fills that silence: a ball being bounced and bounced against the pavement by an unseen hand.

All poetry is witness. Witness to life, to the life force. It is also witness to the great subjects: love, loss, ecstasy, birth, memory, betrayal, desire, death. It asks the great questions: Who are we? Why are we here? Where are we going? And so we are the mortal and fallible witnesses to life, as it is lived, during our portion of history. We imagine other lives, but we live only one, and poetry is often a struggle between those two modes of being. We are unafraid to give voice to what we're thinking and feeling, which, if the voice is strong enough, pure enough, is the voice of many. We watch, often from the sidelines, and take note. We explore the possibilities, the potentials, the alternatives, the options, but we come down hard on the facts, let the image guide us, make the utterance for us. We listen for conversation, between others and between our double natures, we speak from the worst and best parts of ourselves, sometimes from both sides at once. We touch and smell everything—rose and thorn, stem and root, even the deformed and mutilated, even the dead. We dig in with our fingers and work toward the center, onion leaves at our feet. We are the ones who don't look away when we can't bear to look. In jubilance or in sorrow. We lay bare and record. Is this political?

Does it have to do with affairs of state or governments? For the most part, we are ignored or condemned by governments; we are not often invited for comment. And if we are, even by our own souls, we have difficulty taking sides because of our awareness of the dual nature of humanity, an awareness forged by this inward looking proclivity, the inability to interpret what we outwardly see. We know that only in the complexity of things is there poetry. Or as Robert Hass has observed: the Yes firmly embedded in the No. Coming into an embrace with the ambiguity of our nature is the only thing that will keep one brother from killing another, and so in that sense, yes, poetry may be political. It's not in Cain slaying Abel, but in the moment before he does, when he hesitates. That's where poetry lives and breathes.

I'd like to turn our focus a bit more specifically toward your own poetry. What shapes the length of a line in your writing? Tell me about the most important rhythmical and musical concerns for you in a poem.

The first line is often important to me in determining the rhythmic structure a poem will take—a template of the music to follow, but filled with detours and surprises, like a riff in jazz. When the writing is less inspired musically in the beginning, I search through the draft to find a place where the music is alive and work toward a structure from there. Sometimes, I never really find the music and the poem fails musically but succeeds on some other level, and so I let it go. My mother was a classical pianist and has studied music all her life. As a child, I listened to her play but never found an interest in the making of the music—never learned to read music, never learned to play as my brothers and sisters did, at her knee. I taught myself, like many American adolescents, some simple guitar chords, but they seemed only a vehicle for the words I wanted to say that were of far more interest to me. My line is probably nothing special in the scheme of things. Levertov knows how to make a line that is like polished glass, how to make a new meaning ring between the last word of one line to the first word of the next. Forché can do that too. Phil Levine can generate so much out of a four beat line; like a rock star, he just pushes it to its limits. There are many reasons to break a line, and each poem has its own set of reasons. That said, you must remember we're talking here about line breaks. I don't know how I do it, and from what I can see, not many have much to say on the subject unless they are formalists. But it really is instinctive. I rely on my ear. I stumble onto a shape for the poem by rewriting it in as many shapes as will come to me until one seems pleasing, whole, true to the poem's subject and tenor. I don't write in lines; I write for music, image and thought. Later, I break the lines to make them correspond. For instance: "Who would want to give it up, the coal a cat's eye in the dark room;" that was the first line of *Smoke*, written initially without breaks except where the page ended. Now it seems obvious to me that the line needs to be broken at the word coal, not only for rhythm, but for image: "Who would want to give it up, the coal." No one would want to give up the coal of life, the discovery of fire, the core of the earth. Then the cat's eye is a shift in expectations, which I want and will try to follow through on as often as I can.

Yes, I follow that. Can you give me an example of a Levertov line that you find particularly engaging and talk about it?

Kim (Addonizio) and I use a Levertov poem in *The Poet's Companion* to talk about the line. A wonderful poem about the inability to speak or act called "Where Is the Angel?"

> Where is the angel for me to wrestle?
> No driving snow in the glass bubble,
> But mild September.
>
> Outside the stark shadows
> Menace, and fling their huge arms about
> Unheard. I breathe
>
> A tepid air, the blur
> Of asters

The breaks here are wonderful and create rhythm and surprise. What we didn't mention was how her lines often work as discrete units. Take the line "Unheard. I breathe." It stands alone and provides a subtext for the poem, becomes a summation of the poem's subject. But it is also, in and of itself, a beautiful line filled with meaning, yearning, potential, passion and depth. I imagine Levertov as Sappho, only a few lines pulled from the rubble to represent a lifetime of work. If this line were all we had of Levertov, we would be assured of the poet's worth.

And since you're a Levertov fan I'll talk about a few more of her techniques from a poem called "The Dead Butterfly."

> Everywhere among the marigolds
> the rainblown roses and the hedges
> of tamarisk are white

butterflies this morning, in constant
tremulous movement, only those
that lie dead revealing
their rockgreen color and the bold
cut of the wings.

Beyond the gorgeous imagery, one thing you might notice is all those o's. It's a poem of grief and death so the o sound makes sense here, which is something you can count on with Levertov. She's so good at fitting the sound to the subject, marrying music to meaning. What's also interesting is that you can shift words into groupings or constellations: Among marigolds rainblown roses morning constant tremulous movement those bold. Stripping away the connectives doesn't harm the core of the poem—the groupings are strong in themselves. Roses, hedges, dead is also a nice grouping. Revealing green wings. Tamarisk and tremulous. Her word choice continues to disclose. The more you strip away or regroup, the richer the poem becomes. The only word that doesn't have a mate of some sort is the subject of the poem: butterflies. It stands alone. Levertov poems make sense in a highly structural way. She's precise as hell. A great teacher of the delicacies of craft.

You have spoken quite a bit to the musicality of the line— mentioning piano, guitar, jazz. What are the most important elements in your poetry's music? Alliteration, assonance, variation of vowel sounds, percussive stresses, what else?

I'm not sure. Probably assonance is my trigger—similar sounds that can pull me through a line. Like those o's in the Levertov poem. Alliteration is probably what I feel for next, both ways of weaving or knitting words together so that they have the feel of the inevitable about them. But these are things I notice later, when I go back and look over what I've written. The trick of course is to make the weave loose so that the reader doesn't notice it consciously.

In his introduction to your book, Awake, *Philip Levine wrote, "This is a poetry of risk: it will go the very edge of extinction to find the hard facts that need to be sung." What do you understand Levine to mean by that? How do you describe the element of risk in poetry?*

What does he mean by extinction? Of the ego? I think more of Levine's poems as going toward that edge, risking what we, as humans, don't want to know about ourselves: our deep wells of fear and shame, but also our capacity for love and joy. We're afraid of ourselves, afraid of looking too deeply into our natures. We want to be liked, admired, thought well of. Levine's poems don't care about that. They shine the light and if it falls into the abyss, Levine lets the light stay there, illuminating both the gold and the bones of those who dug for it.

One of the strongest poems in Smoke *is, in my opinion, "Fear." The catalogs are compelling both for their rich sounds and their litany of, in some ways, survival. Can you tell me about that poem, how it connects to growing up in America when you did?*

I was eleven when Kennedy was shot, when the U.S. "objective" in Vietnam was not "to save a friend" but "to avoid humiliation," when we saw race riots in Harlem, when neighbors were called to their windows in Queens by Kitty Genovese's cries for help and watched as she was stabbed to death on the sidewalk. It was the year of The Boston Strangler. In a few months we would have Pop Tarts and Lucky Charms, the topless bathing suit. In another year the Beatles would write "Nowhere Man" and "Eleanor Rigby" followed by "Lucy in the Sky with Diamonds." By '68 men in white suits were walking on the moon and I was alone in a theater watching *Midnight Cowboy.* I was 16 years old. In another year I would be able to leave home and find a way for myself, get a job, begin to feel some control over my life. But when I think of my childhood, I think of the *Twilight Zone.*

Parents were gone at night, and kids were left to themselves, to the singular humiliation at the hands of the neighborhood brute, head lice, popcorn and canned beans. It was a time of great loneliness and fear, and we were bound together by it. All we had was one another and our pity. We were too young yet for compassion. Or defiance. We were simply children, watching and waiting. That poem, for me, is simply a reconstitution, in tenor and texture, of some portion of what it was like to grow up during those times. We lived on the edge of a canyon in San Diego. After school or on the weekends, we would climb down into it and follow the dry creek bed for hours and never see a soul. Or we'd take the bus to the ocean and stand on the cliffs, trying to imagine a way out. It felt like the end of the earth, and yet we had books and movies and television, and so we knew something was out there, and at night, up there, beyond us. But it was all new and even our parents didn't know what to make of it. Boys were being brought home in body bags, and there were love-ins at the park. It was something about being alone and together at the same time and of having both the bad luck and great luck of being born as girls. I can't speak of that era without using the pronoun we, and yet the fabric of the time is imbued with loneliness and fear.

The poem, "The Line," is, perhaps ironically, a prose poem. Can you tell me about your understanding of the prose poem and that particular poem?

I actually don't think much of prose poems in general. I like too much what can be done with a line. But that particular poem just wouldn't take a shape that made any sense except a box. It's not one of my best poems, but it's another alone/together scenario, and what seems to me a very American scene and feeling.

In "Life is Beautiful," you end with a cyclical vision of us and the world: desire as the hand spinning the top, so to speak. The consuming of beauty—and the emergence of even more of what is beautiful from bountiful abundance—is a recurring thread in

*your work. "Orgasms of Organisms" also speaks to this dynamic:
how do these poems connect to your vision of the world? Are they
a sort of coda to the new collection?*

I learned something about myself in the writing of those poems. I
had always thought I believed that we should stop making babies,
stop bringing so many people into the world. I grew up with the
notion of the 2.5 family that moved very quickly into the idea of
zero population growth. I believed so strongly in this idea, this
vision for how to save the world, that I made the decision to have
only one child. I was appalled, really, by how this poem ended—
intellectually, politically—but something in my spirit was pleased
at this stumbled upon idea of abundance. The back-story is that
my husband and I had come home from a summer away and our
house was filled with flies. At first, I tried using a newspaper to
kind of herd them out of the house. Then I took down the electric
fan and tried to blow them out the front door. The flies seemed out
of control to me, and I began to actively hate them. I finally went
down to the store and bought some fly strips and tried tacking
them up in the breezeway. In the process, I got fly goop on my
hands; one strip fell onto the rug. After a number of attempts, I
successfully nailed one up and went into the kitchen, feeling very
proud of myself. I washed my hands and walked back into the living
room but forgot where I'd put the strip and it got caught in my
hair. I was beside myself with revulsion. By now, I wanted to kill
every single one of them, individually—torture them, hear them
scream. I had moved from a pacifist desire to send them quietly on
their way to a murderous urge to be rid of them. I suddenly saw
myself as I was: an enraged human being fanning the flames of
persecution and death. I did what any poet might at a time like
that: I went to the backyard and sat down to write.

I picked up my journal and saw at the top of the empty page that
I had written a note to myself to rent the video, *Life Is Beautiful*. As
soon as I saw those words, I began to write the poem. I think it
helped that the movie is about survival; about the lengths we are
willing to go to survive, and to make sure our progeny carry on

with their souls intact. I still believe in zero population growth, but how do we turn off that primal love we experience when we see the face of an infant? How to reconcile these things? There was something in that murderous impulse that made me come to terms with life as it is, on its own terms, and concede to the beauty in it. The poems you mention are a coda of sorts, a sudden realization that, when faced with death or extinction, the beauty of life, in any form, stuns us. I'm not sure if those poems mark a new direction for me. I do think that I'm becoming more concerned with the complexities of living out our lives here on this planet, viewing humanity as an organism with a will of its own, an intelligence that lies beneath our conscious awareness. I don't know why we're here. Maybe we're supposed to kill ourselves off, make room for some other species that will continue the work of life. And maybe we're supposed to bring ourselves to the brink of extinction in order to learn something necessary to our continued survival. Maybe the poems will say.

PHOTO BY DONNA LEE

Li-Young Lee was born in 1957 in Jakarta, Indonesia; after several years of wandering exile in Southeast Asia, his family moved to the United States. Driven by attention, passion, and lyricism, Li-Young Lee's poetry has received many awards and high praise from various critical perspectives. He has published three volumes of poetry, Rose, the city in which i love you, *and* Book of my Nights. *Each of these books explores familial relationships, the enduring resonance of memory, and the self's search for the divine. His prose memoir,* The Winged Seed, *recounts his family's flight into exile and Lee's struggle to shape his past and present selves into a recognizable form of which he can make sense. Written in lyrical, sometimes surreal prose, the book probes the limits of language and reveals the tenuous hold we have both on memory and the immediate moment.*

LI-YOUNG LEE

Li-Young Lee and I spoke in Memphis, Tennessee, during fall 1996.

*On the one hand, "The City in Which I Love You" is a very "twentieth-century" poem—a poem of fragmented memories, of exile, a poem that enacts a search for something to shore against one's ruin. On the other hand, the spiritual longing of the poem seems more of the seventeenth century, closer to the work of Traherne, Vaughan, and Donne. Do you think of your work as marrying these two poetic impulses? Or do you see the modern quest poem—*The Waste Land, The Cantos, *and others—as being propelled by a spiritual hunger?*

I feel a great affinity toward quest poetry and certainly a lot of affinity with Eliot's quest, but I feel ultimately that there's an arc, a trajectory that's ancient as Homer. Every time someone asks, "Who am I?" that's the quest, and I'm sure it was asked by many, many people. There's something else, too. I think the impulse to write that kind of poem arises from the disparity that occurs when we realize who we are, but we find we can't live it. So for me, it's the realization of my identity and that identity as the universe. I am perfectly convinced that is what I am, the universe. I can't live it. Why? So the poetry comes out of that. The poetry comes out of a need to somehow—in language—connect with universe mind, and somehow when I read poetry—and maybe all poetry is quest, a poetry of longing—when I read poetry, I feel I'm in the presence of universe mind; that is, a mind I would describe as a mind that accomplishes a 360-degree seeing; it is manifold in consciousness, so that a line of poetry says one thing, but it also says many other things. That manifold quality of intention and consciousness: that feels to me like universe. So that's why I read poetry, and that's why I write it, to hear that voice, which is the voice of the universe.

For many twentieth century poets, that voice only comes through in riffs, fragments, rather than a complete discourse—Eliot's ability to shape only a fractured answer to his quest. Pound's Drafts. *Is this a fundamental change in poetry?*

The way I read that kind of fractured quality—and I don't know if there's any kind of accuracy in this—is this: there's a kind of bad faith that the poet experiences. Say, for instance, religion lets him down. So he turns his back on religion, and he faces the profane life. But there's a danger in that; in a way, it's a kind of death. I see that a poet's dialogue is not with a human audience. Yes, the poem communicates and so on: that's a by-product. When a poet writes the poem, the dialogue that's actually going on is with the universe, and I think if we don't realize that, then our poetry and our art is in jeopardy. When the dialogue is carried on horizontally, that is, with the culture, that is a lower form of art. When it is a dialogue with the universe, that is the highest realization of art.

Would you say, then, that The Waste Land *is a dialogue with culture ...*

Yes.

... whereas, Four Quartets *is a dialogue with the universe?*

Absolutely. We hear big snatches of *Four Quartets* where it's a dialogue with the universe. I think he's most successful when that occurs; I think, though, that every artist, just like every human being, goes through a period where our dialogue is with the culture. When we pick our clothes, it's a dialogue with the culture. We choose our spouse; sometimes, it's a dialogue with the culture. But ultimately, if we don't realize that our actions are a dialogue with the universe, then our actions don't have any power, don't have any capaciousness, capacity to them, because our horizontal dialogue is not as important as our dialogue with the universe.

Let's give the example of two people watering plants. If one person watering the plants realizes that what he's doing is a dialogue with his highest nature, the value of his watering the plant is very different from someone who's watering the plant and his mind is distracted. Two identical actions with different values; I am convinced of this. We can see that—well, look at the example of you bathing your child. If you're bathing your child and you're in a mind where you're totally present to what is going on in its temporal meaning and what is going on in its eternal meaning, the quality of your bathing your son is very different than if you're doing it distractedly. The value of those two actions are very different, just like when a poet writes poetry and realizes, when he's writing these poems, that he's having a dialogue with his highest nature, his true self, which is the universe, or he's just trying to write his poems in order to get into the *Paris Review*. The value of those two actions is very different, and the poem that comes out of them is different. So I would say that, yes, ultimately, all of us when we write poetry go through a period where our dialogue is with the canon—with Eliot, with Dante, with whom—but if a poet doesn't discover a dialogue that is more urgent than that, that is more personal, that is more anxiety-ridden than that, that has a greater tension and whose goal is a greater harmony: if we don't realize that, we're always going to be middle-shelf poets whose dialogue is with the canon.

You have reacted very strongly against being pigeonholed as an "Asian-American" writer. One of the reasons such a title angered you was that you felt you are a poet competing with the other great poets—Keats, Milton, Donne, others. Do you think that

that was your "cultural phase" and you've gone beyond that?

Yes. It's a progression for me. The fine print of that question—"where do you stand as an Asian-American writer"—is a question about one's dialogue with cultural significance. I would say the answer is nil; I have no dialogue with cultural existence. Culture made that up—Asian-American, African-American, whatever. I have no interest in that. I had an interest in spiritual lineage connected to poetry—through Eliot, Donne, Lorca, Tu Fu, Neruda, David the Psalmist. But I've realized that there is still the culture. Somehow an artist has to discover a dialogue that is so essential to his being, to his self, that it is no longer cultural or canonical, but a dialogue with your truest self. Your most naked spirit.

That makes me think of Keats who, in his earlier odes—particularly "Ode on a Grecian Urn"—wrote with incredible attention to the cultural, through allusions and such. Even in the poignant nightingale ode, one eye is on the canon. But this isn't so in "To Autumn" where he changes the dialogue from a concern about being one of "the great English Poets" to something larger and more poignant. He moves past his obsession.

Yes, and, of course, in order to be one of the great poets, you have to move past it. You have to discover a dialogue that is essential to you so that you can sing the songs, sing the poems, that only you can sing.

What other poets would you point to as having achieved that progression?

I see it in Roethke. Many of Frost's great poems. The instances where knowledge is in the way and he's speaking from a state of unknowing—or, I suppose, a state of knowing, because it is a state where you know in a manifold capacity.

The poems where Frost is creating a "momentary stay against confusion"—but maybe not the one Frost thinks he's creating.

Exactly. In poems like "Directive." There are moments in that poem where I'm sure the poem even escaped him, and that's great, that's what I want, that kind of recklessness where the poem is even ahead of you. It's like riding a horse that's a little too wild for you, so there's this tension between what you can do and what the horse decides it's going to do.

So do you return to Frost and Roethke and Eliot frequently?

And *The Epistles.*

What about Williams?

I read a lot of Williams earlier, but lately I find that . . . You see, my assumptions differ from Williams'. I can't tell why this should be, but I assume the spirit, and the spirit is first. Even the body is spirit.

And Williams is a very material poet.

Correct, and I can't see it because there's no ground. For me, apparent materiality has no materiality, especially now that physicists are proving that to us. The spirit for me—there's a lot of materiality there. I can't help but live but with this constant feeling, this knowledge, that everything we're seeing is fading away. So if everything is fading away, there is no ground; there is no materiality to any of this, anything we see or touch. So where is ground? What is materiality? I can't assume the material world. It seems to me then that Williams' poetry is built on sand; it looks solid, but it isn't because it speaks from a self that is grounded in things. But things have no materiality; they never have for me. Things don't have materiality; every time I try to write about a piece of fruit or the body of my father, it disappears under my looking, under my gaze. It literally disappears. There's nothing there; it's all sound, all vibration. I've been looking for many, many years to find a ground, and I guess mind is the ground I've found. Mind is ground. So my and Williams' assumptions are different.

It seems to me that for Roethke there is an assumption, even in his early poems, that spirit is ground. I felt that the voice is ground. The voice of his early poems is present in his later poems, too, except that it is much more capacious—there's more of the voice— but it's there all along. That voice is ground for Roethke, whereas in Williams, he's almost pared it down to something where I don't know if he was listening for a voice. He was so concerned with apparent materiality.

And is the poem on the page that is so important to Williams yet another dimension of materiality?

Yes, yes. I think it has to do with a backward notion of what the past and the present are. The Eastern notion of the past that I believe is that the past lies ahead of us, before us, and the future is behind us. We are moving into the future. If we can see it, it is already gone. To get entangled with what we can see is to get entangled with a phantom. At the quantam level of apparent reality, the most basic level, there is no materiality; it's sound, song. All of this materiality is the past. All of this is the past. We are constantly inhabiting the immediate past. How do we get to a place where that's not going on? And I might add this; the fractured quality of a lot of twentieth-century writing comes about I think because frequently we've taken our eyes off our homeland, our true place, and we've looked at the past. The past—all the material stuff that surrounds—looks fractured and confused; we forget when we're doing mimetic art, we think, "Well, our art has to look like this reality, which is broken and confused and discontinuous. We've forgotten that this is not where we're supposed to be looking. We're not supposed to be looking at this past. We're supposed to be looking forward, upward if you will, not back.

How can one do this?

I suppose that through constant remembrance that all of this [gestures around the room] is past; that all of this is fading away. All of this is going away; this is not what we're working toward. Don't repeat this. It's an exercise of the mind to think constantly that this false identity is fading away and my true self or identity is universe or God. There are certain assumptions that I secretly carry around, and I don't know if other poets share these. I assume that my true nature is God. I assume that I am God, in my true nature. All of this, everything I see here, keeps me from remembering that. I would say that the way I try to do that is to live in constant remembrance of who I am. That I am not this. I am not this stuff that is fading away.

But doesn't God also inhabit all this stuff that is fading away? Is there some differentiation, some hierarchy between the "hum," the song as manifest at the quantam level in this table, versus how it finds expression in you or me?

I think there is. First of all, it's mysterious but necessary for us to probe this assertion. When we say "All of this is God, too," we have to distinguish how God resides in all of this. God resides in all of this in law, which is transparent. So I would say, "Yes, all of this is part of God," because God is the transparent, subtle law that holds all of this up. That holds all of this together. But it's not this [raps on table]. There is no this. All of this is an illusion.

So, logos as shaping force, whereas in human beings, logos finds embodiment?

In poetry, logos finds embodiment.

Just poetry? What of other arts?

I don't know other arts that well. I look at them; my brother is a painter. But I don't want to claim that for other arts, because I don't practice them. Music, certainly. But everything that reveals for us, law, that's what logos is. Logos and law and Tao. They're the same thing. It's iron, absolute iron: autumn comes at a specific time and spring. It's iron. The earth goes around the sun. That's iron, but it's also soft, transparent. You can't point to it. So I would say that all art is yogic in that it yokes us to our highest nature; it reminds us of who we are, so when we read a great poem or look at great art, that's who we are. That's our true self.

The true self is the one that speaks, and it doesn't give a damn about the one that walks around in clothes. Sorry, it doesn't. That true self voice is the only thing that will last. The rest is chaff. Chaff. I'm not going to get caught up with chaff. All of this is chaff. But there is a deep, subtle law. We live in the midst of law all the time. You turn on a light switch, and the light comes on because it obeys certain laws. I talk to you from this distance and you can hear me; if I were to talk from a greater distance, you can't. That is governed by laws. We adhere to them whether we like it or not. Now, it seems to me that we can empower ourselves if we line up with it. And I don't mean by that going to church or not smoking pot or being Republican or whatever. I don't mean that. Those are human things. I'm saying line up with the voice that is greatest inside you, that is deepest and smallest.

In your vision, is it just that God or logos or law would allow cruelty? How do you account for cruelty?

I would say that human cruelty comes out of ignorance of who we are. If we realize that there is only one body and only one mind— I don't mean realize it intellectually—I mean realize it in a more fundamental way. Cruelty is only possible when we are ignorant of who we are and who the other person is. It's God we're speaking of. Tod, there are not two minds here. This interview is one mind speaking to itself. Do you understand? This is one mind reminding itself, by question and answer and so on, of what it is, of who it is. This is what I believe. I don't experience this; there is a double experience for me. On one level, I experience "two guys talking," but on a more important level, there are not two people talking here. There's one mind trying to figure this out. That's my experience.

Cruelty is when I mistake you for something other than God. Or I mistake myself for someone other than God. If I practice our mutual divinity, there is no way that I could be cruel. It's all practice. God is practice. Logos is practice. The logos is constantly enforced; it is enforced all the time. All of this is fading away; that's part of the logos; that's part of the iron law. The words we spoke five minutes ago are irrevocably gone. Except as recorded here, but they will soon be gone from even this recording, even this text. That's part of the law. It seems to me that we must align ourselves with that logos, if we don't realize our true identity that we are the logos, we are the law, we are God. We have to practice mutual divinity.

Sure, but there's that skeptical voice inside of me saying that Li-Young Lee and I can agree about this all day, but if we go out on Central Avenue in Memphis or Michigan Avenue in Chicago, there will be human beings bludgeoning one another, and there is not going to be a revolution in consciousness that will allow for the mutual appreciation of the godhead. And so we enact religious and governmental contracts in order somehow to mimic—maybe even parody—the law you're speaking of.

What I'm trying to say is this. If we think of ourselves, for instance, as separate countries—each person is a separate country—then I would have to say, "Well, I can't govern anybody else; I can't decide what anybody else should think." I only know what I feel and intuit. So the only thing that I can do is practice. I can practice mutual divinity. I can't ask anybody else to do it. It means, of course, the minute I wake up, I say, "Thank you." While I'm brushing my teeth, I'm saying "thank you." I'm pouring cereal for my kid, I'm saying "thank you." We have sixty-thousand thoughts a day. How many times can I say "thank you" every day until my mind becomes blank, empty, nothing, and God can enter it?

Part of the practice of mantra, an Eastern practice, is the practice of emptying the mind, getting those sixty-thousand thoughts so that they're not various thoughts, but all one thought. And when you can make it all one thought, there is no thought, there is something larger coming to inhabit you. So, in a way, I think of poetry as mantra work; you're trying to hit that one note and keep that note. "Back out of all this now too much for us, / Back in a time made simple by the loss": That's a mantra. "Time past and time present"—it's like a mantra. That's what it is to my understanding. So the only thing that I know I can do is practice it. I practice it. I'm not saying I've accomplished that; I'm saying I can begin again today. Ever since I was a child, that was a practice of living in constant remembrance of—call it whatever you want. Call it what the Sufis did; they picked the word for "fading away." So they're thinking it while they're drinking coffee, "fading away." "Fading Away." They're looking out the window, and they're thinking "fading away." They get up and go to the bathroom— "fading away"—they look down at the table, and so on. That's all they're thinking. Some Buddhists think "thank you" constantly. It seems to me that all of that is yogic. It's exercise. It's making the mind.

You have a rich ear, I think, and it's reflected in your poetry. I wonder how those two things fit together: the desire to capture that "one note" that is the God, that is the universe humming, and the desire to write something like your line "the round jubilance of peaches" that is so full of luscious sounds. In earlier work, were you more concerned with creating an aesthetic texture than capturing this mantra quality?

No. I've always felt that aesthetic thinking was the highest form of moral thinking. It is the highest form of ethical and moral thought.

The beautiful and the good as one?

Right. I still believe that. I think it's bad when poets say, "I don't believe in the beautiful anymore. Look at the world." Well, I say you're looking the wrong way. You're looking at the past. Poets should traffic in the ideal. That's what a poet is; a poet is an angel who traffics in the ideal. You don't traffic only in the past. For me, as far back as I can remember, I was trying to hear a kind of hum, trying to feel it, and if I could hear or feel that hum, then the words just came and perched on that hum. If I don't hear the hum, then I have to make the poem out of words. But if I'm hearing the hum and I hear it very clearly, then the perfect words like birds will come and perch on that line. They will be the perfect words. But if my hearing is off—if it's a little broken—and I'm faking it, then I'm putting words in there, kind of making the illusion that there is something underneath. No. I'm interested in the frequency under those words.

Is there that humming? And the humming, of course, is not only in the ear, it's your whole body. I don't write poems with my mind only. I know there are a lot of poems that when you read them you say, "Well, this is a mentality writing," and it may be a very great one. But it seems to me that poetry comes from my elbow, the ache in my knee. My hip. The soles of my feet. Literally. And whether or not they ache will determine what kind of language I'm using. The way my scalp feels. Whether or not I'm sexually aroused when I'm writing. I need to feel it with my whole being. You see, language for me isn't a mental thing; it's like your whole body. Lawrence said that every man just writes with his penis, but you don't just write with your penis, you write with your whole being. Your fingers, your hair. That's what language is. It isn't some flaky dandruff; we keep thinking that "there's the world and there's language that's like some flaky dandruff that lands on it." If that's the way you think of it, then that's the way it is for you. But that's not the way that I experience language. Language feels to me like milk.

Nectar.

Yes, like nectar.

What of the formal impulses—you use couplets and other traditional forms, even poems that could be called sonnets?

But that's a belief in the law of sonnets. The sonnet is a law. It's a shape of law. We think it's a literary form. No! It was first a law, and then it became a literary form. But there are certain laws: you can make this move, you can make that move, and you can make this turn in a sonnet. The *volta*. That makes the turn. That's law. But some people treat it like it's an empty shelf, a shelf of books and then you add the books and then you've got a sonnet. No. It's whether or not there is a certain kind of turning in the sonnet that occurs. A turning of consciousness.

The couplet, the sonnet, the villanelle as Platonic ideals, as aesthetic forms that have worked, that have successfully rendered the beautiful?

Exactly. And you know, when I did those poems, I wanted to use the word "accident," but the word "accident" doesn't have enough fatality to it. It was fatal that "Goodnight" was in couplets; it was coming down in couplets, and I have no explanation why it was coming in couplets, but I knew that the minute I tried to understand, the poem would stop, so I didn't try to understand. I let it come. Or, let's say I write a version of a poem and something's missing. I ask myself, "What's the law here that I don't see?" And then as I'm walking around one day or looking at the draft, I see "the couplet version," the actual poem, as though something in front of my eyes disappeared and I saw the law under it. And it was saying "couplets." So I put the poem in couplets and it works.

We deal in the invisible, not in the visible. That's what a poet does. It's not the visible world we're dealing with. And that's my argument with Williams, I guess. Though I have to tell you that I love him; I love him. But he practiced poetry as though it's a secular art. It is not. It is the practice of the sacred. I would say that all religion is fossilized poetry. Poets are the real practitioners of the sacred. The priests, churches, they come after us. Let them build. They are already the fossilized versions of what poets come up with. That's the greatest calling for poets. Or we can write ditties. Or we can—and I see Eliot going wrong by putting himself in service to the church. That's where he went wrong. He should have realized that the church comes from him; he's prior to the church. The church is for him, the way King David said the Sabbath is for man. He put man ahead of the Sabbath. The church is for us; we're not for the church. When we make poems, that's what the church is referring to. The voice that we hear when we write poems or the visions that artists see when they make paintings. The invisible. Rilke called us "bees of the invisible," and he was right. It's not the visible world we're dealing with, because the law is transparent. You can't see a transparency, but we put words there so you can kind of feel the transparency.

It's like this. There is a body prior to the words; words clothe that body. But it's not arbitrary; it's not "body" and then "words." If that body is humming, erect, it will magnetize certain words to it. Other words it will not magnetize to it. It's a kind of magnetism; which is vibration: this table, my words, everything is vibration. Thoughts are vibration. You can't see radio waves; you can't see microwaves, but they're there. And there are these other waves: the great voice.

What is the poet's responsibility toward the political? What do you understand "poetry of witness" to be? How does it connect to our culture?

I think that's complicated. I think it has to do with forgetting the poet's mission. I think we have a mission. When I first saw "poetry of witness," I said "Wow! Now here's something right up my alley." And then I looked at it and thought, "Oh, they're not witnessing the invisible. They're witnessing the visible." I wasn't interested in that. When I hear poetry of witness, I think of the poet witnessing the invisible. The poet shows how the invisible is more real than the visible. That the visible is merely a late outcome of an invisible reality, an invisible reality that rules us the way the subconscious rules us. Our dreamscape is larger and rules us more than this waking state. Beyond the dreamscape there is another consciousness that rules us. I thought it meant "poetry of witnessing the invisible," of witnessing our true nature—like Whitman was doing.

I think the poets of my generation have to make a break. We have to realize that the visible is not the material of our work. We can't be poets witnessing the visible; we have to be poets witnessing the invisible. Or else there's no other hope. We know how the mind works. You keep witnessing the visible, then it will keep happening. So in a strange way then, a poet comes in cahoots with what it is he or she is putting down. They're saying, "This is terrible! Look at it! Look at it!" It would be like taking an abused child and keep replaying in his mind his father abusing him. Would that have a good effect or a bad effect? We know now that that repeated behavior in the mind makes it so he can't help but act it out. We've got to find a new recording for him; you've got to put something else in his mind or he'll keep perpetuating it.

So, the poet becomes a perpetrator of those crimes when he or she reproduces those crimes in his or her work. I know that I have done the same thing, but that was out of ignorance or a fear that the invisible doesn't exist. In a way, Tod, I feel a kind of acceleration, a need to disillusion myself and stop thinking that the visible world is all that dear and that we can't lose it. That's a romanticism. We're losing it. From our body, three billion cells a minute are going! And it's faster than that three billion cells a minute rate; I just keep using the body as a point of reference. My words are disappearing faster than the cells in my body are reproducing, so all of this is going away. It's romantic, stupidly romantic, naïve, ignorance. It's ignorance for us to think that we have to somehow witness all of this. No! That's not our business; the poet's business is to witness the spirit, the invisible, the law.

What is the poet's relationship, then, with individual words? What sort of referential connection do you think they have to this vanishing world?

Language's mystery doesn't come from the notion that it doesn't refer to anything. What I find mysterious in language is that it's involved in a state of infinite referral. A flower isn't even a flower; it's a referent for something else. A flower refers to something else; each animal refers to something else. The whole universe keeps referring infinitely back. That's the way I experience it.

An infinite regression of symbols?

Of referral. Every word refers infinitely for me. Certain words are more powerful. Because of my limitations—my personality—certain words have higher vibrations than other words. Because words have vibrations to me. I don't experience sentences as a string of words. I can't explain to you how concrete this is for me. This is not a theory. I experience the length of a day, literally, as a sentence. One sentence. Or, I should say more clearly, as a unit of meaning.

A measure?

A measure! I experience it as a measure. A sentence is a measure. But of what? It's a measure of information; it can carry information; it can carry time. You can write two sentences using different words, and they'll carry time differently. It can carry consciousness; it can carry different modes of consciousness. Certainly the way Neruda uses sentences is different from the way Frost uses sentences. Let's say there is more manifold consciousness in most Neruda sentences.

You say a day is a measure—from rise to sleep. But there's overlap.

Right. Beautiful. So it's like sentence within sentence within sentence. A life is a day. In a way, during a day, from waking to sleeping, you get to enact your whole lifetime.

The past overlaps into the future, then, in a continuum, and thus it's very difficult to pinpoint and capture the present, the essence, the eternal moment crystallized.

Yes, no one is going to capture it. Especially if they're talking about it. Because as long as you're talking about it, you're facing it. But I want to say something else about sentences. Sometimes you write three syntactical units called sentences, but the three of them actually create "a sentence." The sentence I'm talking about. I heard somewhere that the word "sentence" used to mean "truth." That if you said to someone "You spoke sentence," then you meant that he or she said something that had authority. I guess what I'm trying to hear is that authority. So you might actually take three grammatical sentences in order to make a "sentence."

Is that how you understand the movement of The Winged Seed? *You composed that in one movement, one measure.*

There were a lot of contradictory things I was working with, so I felt, in a way, ripped apart.

Why did you use prose?

I didn't think of it so much as prose. The thing that I saw was a unit, a written unit measure that went from one end of the page to the other. Nonstop. So basically what I saw, what I wanted to write, was one continuous sentence. That's what I wanted to write. Two hundred pages, one sentence. I knew that, realistically speaking, I would have to have many grammatical units. But I wanted to say one sentence and it would be long. So the particular sentences would have to embody that length. Thus, I had an interest in sentences instead of the poetic line.

Yes, in many of your poems you use a short line; so a vision of the words stretching across the page is quite a departure from that. Can you talk about your lineation?

When I wrote those earlier poems, I was actually thinking in lines. So the hesitation you experience at the end of those lines, I experienced. That's the way I understood those lines.

I feel those poems as moving vertically, down the page with a push. The movement in the memoir—we're pushed along in a similar way, but the pace is much slower.

Even now, in the poems I'm writing, although they have longer line breaks, I can see now that the sentence is my concern. I like the idea that the line breaks make notation for the mind actually thinking; I like that. But it's ultimately the sentence that I'm writing. Not the grammatical sentence, the measure.

You mentioned earlier that—as you approach forty—the serious literary or cultural work that engaged you when you were younger is not important. And you also mentioned a desperate need for contemporary poets to reorient their work. What best captures the invisible? Do you ever feel that poetry, that language, isn't up to the task?

I'm writing more than I ever have. My experience is that everything is discourse; it's like a big roar, a big hum. Everything is language. Trees are language; birds are language. A bird is a little cipher. A bird is a word. Beyond the word for bird, bird is a word. That's my experience. A tree is a word that refers to something else. The ocean is a word; each wave is a word. The whole world is language to me. Now what I need to do is figure out what I do with this richness. Well, of course, praise. It's the hardest thing to write, praise. What I've been writing, I hope, is just pure praise. That's my hope. I've been writing a lot, and I hope when I get a little time and go back to see what I've done that it's praise. The language of praise. I literally feel Wow! Every leaf—and how many leaves are there in the world, Tod?—that every leaf is a word. A vibration. A word is a vibration; a leaf is a vibration. Physicists have been telling us that: material reality is vibration. A leaf is a vibration: it's a word! Branches are words!

So you don't see yourself as ultimately despairing that you can't capture this litany.

No, no! I feel just the opposite. I feel grateful because there was a period I went through, thinking "it's all nothing" or something like that. But now, I don't know what's going on, I feel like it's all language. It's all conversing. Apples on the trees: I look at them and see all these words on the trees. It's all language. All of it. This table is a very bad form of language. This room is language; when you walk into this room, it's saying something. Your body reads it—whether you're comfortable or not. You're reading constantly. You walk into a restaurant: you know whether you're comfortable or not—by the lighting, the people, etc. You're reading. We're reading constantly. We're walking through the world reading. By the time of day we read, "Oh, I should be home now." We're reading our children's moods, our wive's actions. We walk into a place like this, and think, "Oh, I don't mind talking here, but I don't want to sleep here." Everything is language.

I should add this. It isn't a big turning that I experienced, a reorientation from the visible to the invisible. It was a realization that that was what I was always doing. That that's what I was always hearing. I started to entertain some of the "stuff" that's in the canon; I forgot for a little bit that that was the horizontal, the cultural, and that wasn't the richest mode for me. If you look at the earliest poems in *Rose*, you'll see the vertical assumption. The assumption that the vertical reality was the primary reality and all of this was fading away, just "stuff" spinning off of that more important reality. The change was just in the realization.

> *You haven't published much poetry for the last few years. Your first two books were quite celebrated, recipients of awards and such. How does the "award" and "prize" culture of the literary world affect one's work? Roethke, Yeats: you can point to numerous examples of poets who clip the articles and invest so much in reception.*

I don't do that. I'm not patting myself on the back; I'm just saying that I find it boring. I don't clip reviews and articles and whatever. My wife did for a while, and then she stopped, too. She got bored, too. I think that dialogue is with the culture; I'm not interested in that. Look at it this way: it's like if you and I are having a serious conversation and someone over there keeps wanting to talk about *Laverne and Shirley*. We could engage that or we could just say, "No, I realize that this is what we're here to do." I see that horizontal dialogue with the canon, with the culture, as a waste of energy. I'm being very practical; it's a waste of energy.

On the other hand, you rely, as someone who doesn't teach, on people celebrating your work and awarding grants and inviting you to give readings and such.

I'll tell you this. Let's say there's a man there and he's carving cork. Little pieces of cork. Someone comes up to him and says, "What are you doing?" "Carving cork." And no one pays attention to him. And he does whatever he wants: he wants to do a grasshopper, he does a grasshopper; he wants to do a cup and saucer, he does a cup and saucer; he wants to do a toilet, he does a toilet. And then one day, someone comes along and says, "My God! Those are beautiful; I'll buy them all." It would be foolish of that man to change what he was doing. Why should he change his orientation? The dialogue for him was with his work and he should continue that way. Why should he change?

I see your point.

And I think it's the same mistake as when we think our dialogue is only with the visible. Let's say the poet keeps telling himself, "I am a good poet, I am a good poet." And he works and works and works and his book comes out and he wins the Pulitzer. Suddenly, the temptation is to put everything in front of one, to embrace the cultural dialogue, when the poet should be saying, "Get behind me; I knew I was good. You're late! Stay behind me! I'm still the beginning here. I am the master of this dialogue."

Now that might mean everyone goes away or whatever, but I don't believe that that's important. I believe that when we line up with the law, the law wants to be revealed. It wants to be revealed; it needs to be revealed. It wills its own revelation; we're in service to poetry. Poetry is something greater than us. You see, the whole universe is a poem! It has no rational meaning. It has no reason for being. Yet it is. All of the laws, all of the universe's laws, are poetic laws. None of them are logical; all of them defy understanding. All of them are great. Everything we say about a great poem is true about the universe. A poem is a little universe. If we line ourselves up with that, then the universe—God—can't help but support that. It supports itself. I don't mean to sound crazy, but I can't help but think that—let's say I publish a third book of poems, and I think it's my greatest work. Nobody reads it. That's too bad. There may be a sub-personality inside of me that says, "Oh, gee, I'm sad." But the me that works and loves poetry will look at that and say, "Whatever. My dialogue is not with that. I'll have to be supported some other way. Go back and work at the warehouse. Whatever it is I have to do." Whatever my life, this huge momentous life of mine that is beyond me, whatever it offers me, that's what I'll do.

So I don't like the idea that I depend on that culture. They depend on us, Tod! I'm going to tell you something. When a poet writes a poem, he or she has already created something better in the universe. By writing it! If he never publishes it, he's already created more value in the universe than someone else who didn't write it. That value comes back; it precipitates out into great things. Great things. I don't believe the writing of poems is unrewarded if you don't publish them. So it doesn't get rewarded "that way," which is the most direct way we see. It gets rewarded other ways. Your health— the health of your children. Your mental health. The wholeness of you and your children.

There's nothing more heartbreaking than seeing a child suffer. And we think about the suffering that might be in store for them when we look at this culture. The most we can do—the highest thing we can do—is practice art. There is only one mind, and so whatever we do in that mind—when we create more beauty there, more opening, more understanding, more light, when we shed more light in our own mind—affects the great mind. So you're creating value when you write a poem. And I don't mean immaterial value. I mean material value! I mean someone in China—and they've proven that on the physical scale, that when a butterfly flies across Tianenmen Square, it affects the weather in Florida. In minute and inevitable ways, everything is connected. In the invisible realm—which has more reality than the visible realm because the visible is dying and without materiality—when somebody writes a poem, when they open themselves up to universe mind and that universe mind is suddenly present in the visible world, the poet isn't the only one that gets the benefits of that. Universe mind comes down and that whole mind is a little more pure, a little more habitable. A little more habitable. I believe this. That's why we're the unacknowledged legislators of the world. I never understood that until recently. We keep the world from falling fucking apart, and they don't even know this! Not priests. Not ministers. Not rabbis. We keep the world together. If we stop writing poems, you'll see this world go into such darkness, they won't even know what hit them.

Quite an imperative . . .

Yes, and many poets are giving up that large mantle; they're saying, "We're witnesses of the visible." No. That's not our original mission. Our mission is witnessing the invisible and making it revealed in the visible so that everybody can line up and know what they're lining up with. Like Whitman—lining up with the cosmos that they are. They aren't lining up with the Pope or with "good behavior." They are beyond good and evil. The true self is beyond good and evil, and all poems are the voice of the true self. It's real simple. All poetry is the voice of the true self. So, when you read a poem, you're hearing your true self. The more true self we get into this world, the better for all of us. The more true self we uncover, the better for all of us. If you never publish another poem, but you write those poems, you're already doing work in the spirit world that is absolutely necessary. So when Li-po wrote his poems and sent them down the river, what do you think he was doing? You know, he wrote those poems and folded them into little boats and sent them on their way; he was in a great state of enlightenment— "If I never show these to anybody, I'm doing the work." I'm doing the work! Because there's one mind, I'm doing the work in that mind!

So what would you say to a pessimist who says, "OK, Li-Young, but what about all this tawdriness—Baywatch, Las Vegas, the OJ trial—that commands such popular attention? Do you really think that this 'invisible' stuff affects that?" What of the skeptic that just rejects the Platonic premise of your argument?

Here's the thing. If all the poets in the world stopped publishing, we would still be doing vital work. If no one read poetry. Nobody. If nobody read it! We would still be the unacknowledged legislators of the world. We are still at the gates keeping the visible crap, winnowing the visible crap. That's what we're doing. The fact of publication is secondary; we're doing it in the spirit realm already. In the world of the invisible, we're doing the work. That's what I believe. If there is a state where no one is even writing, then we're in trouble.

I happen to think that thoughts are like radio waves. They're finer than radio waves, higher in vibration; we don't have an instrument that detects them. Thoughts precipitate into action. If we don't like what we see, we're going to have to change our thinking. The mind is the only field of endeavor, the only field of work, that is fruitful to work in. It determines actions, which determine civilization, which determines health care reform, and on and on. But the mind is the first circle. If we work in the second circle, we don't know the outcome. The poet works in that first circle. All the time. The outcome of invisible things is always visible. But unfortunately, we always want to deal in the realm of the outcome. Visible things are always just a reporting in the visible world; as poets, we want to deal with those things at the source. We should want to deal with the cause, not the symptom.

The poet is the one saying the best and brightest things to a reader: "You're God; you're cosmos; you're universe." The poet is walking around, saying, "We are the universe. You are the universe; I am the universe." That's what Whitman did; that's what King David did. What the hell are we doing? I see our mission as much larger than witnessing only the material world. And it isn't to report on a twenty-years war. Twenty years? What is that? That's nothing. It's to report on something much bigger. There's only one news. This visible stuff: that's not the news. We've seen this! The news is that we are the universe. That's the only news there ever was; that's the only news that the poet reports that lasts. We want to hear the news. We need to hear the news.

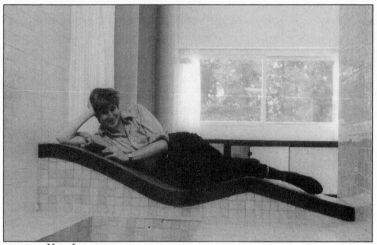

PHOTO BY NICK LOLORDO

Laura Mullen was born in Los Angeles, California, in 1958. She received her M.F.A. degree from the Iowa Writers' Workshop and currently teaches at Colorado State University in Fort Collins. The author of The Surface *and* After I Was Dead, *Mullen's work combines a fierce attraction to experimental poetics with a concrete desire not to slip into pedantic platitudes; that is, she wants her poetry to engage the avante-garde of contemporary American practice with a wit which undercuts the often overly self-assured posture of such theory. Energetic and original, Mullen has also written a book of prose—a "murder mystery"—which like her poetry similarly grapples with narrative conventions. Her writing has won many awards including a fellowship from the National Endowment for the Arts.*

LAURA MULLEN

Laura and I spoke in Fort Collins, Colorado, during summer 1997.

As a woman coming to poetry in the latter half of the twentieth century, what work did you find encouraging? What poetry did you look to for sustenance, what poetry inspired you to try your own hand at the art, or with what poetry did you feel a kinship?

Okay. It's a hard question, it seems to me; I had a frantic dinner conversation about this once you told me that we would talk about it, because, of course, one is supposed to be able to map a (mono-gendered) line of inheritance—and one feels the weight of this: there are some answers one is supposed to have—Adrienne Rich, H.D. Answers like that, and those aren't the answers I have. Of course, Plath is tremendously important, but later: I started writing at the age of fourteen or so because of Richard Brautigan, because of the poem "Rommel Drives Deep Into Egypt," which ends, "How's your ass?" And I thought, "If this is poetry, I can do it." And so I started writing poetry because of Richard Brautigan, but then T.S. Eliot, then it was Ashbery, both of whom I just ate and breathed. Finally, because of the historical limitations of the culture and the academy, I came to the women writers—but late: as an undergraduate student at Humboldt State University where I had a class on women artists and I had a class on women writers. And thank God for the people whose consciousness was high enough to actually be teaching that. And I met a woman poet, Jorie Graham.

I don't think I'd be a poet if I hadn't met her, if she hadn't liked the work, if I hadn't been able to be in conversation with her, if she hadn't showed me the women poets she showed me—I chiefly remember my love of Bishop and Woolf coming out of Jorie's class. But she had me read Heather McHugh; she had me read Louise Glück; she had me read, oh God, she had me read Sandra McPherson, as well as Hass and Hugo. And these writers mattered to me, instantly. So what I finally came to after a long, sort of soul-wracking conversation with myself is that in some ways I still don't like some of the women I'm supposed to like. But there's room to grow backward in time (as in: from Brautigan to Spicer to Stein). I like the women who like those women; for instance, Anne Carson. Now, Anne Carson, I think, has read Sappho and H.D. So I feel like, "Okay, we've got a kinship thing going." But it's not as perfect as I could imagine it being. And I wish I'd encountered Stein earlier—I lost some time in not knowing that treasure existed.

I guess in your response to my question, I found an interesting leap: you went from Brautigan to Eliot, and I wonder if that was because of the academic setting; you initially interacted with some energy, some spontaneity, some fun in Brautigan that brought you to the word, and then you heard from on high what the Word, with a capital W, was, and that shaped your aesthetic.

I think there's something to that. Certainly it occurs to me that when I fell in love with Brautigan as I did, that was because my original influence was Dr. Seuss, who, if I fell in love with the fun of the word, that's when I fell in love: at the age of, what, three? With Dr. Seuss. Then what happened was I ran into Richard Brautigan's books at a free school I was going to (because I told my parents that if I had to stay in a normal school I was going to kill myself). And then I was, in fact, sort of cured of that malaise (because the free school was too expensive) and was back in public high school, getting T.S. Eliot (the gorgeousness of that language contained by a certain pedagogy, poetry as test): so the teacher read "The Love Song of J. Alfred Prufrock," and asked us—I remember this—to identify the two most important lines, and I was able to do it. And it wasn't just that I adored Eliot's images or how deeply I understood (near to the age he wrote the poem, after all) Eliot's sense of desperation and complete hysterical anxiety about time, but also that I'd arrived in a situation where I could get some approval.

Do you still feel as strongly for Eliot's work as you did then?

I really distrust him, but I still love him.

What do you mean by "distrust him?"

I know what's wrong with him now. I mean, he hates the body and fears time—it's very exciting, but I can't live there, you know?

What about some of the other Modernists? Pound, Moore, Stevens, Williams?

Okay. Well, you know, Stevens and Williams: they're my guys. Love 'em. No problem. Pound? Those experimentations are really the original hypertext, but, well, finally I just get, I go to sleep. There's so much of it; it's all over the place, but it seems that you—the reader—can't be: you have to be his good student. And then I think the sentimentality of the early poems haunts and inhibits the thinking. But it's fun to screw around in; I mean, I'm a sucker for the music of it and the largeness of his leaps, though I can't dwell there, or I don't, yet: I'm not getting the energy which makes me want to live and write.

Well, with Williams I can see that energy and the bodiliness of the work. But Stevens is a poet so much of the interior, in a lot of ways, a poet who—you know, I think of one of those later poems, "First Warmth," where he wonders if he's "lived a skeleton's life, as a questioner about reality." That's one of his last poems . . . that poem seems so sad to me.

It's very sad. But he's sad in a way that Eliot is, and he's sad in a way I recognize and struggle to live with. My next book is called *After I Was Dead*. I thought about using an epigraph from "Esthetique du Mal": "The greatest tragedy is not to have lived in a physical world." On some level the question is always how does one live in a physical world while knowing that, as Stevens also says, what we said about it became a part of what it is. To disentangle what actually is the physical world from our ideas about it is so complex and takes so long. I very much identify with the understanding of the difficulty of that quest and the desire to somehow get past what we said about it to what might actually be there.

That certainly is Stevens' quest, and you've got that as part of your work. I can see that in, I think, both books, and the new book more vividly, perhaps. Williams, though, Williams is—?

Well, Williams? For instance, the book coming out after *After I Was Dead*, though it was written before it, is this novel, which isn't a novel, called *The Tales of Horror*. Really, *Paterson* set me free to write that book. I never, never, never would have dared if Williams' work hadn't been there as a constellation, as Michael Palmer says, as a way of showing that anything can go in. I think it's Duncan who talks about recognizing that nothing is trivial, being able to live in a world where everything is part of the art, and that kind of thinking was a (very slow) revelation for me, because I came from a world where there was or seemed to me to be a very clear line between life and art. My grandmother was an art dealer—contemporary art (1960-75)—and though there was a blurred distinction between the gallery (in her house) and her home and while the art she was showing challenged those boundaries in more or less important ways, still, it was all very clean (her house was a Modernist glass box, very white, and the "messy"—self-consciously expressionistic—art was perfectly framed). And in that clean, pristine, perfect display case of a house, I was, at first, just one of the grandchildren who liked to take the silk pillows off the couch and slide down the long polished floor on them—and that gesture (and my grandmother's dismay) intersected in potent ways with my mother's anger and disappointment at not being an artist herself: she didn't have a painting on those walls (much less a show) but these little, you know, trouble makers. So there was the problem of the body; I mean, it was clearly a problem.

The notion that the clean, museum world of the aesthetic object somehow doesn't connect to the mess that is life.

Doesn't connect, doesn't include, can't include, gets upset if life—

Williams realizes that.

Williams makes a space in which everything is colliding.

What about Marianne Moore? She's a poet that brings things into her poems. She's celebrated as someone who brings in these quotations from everyday sources, and yet the surface into which she inserts them is so shaped, so orderly, and so refined. The syllabic matrix.

And for that reason, perhaps—again, it's that lineage thing. I could say, "Oh yes, I like Moore." What I mean is, I like Bishop. And through Bishop, I like Moore. Moore is gorgeous, I read her every now and then, but she's not a poet that deeply matters to me; I think because of that core. It's a bit too finicky, finally, and she revises herself so badly; mostly, it's painful.

It sounds like, then, if I'm hearing you correctly in your reaction to many of the Modernist poets, you appreciate them for the "ground they cleared" or the space that they opened into which poets of the later generation did work to which perhaps you feel more connected.

No. I'm not sure that's true. I feel totally connected to Williams and Stevens. I mean, I'm connected, and it's not because they cleared the ground. Although my quarrel with Stevens at this point is that he said what had to be done, but he didn't do it. He had the realization, but the work does not enact the realization. And what I've come to, what I'm slowly and laboriously coming to, is more and more of a demand that the work enact the realization.

Okay. And in what work do you find that happening? In Ashbery?

Ashbery, absolutely. I just read *Flow Chart*, and I was so, so, so deeply thrilled to be reading that book. I wish I could read it for the first time over and over and over again, because it's such a shock. And I'm reading Lisa Jarnot's *Some Other Kind of Mission*. So good. Let's see, I'll just open it up and read part of Part I [she's playing with the page, in a way that's wonderfully radical]: "Blood in my eyes followed by truck and motel, either severely or proper, followed by police action, followed by truck in, followed by followed by followed by truck in motel at the library, at the truck in motel at the of today there where they're taking me, followed by, I dreamt about and followed by . . . ."

That's Gertrude Stein to my ear.

It's very much Gertrude Stein, although Jarnot's playing with sestinas and collages, and something like the whiff of a narrative is creeping in. So, yeah, it's a bit like Stein (someone who, maybe to a fault, enacted the realization), but also very new.

When you say that you want a poem that "enacts" the realization—I wonder if you could help me phrase this realization: "The realization that we have ideas about the world and yet can never quite connect with the world, and we try to do that."

Well, Joshua Clover puts it nicely in an essay on Language poetry (in the first issue of *Fence*) when he pays homage to whoever first inverted "No ideas but in things" as "No things but in ideas." We have that; we also have the capacity (and urgent need) as a culture to recognize many, many subjectivities, both in the single self in time and across many different selves, different cultures—the objective "thing" is complicated to look at. Or as Michele Glazer puts it, in the title of her book, *It Is Hard To Look At What We Thought We Came To See.* It matters where you stand and when you stand there.

> *It seems that some readers might say that the poets we've mentioned are very difficult. Some people would say that they are very distant from a poetry that could perhaps reach a more general audience, and this difficult poetry is connected to the fact that poetry is such a marginalized art in our culture. What do you think about the notion that poetry is a marginalized art?*

Whoa, let me stop you, because your question had like five layers, and I'm answering all five of them. First of all, let me start by quoting Carole Maso, whose work I adore, who I adore personally: "Then you put me in your box labeled experimental, you put me in your box labeled unreadable, and then I'm safe there." I don't think it's true that the work is "difficult." Hell, Stein is a lot of things, but "difficult"?! Only if you want to test a class on what the two most important lines are!

It's amazing to me that we live in this huge, supposedly free country, and yet—you know this as a teacher—you have students in their early twenties, and as a friend of mine put it, "What happened to them that all the curiosity has been knocked out? What happened to them that they're so worried about experimenting in all kinds of different directions?"

Okay. One answer to your layered question is that, in fact, people are afraid to become imperceptible; they're afraid to go off the map and be where the light doesn't shine, and be where they can't be seen, can't be read, can't be heard. But it seems to me, given the example, for instance, of Dickinson, that it is worth it to not be seen, not be heard now, if you're getting to do exactly what you believe you have to do. So, with *The Tales of Horror*, which is very experimental, it was worth it to just do the thing and not be thinking, "Can I get this published?" because I knew when I was doing it: "No, I can't get this published." And hooray for Kelsey Street, for the courage of those brilliant women, their open vision and the rigor of their commitment to the experimental!

Right. I guess I was hearkening back to some of the rhetoric of Dana Gioia's questioning in his book on poetry as to whether "poetry can matter" in our culture?

I thought that was asinine. I thought that was completely asinine. For one thing, of course, the man who's asking it is paying no attention to the fact of spoken-word poetry; poetry matters a great deal. I mean, whenever people say poetry's marginalized, they're talking about reading-wise. They're not talking about performing, they're not talking about writing, 'cause, man, everyone is writing it.

I think what we're sliding toward here, then, is the issue of what are the formal ingredients of the poem, because many would argue that ingredients X, Y, and Z have to be there for it to be a poem.

I think you're right about their ideas and ingredients. Their reception bandwidth, their spectrum, is very narrow, which makes them see poetry as marginalized, although that's extremely peculiar since the little area that those people are focused on is mostly full of white males who win all the prizes, and how can they talk about marginalization at that level? It makes me giddy. If you look at the wider picture, then you wonder, what do they mean, marginalized? I mean, what do we mean?

Marginalized—well, the fact that Susan Howe—given her achievement— hasn't won a major prize: that's marginalized. But is poetry marginalized? Compared to what? Rock music? Those are the troubador poets of our day! (Bob Dylan slipped me French Surrealism long, long before I went to college to find out there was such a thing.)

Well, what constitutes the X,Y, and Z of poetry for you?

As I said, I was lucky enough to have Jorie Graham as a professor, undergraduate, Humboldt State University: extraordinary, extraordinary experience. And one of the things that she made us aware of was that poetry is happening all the time. I mean, she said, "You go to the supermarket, a poem doesn't stop cause you're at the supermarket." So when you say to me, "What constitutes a poem?" I want to say, "Hey, we don't know yet." I mean, we know everything that's been written so far that we've called a poem, that's what we've said is a poem. But there might be other things that are other poems that we don't know, yet, how to recognize.

Yet, if we look at either of your books of poems, we see language arranged in a certain way on the page—

Although those ways are variable, as you yourself pointed out.

Certainly there's a wide formal range in the books, but you do decide that some things go on the page and some things do not.

Absolutely.

What goes into that decision-making process?

Hmm. Well, it's going to vary from poem to poem. You know? You're cooking something in the kitchen. What makes you decide what goes into the sauce?

I understand what you're saying—it seems like what Jorie Graham was speaking to was being receptive to a constant stream of possible poetry that one might encounter—

Exactly. Yes.

—and yet there's a difference between that receptivity and what

makes it onto the page, especially when you bring revision into the picture.

Absolutely! It has to do, a lot, with what you are able to recognize as poetry, which is why I made the statement that we don't know yet what it is. A student was asking, you know, what's the most anti-poetry thing you've ever encountered, and I replied, "Oh, faculty meetings." One wants to say, "Yes, of course," but that's also my fault, my loss. If I were receptive enough, if I were awake enough, if I were present enough (in maybe a Zen sense), in fact, I would see the poem in the faculty meeting.

So when we talk about what makes it on to the pages in my books, we talk about, in some ways, my flaws, especially with *The Surface*. What got on to the pages of the first book was mostly what I recognized as poetry, given my training, my educational background, and to me just now it seems like a pretty narrow band. I won't disown that book; I like it; but even while stretching the form to fit my needs back then, I was also, unconsciously, compressing my needs and desires to fit the form: I was writing what I knew to be a poem. With *After I Was Dead*, I'm still there more than I'd like to be, writing what I know to be a poem. What I loved about *The Tales of Horror* is that I was writing what I didn't know to be anything yet. And I would aim for would hope to see for myself, further continuation into areas I don't recognize, because that's how the New happens and where life and energy are.

It sounds like you're speaking toward something we might associate with the notion of process, of constantly taking things in and producing poems, sending them out there into the world.

Oh no, I'm not Frank O'Hara. That's O'Hara, really. I'm not there. That's a Zen state of genius that involves or requires more alcohol than I can handle.

Okay, well—on the other hand, this attention, this attentiveness to the world, also has a moral dimension to it.

Absolutely.

A generosity to Being, if you will, and I wonder if the end result of such activity is silence, rather than producing the poem. Because you can't get the constant poem that is Being on to the page, you can only live it, if that makes sense.

Let's see—I don't think so. I mean, one should think of Oppen here, but my first reaction to that statement is, "What about Celan?" I don't think silence and generosity go hand in hand, actually. For me, times of silence are times when I'm saying, "The world is not poetry." They're times when I'm saying, "I have nothing to say, because I'm angry or despairing and thinking what I would like to say is not what the world wants to hear." So, for me, no: it would become more of a time of being aware, being attentive, and also being willing to say, "This is what I need to say now, and I'm gonna let myself say it. Even if it's bad-wrong-ugly. Even if I'm an asshole and a failure."

So when that self of yours says those things, how does it translate onto the page? In your work, we encounter the first-person pronoun, the "I" on the page. I think Sam Hamill once described the "I" on the page as "the first person impersonal." Is that how you would describe it?

My eyes popped open this morning and I said, "I am not the person he's coming to interview!" I was very happy about that. *After I Was Dead* is also a (serious) joke (*a la* Dickinson's "I heard a fly buzz when I died"), in terms of the "I," the particular "I," the singular "I." "I," as Duncan says, "recompose what I like to call 'myself' out of the world."

I'm looking for that line in your poem "sometimes the I, the glue, the poor glue."

Oh, "I the poor glue." Or, the other "I" in that poem, "Structures": "I, the thin ice on this river." It's just . . . selfhood is a very peculiar concept.

So do you see the self as a provisional construct to get you through each day, to that moment of sleeping, and then you wake up in the morning and rebuild again?

No. It's more multilayered than that. I feel I am in an "I," passionately, but I feel its constructedness. I feel both those things at once, which is the duality which afflicts us constantly, which is, "Is there an actuality there? Or, is that actuality made up of the prior ideas I'm bringing to it?" And how am I going to negotiate between those two realities? It's not either completely constructed or just there. I don't know another word for it right at the moment. It's somewhere between the two, the interaction between them, that one lives.

So . . . on the page?

I would say the "I" on the page is like—is negotiating those places, because sometimes it's very, absolutely . . . cry of the heart; other times it's a narrative function.

I felt that in The Surface *the "I" on the page was more cry of the heart, the poems were working a more personal terrain than the newer book.*

But in fact, that "I" from *The Surface*, that "I" which is a cry from the heart, is borrowed from Plath, is borrowed from both my mother and stepmother, who were bitter women, women who felt betrayed by their families and abandoned by men, and it took me three decades to realize, "Oh gosh: I've never been divorced." Because I thought I had, because I was living in their skin—as well as, as Rich points out, the oppressor's language—in some way. And so that cry of the heart is the cry of the heart as in the heart that we've been trained to recognize, the heart of the abandoned woman, the heart of the victim. Is that really my heart?

I didn't mean to imply that I saw "Laura Mullen" as the—

No, no, I'm asking it as a real question. Why do we think that that heart is more real than the heart that is in the next book, the more political heart, and a heart that's beginning, in fact, to accept its role as perpetrator as well as victim?

I don't know the answer to that question.

I know; it's not a question we can answer, exactly. But it seems a useful question to ask.

We're feeling very frightened and very hurt, oddly, as this very wealthy nation.

What is your reaction to what has been called "poetry of witness"?

Well, I don't know. I mean, I don't really have a strong reaction to it, either way. Isn't all poetry, "poetry of witness"? It's like, "Language" poetry. Isn't it all "Language poetry?" On some level, isn't it all poetry of witness? Name a poem that isn't a poem of witness.

Well, there certainly have been those that think that there are poems that come out of contexts of extremity, connected to various political and social movements. And there has been a great deal of debate and a great deal of attention given to poems of that sort over the last ten to fifteen years.

Right. Hanging out with novelists, you see some of them get very upset because novels aren't selling, though memoirs are selling like hotcakes. It seems we want to hear, in poetry—and in fiction: everywhere, we want to hear—from those who've seen the horror and can describe it. And we don't want the horror made up. Now that, to me, is a great betrayal of our faith in the imagination and, finally, sad distrust of what will most likely help us survive the horror. Right now we'd rather hear the "truth." But what is the truth? Who tells it and how does it get told?

So do you think that pressure on "the truth" speaks to a pessimistic vision in the culture?

Well, I don't know, but there are great, celebratory poets, out there (one of the most exciting poets is a Yugoslavian poet, who writes immensely celebratory poems: Tomaž Salamun. I love him), and poets telling the truth of their experience in radically new ways: are they going to get into the poetry of witness anthologies? Maybe not. Because they're not writing narrative poems about, you know, seeing people raped. But does that mean that the poems are less true, less important? I think we're coming back, in a way, to what we started the conversation with, the question: "What do we recognize as poetry?" So let me just say I'm distrustful of the label "poetry of witness" for the way it might cut off parts of the truth it can't bear witness to.

It sounds like, then, that you'd be distrustful of any of those divisions that are frequently trotted out: neo-Narrative, neo-Formalist, New York School, San Francisco Renaissance, and so on.

They're very handy things, and as an academic you really need those tools, you know? Because you can't propose a course without them. But are they in fact useful to you, as a writer? Not for me.

It's interesting how much partisanship in the contemporary scene is bred along those lines.

Oh, it's hilarious. Hilarious. When I was thinking about this interview. I thought that if I had a way to control the world, I would insist on cross-pollination: if you were a San Francisco poet, you'd have to go live in New York for a while, and vice versa. I would insist, as some schools do, on bringing in people from other areas so as to break down those partisanships. They're bogus.

Well, those divisions, it seems to me—and in some ways this is ironic—have also been really emphasized in the last ten years along various social and political lines. Do you have any thoughts on those divisions?

It occurs to me that having just said that they're useful only as an academic—in fact, that's not true. I'm in a privileged position and affiliated in ways so recognized by the culture I can remain blind to them, while for some writers, because of class or race or sexual preference, as well as in terms of experimenting with the medium, it's necessary to have those schools; it's useful to have those divisions because it's very important to have a community. And what we're talking about is made-up communities, when it's not simply a label applied from outside. Then we're talking about people who said, "We're gonna try to make something happen here, together." And that's crucial.

I was thinking of my talk with Li-Young Lee, and I brought up the issue of identity politics, and he got really annoyed—not at me, just the whole issue—he feels that he is wrestling with something much larger than any identity politics, trying to make a poetry that will endure, that touches the godhead and endures. Do you think toward posterity like that?

Well, yeah: anyone who's trying to do this in a serious fashion is thinking about the future, is thinking about making an object that endures, that remains true, accurate, a little longer than most gestures, or opens a space for further truths.

I wondered about reconciling that glance toward posterity with that attentiveness to Being, that openness to the poetic moment. You know, when we think of poems lasting into posterity, we think of art as these holy items, these golden birds set upon a bough to sing.

Sure, but going back to Sappho and beyond: there's complete attention to an absolute present which survives forever.

Would you say that about any of the later poets that we usually trot out as canonical institutions, for example, Dante, Keats, Milton, Wordsworth?

Yeah, probably. I mean, it depends on what happens to us all. Those works are works that still have things to tell us about the heart we recognize as ours, and they're works we will probably want to see, assuming that we still want to read, X number of years from now.

What about the relationship between poetry and other arts? I know that painting is a very large presence in your work. How does painting translate to the written page? What painters have invigorated your poetics?

Well, I'm not sure painting can translate to the written page; it becomes a different thing. Of course, translation, between languages as well as forms, is impossible, period—which doesn't stop us. But growing up around paintings—they were still, and they were perfect, and as Plath says, "Perfection is death." I mean, they were still, perfect, and dead. And meanwhile, life was happening, messily, all around them. And certainly in my first book, there was this attempt to make these perfect, still things, and a realization—with the second book—that it doesn't work. You survive and then that perfect still thing is inadequate. God, is it ever inadequate.

How do you understand the intersection between the lyrical and the narrative? You certainly intermingle those types of discourse. You've written a book that at least has been called, with quotation marks around it, a "novel." What is the relationship between the impulse to story and the impulse to song?

Well, I have to start by saying that I don't really see them as different impulses, and I'm thinking of Walter Benjamin writing quite wonderfully in "The Author as Producer": "All this to accustom you to the thought that we are in the midst of a mighty recasting of literary forms, a melting down in which many of the opposites in which we have been used to think are losing their force." The oppositions we're used to thinking in are (or should be) losing their force everywhere. And certainly lyric and narrative are two of those instances. Narrative has a certain erotic—I would say, a distinctly erotic-power to it: you're waiting for climax, right? So there's that building, that excitement; what's gonna happen next, and I feel like a good lyric needs a little of that in it, you know? Although the lyric is not going to move to a single climax, but we might say— towards multiple orgasms.

Some would take issue, though, with the quotation you just read, ignoring the primary division between poetry and prose. The primary division being a language that has been more crafted, worked harder, is tighter.

Right. And those are the people for whom the definitions are very important. And they're not very important for me. They seem rather silly, outdated. Maso—novelist, essayist—was on the cover of *American Poetry Review* precisely because there's a breakdown between the forms in her work. How can you say, "Okay, this is poetry; this is prose," when they're both getting worked really hard, when they're both musical?

So what compels you, then, when you're writing, to break for a line?

I came to poetry from a drama background. I originally thought of the poem as performance; I'm scoring for voice. I still think of the breath, as Olson said; I still want it to sound to the reader the way it sounds to me, in my head.

*So there's a natural pause at the end of a line. And when the
poem is arranged, more fractured, all over the page, is that a more
fractured scoring, then?*

Sure. As with a musical score; I don't know how else—I mean,
there's punctuation, which is a way of scoring—but to get longer
pauses in, you have to use (Olson again) the whole page.

Like a collection of soundbytes and riffs?

Like jazz improvisations.

*Okay. What about other aspects we traditionally associate with
poetry: the sound of the language, the use of alliteration and
assonance, do they factor into composition at all?*

As O'Hara says, "You want your pants to be tight enough so that
everyone will want to sleep with you." Of course you're thinking
about the sexiness of the language, the materiality of the language,
but this is why I ask if we can really make that the prose/poetry
distinction? Because the prose writers I love are doing and thinking
of the same issues.

*And you would insist that there isn't a different degree to which
those formal concerns are implemented in the art?*

There are a lot of people writing poetry currently where you could
take the line breaks out. I mean, a lot of those "suffering I" poems,
if you took the line breaks out, they'd be very, very dull and prosaic,
and there are a lot of people writing prose that's just searing: people
like Brian Evenson, Brian Kiteley, Theresa Cha, Carole Maso, Bob
Antoni, Thalia Field, or Rikki Ducournet. There are people writing
prose today that seems much more lively, more musical, than much
of the poetry I read.

*You're someone who's bridged life-of-the-writer with life-of-the-
teacher. Can you talk about the relationship between that*

profession and your work? Have you found it a career that you can balance well with the writing?

I think it's varied from moment to moment and from place to place. It's easier with smaller classes, it's harder with larger classes. But those are the obvious points.

What about something along the notion that Donald Hall might write; you know, that teachers of poetry are sort of damning themselves because they're reading the work of juveniles all the time.

Oh. That seems absurd. No. I'm actually working right now—we'll see how far the project goes—but I'm doing some collaborating right now with one of my graduate students. I'm finding it immensely freeing. We've written three things so far; I think we'll go at least a little further. I feel, the Donald Hall quote, the problem with it is, again, being shut down. If you're not paying attention, then of course you'll merely feel as if you're seeing the same thing over and over again, and in some cases, God knows, you might be. But on the other hand, if you are awake and alive and open to new energies, then interacting with very young writers can be extremely helpful. Beginner's luck, that's the cliché that comes to mind: they don't necessarily know yet "what's right" and "what's wrong," and the ways they don't know that, haven't absorbed that, haven't shut themselves down, can be helpful to you.

Something that has had a great deal of impact on many writers in the late twentieth century is the influx of and emphasis upon— in literary studies—literary theory. Can you talk about how reading literary theory has affected your poetry?

There's always theory, whether or not you acknowledge it. So, for me, its helpful to become aware of and read it. And I find it very freeing, someone like Roland Barthes, who was writing a densely poetic text, or Derrida: they're extremely useful to me, as a writer, in terms of their formal experiments and willingness to shift away from the work to the text—you can see how, given my fear of time and my desire for perfection, that's a freeing move.

It seems to me that in your newer book there are more longer pieces. Can you talk about your attraction to the long poem.

My first answer is—the lyric is like an affair. The longer thing, the book-length thing, is like a marriage. You get up every morning and you know what you're doing, as versus, having to meet in cheap hotels and hoping it all works out. So, I like the long form. As in terms of that thing we talked about earlier, in terms of getting to live in the art: there's less separation between art and life. In the longer work more can come in.

So that notion of letting things into the poem is very significant.

Letting things in—making a space large enough to recognize more than you might have recognized. I adore the lyric, but part of what I adore about it is its feeling of constraint, the feeling of how much has to go, to be shucked away, in order to make it intense enough. But I love the long poem for how much can come in, and how much can be recognized and included by the space poetry opens.

You just completed a new book of poems and a new novel. What's next?

We shouldn't really call it a novel. A thingy. I called *The Tales of Horror* a "postmodern Gothic," and I think what D. A. Miller calls "the novelesque" is going to be useful here, but I'm not sure how useful. What am I up to now? All right, two things: *The Tales of Horror* was the first part of a trilogy; I'm writing in the genres that were important to me as a young woman reader. My mother and I would go to the library and fill our arms with Gothics and romances and murder mysteries and bring them back and read them. So I wrote the Gothic, and now I'm working on the murder mystery, and besides that, I'm working on another collection of poems. And the collection of poems might have more prose in it.

So the new work and its allowance for prose and poetry is testimony to the realization that you have to be more receptive, more attentive, in order to write the poetry that will allow for a broken world, the world's wreckage.

Well, to realize our failure is a success. I mean, to realize that there's no success like failure and failure's no success at all, as Dylan says. I mean, the problem is the terms, and that's why, all jokes aside, I said I'm an asshole and a failure: it's taking the words back and saying, "Let's open those up. Let's see what those look like. Let's undo their power over us." I think what we have to realize is the gorgeousness of that wreckage. Failure to recognize that is going to be deadly. Stein says, "If it can be done, why do it?"

Charles Wright has a poem where he talks about what the new poem can't do. What would you ask of the new poem?

I won't know. I mean, part of the reason an interview is difficult is because "my indirection out finds direction out," as Roethke says, quoting Hamlet; I mean, really, what I want the new poem to do, I can't tell you that. I won't know until I sit down at the typewriter.

So no manifestos.

Not now: for a living, I have to try to be smart about other people's work. For my own work—I try to be (I don't have to try, actually, too hard) as dumb as a post, as much as possible. To find my way into it, to stumble a bit blindly. I'm a little afraid of what would happen if I had a large and unwieldy apparatus articulated clearly to myself as rules to obey. So what I have is a lot of fragments of theory and bits of thought, readings, experiences in life, feelings, and I'm letting them all, as Duncan says, recompose. I'm not advancing into the work with the idea, Okay! This is the poem that's going to do X, Y, Z! I'm going to the typewriter to see what happens there.

Lucia Perillo was born in 1958 in New York City. In 1986, she received an M.A. in creative writing from Syracuse University. A 2000 recipient of a prestigious MacArthur Fellowship, Lucia Perillo is the author of three books of poetry, Dangerous Life, The Body Mutinies, and, most recently, The Oldest Map With the Name America. Her poetry frequently uses a long line in order to capaciously accommodate a variety of materials: rumination, narrative threads, contemporary and classical culture mixed dashingly in poems driven by a sassy yet speculative and sensitive voice. She teaches at Southern Illinois University and divides her time between Illinois and Washington State where, before becoming a professor, she worked as a naturalist for the United States Fish and Wildlife Service.

LUCIA PERILLO

Lucia and I conducted this interview in early fall 2001.

Many poets understand recent American poetry in terms of the "lineages" to which they belong, the "schools" or "movements" which have shaped their work. Through what lens do you look at American poetry in the last century? What poets have impacted your work?

It is convenient to look at current American poetic practice as having been transmitted to us via a relatively small number of strands: the cerebral strand (Stevens), the strand of plain speech (William Carlos Williams), the formal strand (Frost). But then we'd have to throw in the discursiveness of Whitman and the hymnody of Dickinson. And then we'd have to add the seasoning of many others, and the strand schematic would eventually break down, so it's best just to throw it out the window at the outset.

Tony Bennett said Sinatra said: "Steal from one person and it's plagiarism, steal from everybody and it's research"—that's the maxim concerning this matter that I've taken to heart. I've been influenced to what is probably a crippling degree by the writers I've fallen in love with, and I have to admit that these are generally people of our era. Early on, I was influenced by the narratives of Robert Browning, but even prior to reading Browning in graduate school, I had been greatly influenced by the dramatic monologues of Frank Bidart and the narrative poems of C.K. Williams' seminal book *Tar*. These long poems were among the first batch of serious poetry I was exposed to, and they appealed to me, an unsuccessful fiction writer at the time, because they showed me what of fiction could be brought to poetry. Plus the poems seemed much more direct and intense than a prose piece could be.

Could you explain a little bit more what you mean by bringing parts of fiction over into poetry?

It's traditional to divide poetry into the narrative and the lyric, with these two being mutually exclusive realms. But I think the realms are starting to hybridize, and that's the aspect of the avant-garde that I'm most interested in now.

Some years ago C.K. Williams came to the university where I was teaching, where he led a workshop in which he cautioned us about the narrativization of our culture, which I believe he thought was being spearheaded by popular media like TV. My version of what he meant is: we watch the Olympics in an era in which the ritual moment of the hundred meter dash is not enough. So we get the narrative of the sprinter's childhood because we've come to demand these narratives. Williams urged us to resist the narrative temptation because I think he felt it would corrupt our sensitivity to the lyric—of course, I could be reconstruing this all wrong. But the ironic thing about his statements was that he made them while, or shortly before, he was in process of writing a prose memoir. So maybe he was deliberately throwing us off his own trail.

One last thought on this matter derives from our recent galvanizing tragedy: the destruction of the twin towers offered proof that we don't exactly have the monkey of narrative riding on our backs. People at this moment of crisis were also drawn to ritual, which is lyric in structure: going to church services or making phone calls to friends, which are lyric in the sense that the same forms are repeated over and over. Even the video footage was delivered to us in the manner of ritual, not narrative, as we felt compelled to rewitness the plane going into the building again and again. The narratives came later. Each person will weigh differently the relative importance of these two realms.

I like your connection between the lyrical and, to borrow your phrase, the "ritual moment." It seems to me that most successful poems draw both from narrative and lyrical sources, as you point out. Could you talk about this hybridization in terms of a specific poem or poet's work? Further, is there a point in time—lit. history time or cultural time—where you see the "mutually exclusive" realms of narrative and lyric start to move together?

I guess the most obvious example of a poem that is a hybrid might be *The Waste Land*, with its hodgepodge of narratives that fuse into a lyric prayer at the end. And that poem might be an inaugurating moment—at least a defining moment—for the breakdown of the separate camps. I'm not that fond of *The Waste Land*, though: it's a little too sterile a poem to get lathered up about. So we could look instead to Elizabeth Bishop's "The Armadillo," which renders a narrative whose purpose is to deliver us to the lyric stanza that ends it. I'm very partial to Bishop, whose most often anthologized work is chiefly narrative but who, if you read more widely into her, wrote often in more songlike forms.

As far as visual art goes, I'm just a dilettante, but I know enough to know that artists similarly speak of the narrative quality or content of paintings, which abstract art would not seem to have. Yet someone like Picasso breaks down the dichotomy. You look at his mid-to-late paintings and they tell some stories, but they are also lyrical in that they seem to be about the act of painting, the way a lyric poem is about the way it sounds and sings. At least in part.

In my own work, I actually just get confused if I make the lyric/narrative distinction before I write the poem.

What do you mean by "the way a lyric poem is about the way it sounds and sings?" Can you show me specifically how you see this dynamic working in a poem?

We could use an example from Elizabeth Bishop, since I was talking about her. It's called "Casabianca" and is a good example of her lesser known lyric work:

> Love's the boy stood on the burning deck
> trying to recite "The boy stood on
> the burning deck." Love's the son
> stood stammering elocution
> while the poor ship in flames went down.
>
> Love's the obstinate boy, the ship,
> even the swimming sailors, who
> would like a schoolroom platform too,
> or an excuse to stay
> on deck. And love's the burning boy.

Now what the hell does that mean? You could do the unlock-the-poem schoolteacher trick and say it's about a shipwreck or an unrequited love or this morning's breakfast cereal. But to me the poem's meaning lies in the sound of it. What it's about hardly matters.

Although there is a great deal of range in your work, many of your poems use a longer line; take us through the formal shaping of a "Perillo poem"—what governs your line length, your utilizing various sound elements, your poetry's rhythm?

I have changed my practices—I try to change my practices—a great deal over the years. Because I was interested in poetry's narrative/ fictional possibilities, a long line at first seemed the most natural. Also short lines are obviously, uh, short, and so what they can accomplish seems limited. Those poems in which you have one or two words marching down the page—with lines like "the"—don't usually interest me. Though one of my favorite poems is James Wright's "Autumn Comes to Martin's Ferry," which I believe has the line, "Therefore."

That said, I am trying now to make a conscious effort to understand white space, which is a mystery to me. The musical pause, the silence. As a person, I tend not to be able to shut up but instead issue a lot of nervous chatter.

Because we have all poetic possibilities at our disposal today, because all roads are open, I think form is the true issue, the agony at the heart of writing poems. I looked into chaos theory because I thought it would help me, and it did, but then my older brother told me that chaos theory has proved pretty much useless when it comes to predicting weather. Same for poetry—theorizing about your neuroses doesn't help you get through them. And every poem is a possibility for new neuroses, for more unharnessable weather.

Really, I don't have any idea what I'm doing and hope that someday I'll get a patron who will command me to write sonnets. Narrowing the field would be a great relief.

Can you say more about your attraction to the use of white space and silence?

I'm not so interested in the poem as canvas—to regard it as such would pull the reader from his or her immersion in the meaning of the words, which we now know, thanks to the theorists, is an illusion, but still the illusion is more interesting than the physical objects of paper and ink (which could be interesting, I guess, but would lend all poems a kind of aesthetic sameness or would convert reading perhaps to a study of font types). I'm more interested in white space as a means of controlling the speed and music of the poem. If the music is the meaning, as I just argued, then the white space's contribution to the meaning is significant.

Your poems frequently use references to contemporary culture; that is, your work definitely does not retreat from the cultural chaos which surrounds us. How do you understand poetry's relationship with culture? Do you believe that poetry has any sort of political function?

As far as poetry's relation to politics and culture (two sides of the same coin), poetry of the moment has zero bearing on the politics and culture of the moment, except within the self-contained system of poetry itself. Poets read poetry, plus there are I would guess a few hundred civilians in this country who are also poetry readers. That doesn't add up to a lot of cultural significance.

Yet we look to the poetry of the past to interpret the present moment, especially moments that have an exceptional gravitas. So, to dwell on our recent crisis again, the now that situates us within the wide shadow of the bombing of the twin towers: the poetry of the not-so-distant past has suddenly become very important in helping us process events. I have heard the line from an Auden poem—"we must love one another or die"—again and again. Also Larkin's "what will survive of us is love." It's curious that both poems have semi-highbrow sources that are probably not part of most people's bedtime reading. And that both poems twine the ideas of love and death. And that both poems are hopeful. And that both statements may be untrue.

This would imply that poetry is a bank of ideas, a basilica of relics. We sense that the relics may somehow and someday be crucial to our processing of events, so we keep them stockpiled like bottled water—the bottles are dusty, but we keep them where we can have access to them in case of emergency. This cultural significance would seem to give poets a civic burden—"I must affirm humanity's capacity for love"—that would cripple their ability to write the next poem. Indeed, I've found it hard to write lately, afraid that what I've said in the past has not been honorable enough and knowing that if I shoot for honor the poem will be doomed from the get-go.

But engaging in this struggle is our job, and the bank of our great poetry is the historical record of how we have wrestled with this burden—of being an authentic individual human soul while simultaneously being one of the chorus of frogs in the swamp.

Bin Ramke was born in Port Naches, Texas, in 1947. A prolific poet, Bin Ramke's most recent book is Airs, Waters, Places. *Other titles include* Wake *and* Massacre of the Innocents. *Recipient of the Yale Younger Poet's Award for his first book of poetry, Ramke has also served as editor for* The Denver Quarterly. *Author of a dark and invigorating poetry that explores the boundaries of formal conventions of line, syntax, and speaker, Ramke's obsessive confrontation of epistemological and ethical questions has shaped especially vivid work in the last three books. He is a professor of English at the University of Denver.*

BIN RAMKE

Bin and I spoke in Denver, Colorado, during summer 1998.

Some poets come to poetry through an attraction to contemporary or Modernist writers; others are initially more engaged by older work. How did you come to poetry?

Very specifically, through the work of Wallace Stevens. It was my sophomore year—no, I guess it was actually the end of my freshman year in college, where I was a mathematics major, and I took a course that involved Stevens and other Modernist writers: Yeats, Eliot, some Pound, Hart Crane. It was an extraordinary experience. I suppose it was the first time in my life that I seriously looked at and listened to poetry, and in some ways I think I was attracted to Stevens because he was the poet I didn't understand. He was the one who offered the most resistance to my reading. In a way, what he offered was a sort of puzzle—I mean, that's kind of a terrible thing to say—but something equivalent to what I was just then learning I was not able to deal with, was not so talented in responding to, in mathematics.

And you've maintained this interest in Stevens' work?

I have. It has increased and waned a bit over the years. Right now I feel a renewed interest in Stevens. And I know that there's a kind of a perversity in my continuing interest in the writing of Stevens. I always like the fact that he had this other life, what some might call a real life, that he was not attached to the academy, and was aware of but lived only on the edges of the literary community. But it's really the work itself, the kinds of issues he wanted to deal with and the way that he, I think, invariably dealt with those issues poetically.

Various critics—Longenbach, Vendler, and others—have considered Stevens' career in terms of different phases; are there poems from certain periods that invigorate you more than others?

Yes, yes. The later work. I actually did an M.A. thesis on Stevens. I concentrated on "The Rock," a section of the—it was not published separately, but it was the last section of *The Collected Poems*, the last group of poems that he wrote that he then supervised the publication of. And it just now occurs to me that, from my earliest interest in poetry I was attracted to the work of a dying man, works which were directly responsive to that. I mean, the name itself: "The Rock" suggests looking at a kind of barrenness, the threat rather than consolation of the world, stripped of decoration and softness; but anyway, yes, that's the work I was attracted to. It may be that the very first Stevens poem that I read which evoked excitement and response in me was "Sunday Morning." But I fairly quickly sort of turned to the back of the book. Later on, I went to the middle and was able to deal with the difficult, for me, long poems: "Esthetique Du Mal," "Notes Toward a Supreme Fiction," "An Ordinary Evening in New Haven," and I've come to like that long, meditative, time-consuming, world-consuming approach to poetry.

Stevens, as you mentioned, is a Modernist poet who has come to be recognized as a very significant force in shaping twentieth century American poetry, but during his career, as you mentioned, he was someone who was sort of "outside the fray." How do you respond to those writers that immersed themselves in the manifesto writing end of Modernity—Pound and Eliot, Williams, even through her editorship, Marianne Moore, perhaps? Does their work attract you as much?

Well . . . I suppose it doesn't. Being involved so much in the academic world as I am, sometimes it's hard for me to get back to thinking about what my own more personal reactions are to some of these people, as opposed to a kind of necessary professional relationship to, say, Pound. Pound's work does attract me, enormously, as a matter of fact, in the midst of a kind of repulsion toward much of the life, of the ego, the ego that is central to the work, to *The Cantos*. But it's an ego that he struggled with, and against, from the beginning. The thing that attracts me the most to Pound is probably his generosity toward the world, that every element of the world can be a part of his poem, which also, I think, means his life and his personality.

I think Jack Gilbert said in an essay in Ironwood, *in the late eighties, that the greatest contribution of Pound for the contemporary poet is that he showed how much could be put into the poem. I guess that's what I was speaking to—with Stevens, especially through a poem like "Sunday Morning," we can trace the Romantic lineage very clearly—*

Sure–

—you know, the luscious blank verse, and such, that we find him using various times over the course of his whole career, whereas we have other Modernist writers making a mission out of disrupting this inherited poetics. So I guess what I was curious about is how you respond to that Modernist agenda of breaking the iamb's back, going in fear of abstractions, impersonality, and so forth.

I suppose I have tended to be a fairly conservative sort of writer, and that bothers me a little bit, you know, and there are times when I won't admit it, but quite frankly, in thinking about this interview I was just sort of going back over what ought to be my answers, and I just had to admit that I started from a position of being fascinated by the accomplishment, whatever that accomplishment was, of previous eras, and trying to retain as much of it as possible. But this is sometimes a deadly attraction, so a lot of what I have done is figuring out ways to work against my predilections, finding ways to . . . well, to make new. It's interesting how that phrase is quoted so much—I do it a lot of the time as well—and yet in many ways, Pound's project is a recovery of ancient cultures, ancient languages, and often bringing those languages indirectly into his work; there's something wonderfully exuberant about how much of what we ordinarily call "the past" Pound insists on keeping and stirring up in the present of the work. Possibly, you could make the distinction between poetry and this world—that is, he's resisting the present tense of the poetry of the time that he found himself in and inviting in the world of the ancient and the foreign.

There's this interesting business, to put it very crudely, a kind of Stevensian and—it's probably more Eliot—Eliotic line from Modernism to the present, whatever we want to call the present. And the Pound line that carries us up to the present; with most of the people who are, very deservedly, receiving attention right now, much more in a Poundian mode, at least they trace their ancestry to what Pound is doing more than Eliot. Of course, Eliot was the first of these Poundians. Eliot was formed by Ezra Pound and was historically the master practitioner of much of what Pound preached.

You're exactly one step ahead of me, because my next question was about lineages and your understanding of how various lineages have shaped contemporary American poetry. It seems to me that we can look at all three of those poets you just mentioned and Williams also as having been the source for various groups of contemporary poets. Stevens, it seems to me, has certainly been very significant over the last twenty years.

I think there's also been a reaction against Stevens over the last twenty years and probably for good reason; he does have a kind of domesticating impulse, which is possibly dangerous. While I would never think of Stevens' poetry as a nostalgic poetry, there is this constant eye toward some sort of preservation that is attractive in Stevens, and also possibly—well, not possibly—definitely dangerous for the writer who's being influenced by him.

I feel a much more physical connection between the poem and the world in your work, as opposed to Stevens' work, which tends to be more philosophically ruminative.

That's fascinating. It's a major question, a major issue. I would approach that issue in one way by saying, I don't really trust the poets that declare themselves—well, we're getting at a word like "political," Stevens as political poet, and certainly in a profound sense of the term "political," every poet, every person is political. The claim to be non-political is itself one of the most powerful and dangerous of those political claims. Stevens never claimed not to be; Stevens did decide not to deal with the politics of the world in a direct, obvious way in his work, and I will say that I tend not to trust a number of—there's an element of a number of contemporary poets which has to do with their declared politics—the declarations that they are political. And they don't know exactly what that means, and I'm thinking of the Language poets. And when I say "The Language poets," I realize that there's no such thing; I mean, there's a kind of element that we will recognize by using that phrase, but no one wants to be completely identifiable by such a term. But there is the declaration that "Language" poetry results from a political attempt to, in some sense, to purify the language, to do something to the language which makes certain kinds of experience accessible again. I don't see why you couldn't take these sorts of declarations and apply them, let's say, to Stevens, and it would be kind of a curious exercise, but I think you could find it happening.

Other poets have assumed a political position based on the subject

*matter of their poetry, addressing oppression and extremity. What
is your response to work of that sort?*

I must say that there are the occasional exemplars of this work that
I admire very much. But generally speaking the success of such
work is essentially nonpoetic success. The poetry of such poetry is
not really an issue, and, you know, I may admire the person, may
admire the stand, may reject the person or the stand, but in all
these cases it's not the poetry itself. It probably has to do with, in a
simple-minded kind of way, that which is external to the language
having priority over the language; we are dealing with language as
tool toward some end, and those ends are, by my definition,
nonpoetic. I don't, however, want to sound as though I believe in a
necessary purity of poetry. I think the poem does respond to the
world, whether we want it to or not. In fact, probably the law I
believe in most is the law—what's it called?—the law of unintended
consequences, and one of the problems I have with a lot of expressly
political poetry is that by going after this subject, directly and
expressly, the poet may end up causing something, or the net result
is out of the control of the poet anyway. Just because you think
you're starting off justifying behavior of a certain group against
another one, that may not be where it ends up, at all. For me, the
random is always a powerful element of a poem, of language. I
guess this is part of the problem with trying to be expressly political,
because there's going to be some random element which will cause
it to be read differently than one might have expected or hoped. I
invite that, I love that, but if I were trying to get some political
issue dealt with, then I have no control over it.

*Your adeptness with traditional form is quite impressive. Can
you talk about what the primary shaping force or impulse is in
your understanding of the poem? How does the poem assume the
shape that it eventually takes?*

I think that when you decide to control one thing, you're also deciding to allow something else, something that you don't know, to go its own way. In some ways, the more tightly controlled the structure, the more another element of the mind is released to go in some strange, other direction.

The poet Christianne Jacox Kyle said something once at a reading that may be connected to this. She claimed that children play more imaginatively and freely within a fenced-in environment—analagous to the imagination working in forms.

Oh, yes. There is that, but there's also a bit of a problem with cliché—I'm not saying that this person was clichéd. What I'm saying is that I was leading myself toward a kind of cliché. I mean, the sort of notion of Venturi effect, that you take all the force and you pull it down into a more constricted area, like you put your thumb on the end of a hose, and the water comes out with more force, more power, and that's possibly true: when you set certain kinds of restrictions, within those boundaries that those particular restrictions set up, maybe there's a greater freedom. It's easy enough to say that, but what does that actually mean when it comes to working with the language?

How do you, personally, decide on the formal shape of a poem?

Well, starting with the most recent—I mean, my habits of composition right now involve long-term projects, and I don't seem to make decisions like that. That confrontation with the blank page is so painful, and sometimes silly, I almost never start with a blank page. I've got lots of failed attempts—I used to actually keep them in a box. I'd cut out lines, stanzas, and just throw them in, and when it was time, when I wanted to sit down and write, I might pull things out randomly and just stick them together. I tend to do this on a computer now—it's just some sort of operation—and see what happens when these bits of language, which I may have composed myself, were randomly juxtaposed against each other;

this might randomly lead me in some direction. There may come a point when—and I can't really say why this would occur to me, but it might occur to me—I want to see what this is like if I put it into something like ballad stanzas, and there may be nothing behind it except "this will provide me another, little point of view" and so I'll just split everything up into quatrains, and I may even decide, "I really don't know what's going on here," so I'll make it rhyme, and I play with rhyme in that way. But I can't say that I make certain decisions that now that this has happened I know where it is I'm going to go. It's almost gotten to the point that I try to hold on to a poem as long as possible, two or three years. I'll keep putting it in another form, changing things around

The title poem from my book, *Wake*, went through some spectacular changes in form, and would probably go through a few more except that publication generally inhibits my tendency to keep fiddling. As it was finally published in *The Ohio Review*, the poem is six pages of unjustified massed text: a block of type. With notes, even. It was once broken into several sections, all now abandoned. It was early on presented in iambic pentameter packets—neat and unchallenging. Once it was a group of prose poems, with prose paragraphs and standard punctuation.

One thing that I learned through the process, the evolution of this poem, was that it is trying to say all things at once, in one breath. It is impossible to read correctly, so among the lessons that it taught me is further humility.

> it mattered matter and the body the coming into one's own.)
> "Safe with my lynxes, feeding grapes to my leopards," Pound
> wrote the man wrote early in a long dangerous career careening
> path (the French for quarry as in hunt or stone) translation is
> hard (crossroad career carriére) the French for anything in his small
> memory of Mom and you'd think he'd grow up by now a life
> "And I worship I have seen what I have seen" he knew so much
> and hated so many he was sad as all get out at the end he ended
> that way famous the cantos "And the frogs singing, against the
> fauns in the half-light, And . . . " So I was only eight years old
> and the night before the trip I was saddened knowing now the
> trip was upon me it was soon to be over and this excess of antici-
> pation ruled my remaining life the next night on the barge I

Are those supposed to be a long-lined lineation? What is the
purpose of long, prose-like lines, versus, say, justifying the text?

It is not justified on the page here. And no, it is not lineation. It's
typing to a right-hand margin and then going back. Again, this is
an element of the random, the randomness of where the line ends.
But I'm not really even going for that. I mean, I see that there are
certain words that sort of interestingly fall at the end of these lines.
But no, what I suppose finally decided what was appropriate to
that poem is a kind of breathlessness and a refusal to make certain
kinds of decisions. I pulled out all the punctuation, so I wasn't even
going to make that decision about where a sentence, or where a
phrase, or any of the poetic units of language, begin or end. Refusing
to decide where one unit would end and where another one would
begin and pulling down all of the paragraphs, so you wouldn't even
have the comfort, you might say, of standard prose, reassurances
that we have completed one gesture and now we're going to begin
another.

Walter Benjamin wrote about the collapse of genres; is this poem
moving toward recognition of that?

Oh yeah, absolutely. In fact, although I probably don't speak of it
very well, intelligently, I do think this business of collapsing of
genres is the most exciting element of poetry of this century. I think
a case can be made for lots of experimentation, conscious or
otherwise, with genre boundaries, in all eras of English writing. I
think we can see this practice happening in Chaucer, and Milton
as well, practices that could usefully be talked about in terms of
some kind of experimentation with genre.

Traherne's Centuries *come immediately to mind . . . these chunks*
of prose that are so full of consonants, alliteration, assonance.

I have another longish poem—and, as I was starting off down this
particular road by describing more recent compositional habits: these
poems have tended to be long, because I have sort of given myself

the luxury of playing around before making these decisions about . . . well, I don't know that I do make these kinds of decisions, but before making the discovery of what the poem is more or less about, where it's going to go.

You know, that poetic seems very different from your first books, where the pieces seem tighter; they seem within an aesthetic oriented toward making a well-closed, attractive work of art.

Yes.

Rather than a haphazard openness to the various elements that you're talking about.

Well, I have . . . I don't have to but I will admit that I am still actually quite attracted to orderliness. You wouldn't be able to tell that from looking at my office.

All the books in your office here are alphabetized.

Yeah, I do think there's something quite wonderful about this sort of neatness, the predictability that comes from recognizing a pattern. It's probably what I actually like about mathematics—I was heavily involved in math—that there is in fact a structure to what had at first seemed to be randomly disordered numbers. Even as I say that, of course, I realize in some way that the inverse is also true; there's a great delight in suddenly recognizing the randomness and the disorder in that which we thought had been contained and domesticated. But in the first three books that I did, I was probably overeager to find a place I could "close it down," where I could shut down what seemed to be happening in the poem and capture it. Maybe if I pushed whatever I was doing too far, the disorder, the chaos, would manifest itself, and that would be scary. So I would try to find a way to end it. On the other hand, I could say that I've probably always been convinced, without necessarily knowing it, that the reason a poem is valuable is that it can be smarter than the poet, that poetry is a way of using language in order to make discoveries, and so I've always felt an attraction to being a little bit out of control. I've always had tremendous doubt about my own mental abilities, my own intelligence, so finding a kind of machinery that led me to discoveries, to areas that I would recognize, but I couldn't pretend I had control over it, a full understanding of it. I found this to be quite thrilling.

> *The question of how poetry matters is one that critics and poets spent a great deal of ink on in the late eighties and early nineties. How did you respond to those various assertions about poetry's significance in a culture where it is a very marginalized art form.*

Well, I don't worry about these things so much—not necessarily in the terms that have been set out. I'm not terribly worried about poetry being marginalized culturally. I don't know if those are exactly the right terms. Here's one sort of response to it. I had a strange personal revelation—probably everyone else in the world realized this long before—but I promise this will be my only sports analogy. I was reading somewhere about TV sports' producers lamenting the fact that women don't like to watch women doing sports on television, that women would not sit down in front of the television set to watch another woman play basketball or tennis or whatever; they'd rather be out there actually doing it. And of course we see the irony here; it's really quite wonderful, and it's something that could be said against men, that we tend to sit down and watch other men doing things better than we can and allow ourselves to be turned into . . . well, it all has to do with—what word do I want?—you know, commodities.

The parallel to poetry is that you find that all kinds of people, under all circumstances in this culture, write what they consider to be poems. There is a tremendous amateur—which, remember, means "lover"—amateur interest in poetry. We tend to get frustrated because people won't sit down and watch us, those of us who are professional poets; we can't get big enough audiences, high enough ratings. Well, it's kind of absurd—if you think of the parallels this way. Poetry, very clearly to me, in some vestigial form, is a necessary part of human existence. And there may be something wrong with what Modernist or Postmodernist—you know, contemporary— poetry, is doing that it isn't recognized by more of the population. I'm not totally convinced that we are absolutely right and that those "ignorant masses" out there, if only they would recognize what we had . . . I don't know. I shouldn't go down that particular road. All I'm saying is that there are elements and aspects of what most people would not even recognize as poetry that continue to be important parts of people's lives. So even if what I do, the particular poems I write, don't attract great audiences, that's not essential.

I also have two contradictory beliefs about poetry. One belief sees poetry as a parallel to mathematics. We don't actually go around testing mathematical proofs by how many people are attracted to them. Now, I will admit to a kind of romantic attraction to the notion of a solitary genius, sitting in his attic, and making discoveries and scribbling in the margins of the text—well, Fermat's last theorem is what I'm getting at. I find it actually very attractive, and if Fermat as a matter of fact did discover a proof for this theorem, and in fact there was no room to write it down in the margin of his book, and then he died, that proof would still, somehow, be correct, even if the world didn't know about it. Part of me liked that notion of poetry: we make these things out of language that have their value or interest or use or beauty, even if there's no one in the world who looks at them. The contradictory kind of sense that goes along with this notion is that I do believe language, as language, is social, and, therefore, it does require connections between human beings.

Many readers come to contemporary poetry and say, "I can't make heads or tails of this poem; this poem is too difficult."

Yeah, well, that doesn't really bother me very much. First of all, I'm delighted that there's so much variety out there, that—first of all, if someone were intrigued by the concept of poetry, she can find poetry which does respond to some of her expectations. And so we can think of the work that is more resistant as being somehow the research and development phase of certain materials. I mean, we understand that you experiment, you try things out in this world and see where they take you, and you do that with language, so I really don't have a lot of patience with that claim of frustration. If a person is actually looking for poetry that's of interest to him or her, that person can find it. Usually, they're not really looking. They're making some kind of point—possibly, some kind of political point. I also do think that sometimes poets, well—I don't have any objection to anything that anyone is doing as a poet. I think it's worth following all of these lines of experimentation to their conclusions or to wherever they take a person, and one of the reasons I can say that is because of the great democracy of poetry that's out there. There's so much that's available. I must say, as soon as someone has identified, named, and denigrated a school of poetry, I have a tendency to want to go back and like it. I'm having this sort of phase right now where I'm going to re-examine Confessionalism. John Berryman, I think, is fabulous.

What a coincidence. I just finished reading Dreamsong, *Mariani's biography of Berryman, and re-reading* The Dream Songs. *What's bringing you back into Berryman. Is it his experiment with syntax? Such language!*

The syntax of Berryman. When he went from the *77 Dream Songs* to *His Toy, His Dream, His Rest*, when I first encountered the enlarged version, there was something very neat—speaking of his structure before—about *77 Dream Songs*. It was an experiment, but there was a constrictive aspect. Each of the dream songs was a kind of variation on the sonnet, and a group of seventy-seven is not overwhelming, and I remember not knowing exactly what to do with the book. He was just doing the same thing over and over again, and I secretly objected to that. I go back to it now, though, and I realize there's something else happening, something profoundly structurally resistant, you might say, in this language, and I think you've identified it: the syntax, not the subject matter, not even the voices.

*Well, what about the "Confessional" label that initially sent you
back?*

I've heard too many times now the word "confessional" said with a
sneer: "None of us 'advanced people' will be taken in by this stuff
anymore." Well, I'm reminded that "Romantic" was also said with
a sneer; it was an attack, a way of denigrating the work of Shelley,
and so forth. So it was that sneer that kind of sent me back. What
I realize about Berryman is the power of the statement made by
the different voices—the blackface—and the interesting sort of
cultural-social commentary implicit in that. But that's not what it's
about for me now; the attraction—you identified it—is that there's
an amazing continual juxtapositioning of what a sequence of words
does. And then the next sequence will start working in another
way, and you can just get carried along with the exuberance of syntax.
Probably being a nonexuberant kind of person, I find the quality
attractive in other people. So again it's this combination of a sort of
control of an apparent movement in certain directions with a kind
of unpredictability that I don't think we'd seen before those poems.
And he kept pushing it, and so he needed to go on and on, and
three or four hundred exemplars of it finally is just about sufficient.

*What of the other poets that are frequently trotted out with that
"confessional" label?*

Lowell—

Lowell, Sexton, Plath. Snodgrass.

I think a lot of people do recognize, though, in Plath that there's a
tremendous variety of skill and, you know, it kind of does maintain,
for whatever reason, some of the reputation she had before. Lowell
is often beaten up on, severely, and Lowell is intriguing to me for
several reasons. I think his various engagements—the Catholic
church, the classical tradition, the enormous changes that he went
through, from one book to another. From *Lord Weary's Castle* all

the way up to *Day by Day*. His appropriation of language, for which he was castigated: taking the words of wife and daughter from their letters, putting them out there in rough sonnet form, but obviously the relationship between that and lots of the experimental work, the collage work that recent writers are doing—it's kind of shocking, in some sense, how advanced, if you want to use that word. I think one of the mistakes that we make is in such words as "advanced." I mean, I do believe in a kind of avant-garde, I do believe in the necessity of thinking that you are moving out ahead. It's an interesting military term, of course, avant-garde; but simultaneously I also believe that in literature there is no progress. We are not better writers than Milton was, as poets (we are, as prose writers, but worry about that later on). There's something—and I guess the genuinely literary, and I have no idea what that means, but—that does not progress in the way that science claims that it progresses or engineering. "You can't say it that way anymore: yes, that's absolutely right."

Ashbery is a person from whom I've learned tremendous amounts, and I have much more to learn. But that statement, "You can't say it that way anymore," doesn't mean that we have superseded the ways set before. Anyway, one of the delights that I take is going back and finding surprising—and finding, as Harold Bloom once said, how Stevens is influenced by Ashbery: the new work gives us a new way of going back and reading the old work, seeing what we didn't know was there.

One thing that you've spoken to a number of times during our talk are various schools and partisanships. It seems to me, at worst, those schools and partisanships can lead to very parsimonious readings that condemn. One thing that I've found to be true in the Denver Quarterly, *which you edit, is there doesn't seem to be an adherence to one school, one movement; you'll find Claudia Keelan and Dave Smith in the same issue. Can you talk about your role as an editor, what you hope to do in your journal?*

Yes. I delight in that description of the journal, that description that you just gave. I enjoy the random mixing of these various kinds of writers. I can understand, I must say, that other people won't necessarily agree, and I can certainly see the value of establishing a set of principles and following them through as far as you can, in say, setting up a journal. This is one of the uses of literary journals, as an extended manifesto.

In early Modernity, Blast, *for example.*

Right. In some ways, though, those are often the most interesting journals, which probably have fairly limited lives, too, because you set out the limits and you push them, as far as you reasonably can— and then probably lose interest or funding. But, as far as my own relationship to this journal, the *Denver Quarterly,* what I hoped to do—first of all, I have to say, I hope to keep it alive. The plight of the literary journal, of course, is typical; just the sheer work of day-to-day, keeping up the business of it is, is sort of appalling. I wanted to also make myself aware of its own tradition and to see if there wasn't something I could do with that. I mean, the journal is thirty-something years-old, and it seemed to me I owed something to the founder, John Williams, and to the previous editors of the journal, so I made a fairly intense study of what was in there before. And, in some ways I found it almost comically conservative— politically. Occasionally, you'd find the most outrageous statements: almost anti-feminism, this-that-and-the-other, and yet, there were some fascinating essays by Laura Riding Jackson. I guess what I'm saying is that I found that it had a sort of traditional bent along with that attitude of taking on all comers and of just trying to present material that might be interesting. I found that an inspiration.

The other thing is, I genuinely like an awful lot of American poetry, fiction, and thinking—I shouldn't say American, because we have a strong international element, too—and it seems to me that I have to be honest about the material that we present in the magazine, and I sometimes will like things that seem quite contradictory, and I'll just try it out. See what happens. I do make some efforts, like trying to be sensitive to the newer, younger writers—or the newer writer, not necessarily the younger—who have not published a lot, and occasionally I take something because it looks intriguingly promising. I hate that word, "promising." It's a terrible thing to be "promising." What comes after is so difficult. And anyway, what I'm saying is that I try to take the magazine in some direction, but I try to maintain some kind of balance: with new and established writers, and with a look in various directions in the United States. And not so much geographically—one of the things I resisted was any sense of its being a regional journal.

Well, as an editor, you certainly see hundreds and thousands of manuscripts, so it might be fair to say that you might be able to give some insight into—approaching the end of the century— American poetry as it evolves into the first years of the next century: what do you see happening to the art?

Hmm. I resist thinking of the end of the century as a significant demarcation of any sort, except that the more people say that, the more people focus on it, the more it does bring about a sort of self-consciousness, and I do see that coming about, as a matter of fact, a kind of self-consciousness of artistry, a sort of examination of who we think we are as poets and fiction writers. I don't know whether this is always good.

Who do you think we are as American poets in 1998?

A pretty varied, an extraordinarily varied collection of individuals who enter into temporary alliances and break up and reform into other alliances, probably more quickly than the people in them realize. It's a cliché, of course, to say that the speed of life has increased as the century has gone on; I don't really believe that, necessarily. But the process of looking back and saying, "Here's who we are" seems to have rapidly increased. I'm thinking of the influence of several major literary anthologies over the past few years, and the recognition of what has happened with the Norton anthology. I mean, a publishing house got itself a position of near-monopoly on the education of American youth, over what was canonical literature, and then over a sequence of reediting and re-publishing this tome, this work, more and more rapidly it expanded, it broke into sections. There was the Postmodern one— then that was more or less simultaneous with the publication of *Poems for the Millenium*, I and II, which were both very self-conscious attempts to say, "Here is the dominant poetry; here's what has been happening, which has been ignored by dominant people in power." Well, there are no people in power. There's also a considerable uproar about, say, what's happening with commercial publishing, the buying up of publishing houses by other publishing houses, and oil companies, German manufacturers, whatever: drugs and newspapers, as if this says something about poetry, and the limits of the ability to contact each other, and I think it doesn't. It really has nothing to do with literature, and that may seem to have nothing to do with your question, except that as the century draws to a close, there's a fair amount of a kind of hysteria that may not really have much to do with anything that comes out of what we go to poems for and why we make them in the first place.

Wringing a sort of identity out of these various conflicts?

Ahh, and that, too! Yes, I've sort of avoided talking about that . . . identity. The poetics of identity, particularly when it comes to the fragmentation of what we pretended was a more or less monolithic culture, through, let's say, the fifties. In the time of World War Two we seemed to need the consolation of feeling that we've made the world safe for democracy, and then you can say it was all split up into ethnic tribal interests and concerns. Maybe it was a certain kind of consciousness that began to get split up; I don't know. But poetry's always full of contradictions. I think poetry always depends on ambiguity and contradictions, and I think the poet may be driven to defining a group—a tribe, or a culture, an ethnic identity—that she or he belongs to, to separate out from, to say: "This does not say who I am; I am more than, less than, or other than this identification." And whether this has to do with family, with religion, or political or ideological conviction, as we spoke of before, I think it's the tension, the conflict, that matters and not the particular identities.

I came to realize at a certain point in my career that one reason I feel so uneasy about connection to any literary group is because I came to writing not from a literary background. My mother's Cajun-French, and her father, my grandfather, spoke English, but he didn't like to; he didn't speak it very well. So on one side of my family I heard this foreign language, and it remained foreign, because my mother didn't teach the five of us Cajun. I had my own theories about that, and I think she'd probably disagree, but I think it had to do with her growing up in a time when she was supposed to join the mainstream, and she was punished for speaking French—even on the playgrounds in school, in south Louisiana when she was growing up. My father was from a German immigrant family, also farmers in south Louisiana, and also, we were Catholic, but I grew up in East Texas, and while there was a strong Cajun and Catholic population, I was very aware of what I interpreted as a very hostile Protestant culture surrounding us. The Catholicism of my youth was that of Latin—the Latin mass and ceremonies. It occurred to me, not too long ago, that there were these languages going on around me, the Cajun French of my mother and the Latin of the mass, and these were connected with—well, you might even say the political—that is, the conflicts and the hostilities between Catholic and Protestant families. My father's was originally Lutheran. And yet rituals and ceremonies are associated in my mind with the Latin, a certain kind of maternal something or other with the French, but all of these sounds didn't necessarily deal with meaning.

Well, the assimilation of this polyphony seems directly in alignment with what you've been talking about in terms of your attitude toward schools and movements. The more languages, the more echoes, the more rhythms, the more poetries there are, the better.

Absolutely, yes, I think that's right. I like that, because otherwise what you have to do is say "Yes" to one group, and "No" to another. This is not at all the way it was in my family, but in a symbolic way: say "Yes" to my mother, "No" to my father. Now, my father didn't do that, but in some ways, to say absolutely "Yes" to one culture, occasionally, would be to reject the other culture, which is fairly complicated. So it's not a matter of yes or no, but of trying to bring them all in. In addition, I was also growing up in this region during the time of the civil rights movement, as well as of the Vietnam conflict. So there were quite a number of well defined forces: integration versus segregation; being for the war or against it. Not a lot of room for nuance there, but all I was interested in was nuance. I mean, I'm still confused by Vietnam, the conflict, and so I see that as part of this search for language and ways of taking positions, making gestures . . . .

Well, a Stevensian long poem is a poem of ambiguity, revolving around an idea, rather than reaching a conclusion.

Exactly, absolutely. I mean, just thinking of a title: "Notes Toward A Supreme Fiction." On the one hand, this arrogant notion of a supreme fiction; you know, what could that mean? On the other, all he's doing is taking notes toward . . . he can't make that final plane, final position. Yeah.

For Stevens, poetry had the role of replacing "empty heaven." Do you elevate poetry in a similar manner?

Not exactly, although religion is a very big part of what I feel that I'm doing. I mean—I may be sorry for having said this—I probably think of myself, in some ways, as a religious poet. I am not religious, a believer in any sense of that term, and I've always relied on a scientific approach to the world, to any of those orthodoxies of spirituality. But I do think that this is one area that people are becoming curious about, and curious in their responses to: the millennium as a time for a kind of reexamination of faith. Whether it's faith in the spiritual sense or in terms of politics and social concerns and so on like that, there does seem to be a kind of self-consciousness about it all. So faith at the end of this century is fascinating. I recently wrote a statement connected to a poem that appeared in *New American Writing* which essentially said in some ways I want to write a kind of scripture. There's something terrifyingly fascinating about the Bible (and probably, more or less, the King James version of the Bible) and the way in which it continues to be alive to those who, for whatever reasons, feel this strong attraction to it. I have no patience whatever with fundamentalist religions. I find them scary and enormously dangerous. And yet I find something fascinating about being able to go back to this old language, this translated language, you know, and find some tiny text, and one can weave enormous sermons out of it, picking the text for the day. The density, the complexity of this language is what I look for in poetry, try to make in my own, and try to recognize in other people's. There is structure, use of narrative, but narrative is wonderfully fragmented, contradictory, and yet insistent in a strange sort of way in these texts, both Old and New Testament. There's a lot of promise also that may or may not be fulfilled, in the sense that you're getting somewhere and yet you don't, actually. At any rate, I find lots of that to be very attractive, and what I think poetry can provide. I think there probably is value in complexity itself.

I love being in the presence of something that suggests and in which the rhythm of the language, the very sounds of the words, has a kind of sacredness. Another last thing that poetry is about for me is providing necessary distance from the world, from experience, from each other, so we can examine—as we say, "come to terms with"—the rawness of the present tense.

Donald Revell was born in 1954 in the Bronx, New York. He received his Ph.D. from SUNY Buffalo in 1980. Drawing from diverse traditions, including French Surrealism, Poststructuralist theory, mystical and antinomian thought, and various musical forms, Revell's poetry exhibits both radical experimentation and a deep connection to American traditions. From Anne Hutchinson to Thoreau to Charles Ives, exploration of the unsayable and the erased have engaged Revell's thought and found expression in his work. Revell's first book, From the Abandoned Cities, was selected for publication in the 1982 National Poetry Series. Since then, he has published five additional books of poetry, including New Dark Ages, Erasures, and There Are Three. He has also published a translation of the French poet Guillame Apollinaire's Alcools. Revell presently teaches at the University of Utah.

DONALD REVELL

This conversation occurred in Iowa City during fall 1995.

You've spoken of a "lack of generosity" as a failing point for some poets and poems. Who among the Modernists do you see as least generous and why would you dub them so?

The Modernist enterprise is fundamentally ungenerous because it is conceived in opposition to time. And since time is where we live, is what everything we do is made of, setting up shop contra time is explicitly ungenerous. I find myself moved by how several of the Modernists became Postmodernists, sort of understood that their original idea of time as degenerative mode, time as destroyer, as chaos, as unmaker of civilization, needed to change. Ronald Bush's book on Eliot talks about this a lot, how the Eliot of *The Waste Land* is a very different creature from the Eliot of *Four Quartets* because *Four Quartets* moves toward an affirmation of time. April is not the cruelest month; there is no such thing as a cruel month. Whose ruins are they and who says they're fragments? To say the word fragment itself is to imagine a preexisting whole, and what was that and why are we privileging that which does not exist over that which does?

Stevens I find, because of his insistence that art provide durable forms of happiness and pleasure, ungenerous. I think he's so fundamentally disappointed with the world that he overprivileges art and, in doing so, is ungenerous to what actually happens. And I believe he realizes this in his later poems. What makes Stevens' later poems his best is the fact that they confront the failure, the parsimony, of his attitude towards change and the world.

On the other hand, Williams understood that time is a mess, the world is a mess, and therefore time and the world are simultaneous. To affirm anything real, whatever it is, whether it's a painting or a piece of broken glass in the gutter, is to affirm time. Williams is generous to the medium that includes all media. It's in useless opposition to time that Stevens and Eliot take themselves out of the creative, i.e., the generative, genital realm. Eliot is an uncreative writer. Stevens, until late, is an uncreative writer because he abjected the very medium in which creativity occurs. It's like saying, "I love to study fish, but only when they're out of water."

And The Cantos?

If you read *The Cantos* you can see a progressive change. Pound is in hell when he opposes time. The first movement of *The Cantos*, which Pearlman calls "the inferno cantos," is hell because of Pound's attitude toward time. And as the poems go along they reach *Paradiso*, they reach paradise which is a paradise of the affirmation of time—in *The Pisan Cantos* he looks out of the cage and says, "O Moon my pinup / chronometer." That's when he gets it, that time is all right, and then he can go on to write those beautiful *Drafts and Fragments*. "I cannot make it cohere; i.e., it coheres all right." It was a Modernist fantasy that order could somehow be imposed upon reality, when in fact reality always imposes order of its own, and if we fail to see as much, that's our problem; Pound is happy in the later cantos because he loves time. Time works for him; he understands it as a benign, loving process, and that's where Eliot was beginning to arrive in *Four Quartets*, understanding that eternity exists only because at certain points it intersects the temporal.

Certainly someone who changed her work over the course of her entire career, who revised incessantly, is Marianne Moore;

Marianne Moore was very resistant to the notion of finishing the poem, of putting a final layer of finish on it. How do you read her? How does she fit in?

I like her mind better than her poems. I think she was trapped because she was such a counter of syllables. She never trusted her lines to duration. She had a musician's heart but a sculptor's craft.

The matrix was made before the music came into being.

Yes. She never was trusting in that way. I think there is something self-mutilated about Marianne Moore. I like the idea of her better than I like any of her poems simply because all the poems panic and fall back onto number, onto counting, onto some sort of sculpted—however eccentric, however unique—form of aesthetic.

Do you see her use of quotations as a generous invitation to enter the poem or as an exclusionary act?

I like the fact that she is willing to find and understand that art is more finding than it is making. I think a lot of what differentiates Postmodernism from Modernism is this understanding that mostly we find things because if you say that you find your poem then you've already said that time is where it happened. Anyone who finds anything finds it in time. So Marianne Moore, like Joseph Cornell, has this trouvere mentality that is wonderful. But then they put it into boxes. They somehow panic at the critical moment and seek to contain. Marianne Moore containing it through her numbers, counting syllables; Cornell literally containing it in boxes; whereas you get someone like a Rauschenberg or a Jasper Johns and he's not interested in containment. Just put it out there, put it on the floor, tack it to the canvas.

Containment is the great contrast I see between Stevens and Williams. In early Stevens we have a sort of clipped-wing Epicureanism sinking "downward to darkness" and landing time and time again in a gorgeous yet static "Palaz of Hoon."

Well there's something very Mandarin about Stevens. Until those later poems, when he finally realizes that everything he'd written was a dismal, morose failure, and he throws open the shack in *The Auroras of Autumn* and steps out and sees the northern lights and they just extinguish, they exterminate him, and he realizes that the music of time, the music of change, is so much more beautiful and durable than any of the brittle little squeakings he's produced.

Williams' notion of the imagination—as he articulates it in Spring and All—is so very different from Stevens'; so many of his poems are of the moment or multiple takes of the moment, of, to borrow Breton's phrase, the "magical circumstantial." Could you elaborate on this?

Circumstantial is the word. What excites me about Williams and why I always go back to him as our best poet of this century is his fundamental discovery. In *Kora in Hell* as well as *Spring and All*, he realizes the uselessness of the Orpheus myth. The idea that the poet is looking back or not looking back, that the poet therefore is in charge of the circumstances, of the circumstantial nature of the poem, is just wrong. The poet's not in charge. That's not the poet's role. What happens in *Kora in Hell*, what happens in *Spring and All*, is that Williams sees that Eurydice had better be in front of Orpheus, that if she is in front of him, everything is going to be okay. The reason everything went wrong in the myth is that Orpheus had Eurydice behind him, whereas the poet should always keep his subject or her subject out in front. Poetry is a way of getting to the world, not a way of getting out of it or beyond it. It's a way of just getting there. Poetry is a vehicle by which we hope, nearly, to arrive at reality. In *Kora in Hell* and *Spring and All* and all the best of Williams, that's what's going on. The understanding that the world is ahead of the poem and that what we have to think of as poetry is an order of words, an event of words that will very nearly get us there.

That's why Olson is always writing about cars. He says near the end of *Maximus*, "trouble with the car." Or as in *Spring and All*, "No one to drive the car."

Or Creeley.

Yes, exactly: "I Know a Man." Get there! Poetry is the vehicle; the world is the purpose. The world is not an afterthought of the poem.

In Spring and All, *Williams uses the expression "the eternal moment." His notion of the eternal moment seems very different from, say, Czeslaw Milosz, who also uses the expression.*

The moment is eternal; that's just a fact. It's not a question of "Ah, what we want to do is find that moment which has the potential for eternity." Eternity is a moment. And then it's the next moment, and then the next moment, which is also eternal. So it's this whole endless sequence of eternities, not an eternity that hovers around like some besotted psychiatric angel on the outside of reality.

With Williams, though, there seems to always be that forward vision whereas Milosz seems to want to look back and find an eternal moment that he can pluck from the past in order to make meaning.

He's fundamentally a Classicist. This is not the case with Williams. Williams does not locate the golden age anywhere except out in front.

A concordance of Williams' Collected Poems would surely uncover that two of his favorite words are "edge" and "edges." I certainly see a connection between that and what you've just been saying—that awareness of what is going to come next. Such a movement toward the future certainly manifests itself in his line break. Do you see any point where he suddenly became more aware of this and began using the line more conscientiously toward this end?

I think it's in *Spring and All*. It's so sad that most people know Williams through the *Selected Poems*, the one that Randall Jarrell assembled. Why would anyone trust Randall Jarrell's selection of William Carlos Williams? It's almost as bad as what happened to Poe in the nineteenth century. *Spring and All* is a poem and there's no sense pretending that it's a book of poems from which you can excerpt. In there, in the throb and pulse and throb between the prose and verse, we see Williams discovering his "edges."

In Williams' poetry, although there is this "beautiful carelessness," as you've called it, there also seems to be a contradictory compulsion to fulfill more rigorous demands or at least more expected demands of what a poem is. For instance, "The Poet and His Poems" seemingly began as a very spontaneous outburst:

The poem is this:
a nuance of sound
delicately operating
upon a cataract of sense.
Vague. What a stupid
image. Who operates?
And who is operated
on? How can a nuance

operate on anything?

and was clipped to the much shorter, much more recognizable:

It is all in
the sound. A song.
Seldom a song. It should

be a song—made of
particulars . . .

Well, I agree with Marjorie Perloff in her understanding that the later Williams was a falling off, but why I continue to honor Williams is that he knew it too. What I love about the second half of Williams' career is its honor to time. He understood that one's abilities, one's nerve, one's courage were nonrenewable resources, and it's almost as if he wrote the later poems in that understanding, saying, "Look, I'm getting older, I'm frightened. I'm panicked, and I'm doing all sorts of things that I'm not really proud of but I don't really have any choice because that's what happens in this phase of a human being's life."

I'm not one of those who says, "O Asphodel . . . how spiffy." I prefer *Kora in Hell* to "Asphodel." I prefer *Spring and All* to *Pictures from Brueghel*. I agree with Marjorie Perloff when she says that *Paterson* was the poem everybody was ready to read, that it's not really the great Williams. The great Williams is the stuff that's in New Directions' volume *Imaginations: Kora in Hell, Spring and All, The Great American Novel, The Descent of Winter*. But Williams was a good doctor and he understood that the body starts to deteriorate before it dies. Why shouldn't the poetry? The poetry which understands the process of its own deterioration, its own death, can be beautiful if it doesn't pretend that something else is happening. So many poets pretend that the withering away of their gift is actually a form of wisdom. I don't think Williams was fooled. He understood that his loss of courage, his loss of nerve, were part and parcel of the aging and dying process. His poems age and die. They lose their "edge," to use your word, and they talk about it forthrightly and candidly. I never feel deceived in Williams.

This century certainly has been one in which we've seen the influence of many imports upon American poetry: from Pound's efforts at bringing Chinese poetry into the Modernist scene through Cathay; *the impact of several French poets including, for instance, LaForgue, Eliot's great stimulus; and various Eastern European poetries, to name but a few examples. What influences from abroad do you think have been most productive? Which ones do you think have been the most destructive?*

However inaccurate it was, what Pound was doing with the ideogram was very helpful for reasons that I don't even think Pound predicted—let's treat words as physical things rather than as symbols or totems. Poems are things made of stuff. The stuff is words. The fundamental demystification was enormously helpful, but the idea that the ideogrammatic method was possible in English was not so. We see the same input having both deleterious and salubrious results. On the one hand, we strayed off into thinking we could write ideogrammatic English; English is not an ideogrammatic language. But we could begin to think of our words as things, as objects in the field. And that's what led to Olson, Creeley. Very helpful.

We like to think of French as one thing, but French is many things. I adore Rimbaud. I do not enjoy Baudelaire. And normally they turn up in the same anthologies. They have nothing in common. Again, Baudelaire is looking at the world, in that central poem of *Flowers of Evil*, "Correspondences," as if somehow these symbols, these clusters of words made reference to some eternal world outside, whereas Rimbaud knew that poetry does not go all the way, language won't go all the way. Language won't solve anything. It ends as an "O" which is why Olson picked up that best of Rimbaud's poems "O Saisons O Chateaux," because it's "O, O, O," the language just falls apart.

And of all the French poets, Apollinaire shines most brightly, most instructively. In *Alcools*, language celebrates the fact of our being, the malleability of all things, words included, the endless multiplication of perspectives that occurs in any act of saying. In *Alcools*, materiality and temporality become the perfect expressions of human love and of the possibilities of joy.

I found the ideogrammatic method enormously useful because it insisted upon the materiality of language. That helped. Poets like Apollinaire and Rimbaud, who insisted upon the fact that language is just one of many things in an enormous field of things and that to rely upon it as some sort of key is ludicrous, were also helpful. So whatever came in and chastened us, humbled us, worked. Whatever came in and offered us shortcuts, offered us alternatives to responsibility of presence, proved to be a curse.

Same thing with Eastern European poets. They're not a single category either. I think of Attila Jozsef, who's about ideology breaking itself into pieces against the facts, the coming apart and exposing of the nakedness of language in ways that I don't think occurs, necessarily, in all Eastern European poets. I think Milosz still trusts language to convey something. Jozsef fell to pieces because he knew it didn't. You think of the difference between Akhmatova and Tsvetayeva. Akhmatova still had a certain confidence in what poetry could do; Tsvetayeva lost it. I honor Tsvetayeva over Akhmatova for that reason. She understood that the necessities of humanity could not be satisfied by poetry alone, whereas Akhmatova really thought she could describe the Stalinist terror. Tsvetayeva screamed, which makes more sense to me.

And you can do the same thing with almost any European poetry. There were people there who exaggerated the possibilities of what poetry could contribute and those who painfully, but voraciously, admitted that poetry has fierce limits. That's why I really can't love Rilke. Rilke had too high an opinion of poetry. He thought it could do too much, that its role was too wonderful. But someone like Trakl understood that poetry would never suffice, that it wasn't enough, that human suffering was larger than language and that language was no balm for catastrophe. And so I honor him above Rilke.

Another "import" in a very different vein is Auden who wrote the famous line "for poetry makes nothing happen." What do you understand as the limit of what poetry can do in the public sphere? What do you think its role is?

I think that by the time Auden was writing that poem he'd already shrunk from the "low, dishonest decade" of the thirties. Understandably so; it was a horrible time to be anybody and to understand the criminality of language. English as a language was an accomplice of Fascism; it was an accomplice in the whole horror of Hitlerite Europe. To feel disgraced and to want to just take language out of it all was an honorable if flawed intention.

Poetry is where the language gets made. It's where the language gets examined, where, if we're lucky, the rigors of truthfulness and responsibility are applied to words. Consciousness is made of language; therefore, when we subject language to rigors, we subject consciousness to rigors. It is the fundamental building block of what people think and what people see because they see everything through a filter of words, they see everything through a screen of words. The world comes to us through words and is expressed by us in words. Therefore, poetry is tinkering with a primary material of human activity, language. I think that terrified Auden. I think it ought to terrify everybody. Nobody much reads poetry, but that's not the point. Nobody much knows about genetic engineering. We're all affected by it; the history of the species is going to be changed forever by genetic engineering. It doesn't matter that people aren't lining up in bookstores to buy the latest book by a genetic engineer just as it doesn't matter that people aren't lining up in bookstores to buy the latest book of poetry. Poems are where the language gets made. It gets cleansed or it gets soiled. It gets healed or it becomes sicker through poetry. When something goes right or wrong in language it goes right or wrong first in poetry.

Poetry is not about making things happen. That's what language does. Poetry is about making language happen. People make language do things in all human spheres.

So the conflict is at the level of the word, syntax, grammar rather than within any specific political upheaval.

Yes, poetry is prior to all that. Poetry is language languaging. Which is why it's so silly that they call some poetry "Language" poetry. All poetry is "Language" poetry. The subject matter is incidental. What's really happening is that language is becoming its next self in poetry and if that next self is depraved or mendacious, things are pretty bad. But if that next self is forthright and clear, perhaps things get better. I honor Williams and Creeley simply because, in their poems, language becomes a cleaner next self, a clearer thing, a more honest thing, not a more swaddled or concealed or duplicitous thing. Poetry is political the same way that poetry is biological, the same way that poetry is agricultural, economic, philosophical. Everything that human beings do is made of words and the words come from the workshop of poetry.

How then would you articulate your attitude toward the trend of appropriation of certain political upheavals, the wreckage of history, by American poets in order to assume a political stance? Do you think it irresponsible, immoral, or perhaps just irrelevant?

It's most often adolescent but sometimes immoral. No one should ever feel sad that the secret police aren't breaking into his apartment, thus depriving him of poignant material. The fact is that we all participate in these catastrophies anyway; but we shouldn't be distracted by the glamor of catastrophe, the easy, outward, identifiable enemy, because the enemy in Eastern Europe, the enemy in Tianenmen Square, the enemy in Palo Alto, is always the same. It's people lying to themselves. Poetry is about trying to put a stop to people lying to themselves. Before a tank can run over a boy in Tianenmen Square, before someone can be tortured to death in the Gestapo basements, somebody has to lie to himself. Poetry works at the sub-atomic level. Things go wrong when you tell lies; language, when it goes wrong, is a lie we tell to ourselves, and I think that an infatuation with history avoids the central issue of history in a weird way. Writing about "bad stuff" that happens in—fill in the blank, Central America, Eastern Europe, Mississippi—that's not the issue. Something more fundamental went wrong before that stuff went wrong and you don't have to go out of your own room to see the holocaust happening. The holocaust happens when someone consents to lie to himself, and he lies to himself in the form of words. Therefore, we should sit very still and be very rigorous with every syllable we pronounce. That's a way of participating in the resistance to totalizing inhumanities whether they're happening in China or in the pet store down the street. It doesn't really matter.

> *So whatever misdirection his enthusiasms may have caused, Pound's Confucian notion of "Calling things by their right names" is fundamental.*

Right. As he said, "Abstraction is a greased slide." If you can tell the truth to yourself about your daily life, you are in the resistance. It's adolescent, this desire of American poets to vampirize other people's suffering. Sure it's easy, but it has nothing to do with what's really happening, and the people who are there would be the first to say it. That's what we were speaking of last night, Miklos Haraszti's beautiful book, *The Velvet Prison*. It's happening everywhere. There are certain hallucinations called Stalinism, and there are certain hallucinations called free market economy. The issue is to demystify the hallucinations, whatever they happen to be. Whether they are fast food franchises or five year plans, it doesn't really matter. Somebody's using a lie to conceal a truth. Language is there to debunk lies in real poetry.

> *Speaking of real poetry and its impact, you've written of being "floored" by* The Double Dream of Spring. *Can you think of other moments of being floored by a poetry when you first encountered it?*

Besides Ashbery? I would say when I read Olson's "The Distances," that poem. "So the distances are Galatea / and one does fall in love and desires / mastery." That astonished me. Jorie Graham's second book *Erosion*. I was on my way to an opera in Virginia, and I stopped at a bookstore and there was *Erosion*, and I bought it, and I sat down and read it and wept on the sidewalk. Ashbery again with *Houseboat Days*. When that book came out, I was at the bookstore before it opened, knowing that they would have *Houseboat Days* that day. These books have simply taken the top of my head off.

Jabbes, when I first read *The Book of Questions*. I had no idea that such things were possible—that writing could be writing. It didn't have to become something; it could stay writing—for a long, long time. And Breton. When I read *L'Amour Fou, Mad Love*. The idea that the only thing worth doing was keeping oneself in a position to fall in love, that the only thing worth doing with your life was throwing it away with both hands. Marvelous.

In the same essay on Ashbery you describe his "spontaneous interiors." In Williams one might be inclined to describe his "spontaneous exteriors." I wonder if they have become two poles of a dualism, two different guides for you?

People are always talking about how much Ashbery comes out of Wallace Stevens, and of course, Ashbery benefited enormously from Stevens' project. Yet I see Williams in Ashbery as much as I see Stevens. I think it's part of Ashbery's genius to understand that the inside is outside too. Part of what happens in the making of poems and the reading of poems is the understanding of one's inner life as being outside and all around you. So I don't see them as being poles at all; I see them as being orchestrations in the same moment of music. I think Ashbery daunts people in some ways because he is so accessible. They can't quite cope with a poetry that is so on the page. In a sense he is the most approachable of American poets because nothing is being concealed, and that's why I'm always astonished when people say Ashbery is a difficult poet, because he's not. He's quite the opposite. He's the most available, the most welcoming of poets I know. Everything is what it is. It's not a symbol for anything else. It's this entire exteriorization of the inward life, this humility that says there is nothing in me that didn't come from the world. It's not as if the world were some pale substitute for my splendid inner life. If I have an inner life where do you think it came from? It came from the world.

If you can make such a choice, which of his books have meant the most to you?

Well they change all the time, which keeps me nice and humble. I think when I started reading Ashbery it was *The Double Dream of Spring* and *Self Portrait in a Convex Mirror* that most mattered. As I get older, I love most of all *Three Poems*. I don't want to call them prose poems but we'll call them prose poems. What happens in there is so enormous I can hardly begin to speak of it. All I know is that Ashbery is the first poet who taught me that the poem begins when you stop reading. You read Ashbery and it's beautiful and it's lovely, and then you look up from the page and realize the world is different. What happened as I was reading is that my eyes were changed. My head has been changed and now I'm a different person in the world. So I guess now *Three Poems* is my favorite, along with *Hotel Lautréamont* where he seems to give authority away with both hands. I don't know of a poet who can be considered more generous than Ashbery. His learning is enormous. His wisdom is enormous. His memory is capacious, and he never asks to be admired for it. He just gives it away.

Which connects to what his poems have to offer through their resistance to tight closure.

I think Ashbery has said in a variety of circumstances that poetry is continuous. Any given poem is just a cross-section of what was going on before the poem started, and it continues long after the poem ends. It's almost like poetry is a coming attraction for poetry.

You've written of "the need to recapture largeness . . . a revival of the grand gesture." How does Whitman figure into your notion of largeness. Is the Whitmanic presence and its vastness of gesture part of your definition?

There's no way around Whitman. He's both a blessing and a curse. One that I suppose every poet, especially an American poet, has come up against. On the one hand he understood that things like "a self," "a voice in a poem" are always in the process of being put together. He understood that these things were always under construction, and therefore, any gesture had to be large because it was part of an enormously long project. We weren't beginning with little lyrical exposures of an already completed self. We had work to do; we had to make a self. The genius of *Leaves of Grass* is that the self is something you make. A soul is not something you have and then understand. A soul is something that you put together as a result of living in time.

The trouble was Whitman believed you could finish the job, that eventually you did put together a soul. That led to a political creepiness, a sort of manifest destiny idea that, once you had put this soul together, you could use it as a form of authority. Ashbery goes beyond the limits of Whitman because of this. He understands that yes, the self, whoever you are, is something you're always putting together from pieces that float along toward you, and that you never finish the job. I think Whitman thought you could finish the job, that eventually you got someplace where this was "I." Ashbery realizes that it's an endless improvisation until you die. The job is never completed, the task is never completed. The gesture is never finished. Whitman held onto the idea that, well, I'm starting from zero and I'm the new man in the new country, in the new place, and I'm going to put together this thing—I'll call it "Walt." His insistence upon revising and changing *Leaves of Grass* instead of just writing another book betrays that. Ashbery knows that nothing can be perfected, and that's perfect. Everything we have is perfectly fine, and then we're going to have something else that's perfectly fine, too.

The notion of the "unfinishedness" of the soul is important to your essay, "The Moving Sidewalk," a very powerful autobiographical piece. In that essay you argue against any notions of essentialism in regards to class. Do you think your arguments are applicable to a debunking of those same beliefs in regard to, say, gender or ethnicity?

As I get older I become more and more of an antinomian. I distrust any name. I think it's the project of poetry, the project of writing, the project of reading, the project of doing almost anything to

unname things. I get very sad when people latch on to names because
I know there's one way of being sure that someone is wrong and
that's if they're trying to make the world smaller. I'm not really
good with ethics, but I know diminishment is always wrong.
Somebody does something the result of which is a world smaller
than the world he received, that's a bad person, that's a bad activity.
And so I oppose anything that seeks to define because I think poetry
is about undefining. And not just poetry. I think that being human
is about that. The more you live, the more you understand the
uselessness of definitions and the inutility of seeking to make
definitions. All human beings transcend class, all human beings
transcend gender, all human beings transcend race, nationality.

*The willing indeterminacy of your poetics, the provisionality you
were just speaking of and have written of as "nextness," revisionist
approaches to genre, the paradoxical openness of the most generous
closure—I understand these as profound gestures of humility. Is
humility the building block of the creative process? A necessary
step toward transparency to the world? What role do you think
you play in the creation of the poem?*

I think that I'm a better poet the more I unbuild myself.
Transparency is something that fascinates me; it's my career goal.
It's wonderful that Wittgenstein's last book, *Remarks on Color*, was
a hymn to transparency. The idea that if I can be something through
which light passes undamaged, I'll have done a good job. If somehow
truth can go into my work and come out of it unharmed—because
that's the original meaning of innocence. Innocence does not mean
"not experienced." Innocence means "I do no harm." If I can
somehow put words together that do no harm, allow the free passage
of the facts, of the real, it's a Raoul Wallenberg kind of thing. If I
can get people out of danger, if I can get words out of the camps, if
I can rescue a few phrases from becoming murderous or murdered,
how wonderful! And to the extent that I can become transparent,
to the extent that I'm not there at all, I'm doubly honored by my
Guggenheim fellowship because what I asked the Guggenheim

people to fund was a project in which I would look for ways to write poetry as if I were nobody at all. And to my delight they funded it. To my delight also, it helped. What I found living in regions of Europe where no one spoke any English at all, where I did not come in contact with English on a daily basis, was that I became no one at all, that I had no marketable, commodifiable self. All I could do was invent something every day. Whatever language I spoke on any given day was something I made from my useless English and my inadequate French. It was marvelous.

Everything is about free passage. Wittgenstein talks a lot about prisms. What does a prism do? It does not create. It does not contain light. It is not a creative thing. But light, passing through a prism, is revealed as itself. The light comes in and then emerges as its entire spectrum. Nothing is in the prism, nothing has been created by the prism, but because the light passed through it, it became knowable as itself, as being a spectrum of red, orange, yellow, green, blue, indigo, violet. I would love to know that someday I could write a poem that was prismatic in that way. We're back to Marianne Moore and "In the Days of Prismatic Color."

The idea that language would somehow come into me, since I didn't create language, I didn't make any language, I didn't invent a single word in the dictionary, and that language passing through me, not remaining in me would, as a result of passing through me, be more visibly itself.

This goes along with what I've been trying to teach my students here at Iowa: that meaning does not reside in poetry, meaning passes *through* poetry. The point of making a poem is to make something out of words through which meaning can pass without impediment and without significant loss of energy. It's like when you design an electrical circuit. You want as much of the energy that leaves the battery to arrive at the light bulb. The best circuit is the one that allows the least loss of energy. Same with poetry I think. Whatever truth the language had coming in, you want the greatest amount of that to arrive at the other side of the poem. And to that extent, the poem is best that draws the least attention to itself as a form. It's a middleman, a poem. A prism.

Do you see your four books as progression, revision, retreat? Or
perhaps you can supply a more accurate word?

Well, it's in hindsight, so any such gesture is going to be self congratulatory. I'm not about to say that they've just gotten worse, they've deteriorated over the years. *From the Abandoned Cities* was in a lot of ways a very, very formal book. Formal for the reasons that you would expect: I was young; I was insecure; I was coming from a physically very bad circumstance, the environment I grew up in was a chaos with which I was unable to cope. I found in the ritual of ordering words a way of coping, a way of not drowning. The Bronx is a beautiful, terrible place that is so much larger than an individual that you have to talk yourself out of it. So that first book was sort of "whenever I feel afraid I hold my head erect and whistle a happy tune." Whistling, formalism, as a way of talking myself out of the dark. I'm not ashamed of the book at all; I'm very pleased with its reception and what I was able to do. But I think it shows youth, the idea that I needed to wear a magic coat, I needed to have a decoder ring—all the things that are in contemporary boy mythology. You know, we have to have some sort of talisman to get us out of a scary place, and I got out of the scary place through the talisman of poetic form.

The Gaza of Winter was very much a transitional book where I was trying to exorcise my feeling that personal tragedy was unique, that somehow it gave me super privilege or that it was enough to make poetry from for the rest of my life. What *The Gaza of Winter* finally sees is that all the terrible things that happen to me happen to everybody and that I had better find something else to talk about because it's not really news. That's why the book ends with a poem about the raft of the Medusa, a group of people exposed to an extent to which I've never been exposed and reduced to circumstances of violence and horror to which I've never been reduced. Subject matter is not what poetry is made of.

Realizing that, I was able to write *New Dark Ages*, a more explicitly political book. Still very much understanding that there is no such thing as a distinction between private and public life, but rather that there are certain nightmares that result when we treat public life as though it were private and private life as if though it were public. When we try to blur the words, we become irresponsible. Taking history personally and thinking of your girlfriend leaving you as some sort of political catastrophe, that's what makes a "dark ages." The first dark ages were made by a failure of nerve. These days are our "new dark ages" because our nerve has failed again. In the middle eighties, historically, whether we deserved it or not, we were presented with an opportunity to do things anew, to make a new polity, to make a "new world order," as they say. We panicked and decided "well, the old world order was pretty good. If it wasn't for these guys like Stalin and Karl Marx and Adolph Hitler everything would have been fine so let's just go back to the old world order and pretend none of this ever happened—" Which means, of course, that it's all going to happen again, and it is. Failure of nerve.

Erasures is a book of despair about that. The presiding genius of that book, the consoling friend, was Karl Kraus whose line, "Let him who has something to say step forward and be silent," inspired it all. The idea that something so horrible has happened in this failure of nerve that the results are going to be incalculably awful.

And yet through the book you step forward and speak, so there are grains of hope . . .

I don't know if I'd call it hope. There are certain circumstances where it is possible to say something not untrue. There is no moment in *Erasures* when there is any expectation that that event will have consequences. The book ends with the line "The unborn have been revoked. They will not be kind." Yes, from time to time we can stand up and say something that is not untrue, but I don't know that anything is going to come of it. To me, if there is one great work of literature in the twentieth century, it's *Endgame*. If anything survives from the twentieth century, I hope it's *Endgame*. That moment where the one character says, "We do what we can," and the reply is, "We shouldn't." That haunts me. I know that in *Erasures*

I try very hard to say things not untrue, and I don't know that I should. I don't know that I wasn't congratulating myself for being able to say something that was not entirely false. Hubris? Ego? Narcissism? In my work now I'm trying to explore ways of saying nothing at all. We'll see what happens.

PHOTO BY DEE SMITH

PHOTO BY DEE SMITH

Dave Smith was born in Portsmouth, Virginia, in 1942. He is a prolific writer whose poetry, fiction, and criticism form a substantial body of unique work. His books of poetry include: Drunks; Goshawk, Antelope; In the House of the Judge; Cuba Nights; Fate's Kite; *and* Tremble. Louisiana State University Press *recently published his* The Wick of Memory: New and Selected Poems 1970-2000. *By continually exploring how to conflate the immediacy of the lyric with the meaning found within "a tale," Smith has shaped a lasting body of writing. Winner of a variety of awards—from an National Endowment for the Arts grant to a Guggenheim fellowship— Smith's impact on contemporary American literature, as an important poet, critic (his collection of criticism,* Local Assays, *is an insightful exploration of the art) and editor (he has edited* The Southern Review *since 1990), is substantial.*

DAVE SMITH

Rob Carney and I spoke with Dave in Baton Rouge, Louisiana, during spring 1995.

You've written short stories, novels, and many "narrative" poems. What do you think the difference is between how narrative works in poetry and how it works in other genres? Exactly how detailed a "story" do you feel compelled to tell in a poem? When does exposition, in poetry, become tedious?

There has been an abundant discussion—particularly among lyric poets—in recent years about narrative and lyric as genre definitions. I think of narrative as essentially "what happens," the narration of a sequence of events. As a poet in some ways identified with the characteristics of the regional literature of the South, to be called a narrative poet came to feel to me as something of a limiting jacket. I think any writer is likely to bristle, maybe unfairly, at what he or she is labeled. So sometimes when I speak about narrative, it sounds like I'm rejecting it. I don't mean that at all. Robert Penn Warren, in his great poem "Audubon," says, "Tell me a story of deep delight." The recognition behind that is that in some way all experience is organized, made acceptable, made accessible when it's given narrated shape. I certainly feel the interest in narrative or story or tale that perhaps has been identified with my writing. On the other hand, even my longest poems, if distilled to the plot, would take only a few seconds to say, whereas the poems themselves may take ten to fifteen minutes. That is indication that they are not essentially narrative poems, but in fact lyric poems that take narrative occasion to play with the language.

I'm much more interested, ultimately, in quality of expression, in the way something is said, than in what is said. I don't reject narrative. Ellen Voigt and I have been having a running dialogue about it. Ellen feels that there is too great a propensity among younger poets now to move in the direction of narrative. And that may very well be true. If it is true, then I may have had something to do with it because in the mid-seventies, when I was beginning to write seriously, everything was image and lyric and there were only a few of us who were interested in what's come to be called the narrative poem.

Part of the reason I bristle now is the so-called "neo-Narrative" movement with which I have nothing to do. I think what they are interested in writing, in so far as I understand what they're about, is not at all what I am interested in. Stanley Plumly, in the late seventies, identified something in *APR* he called the prose lyric. I don't think Stanley went far enough in the way he defined this, but I agree with his principle which was that some of us were trying to write a poem which attempted to marry what Robert Penn Warren called "the imperfection of experience," and which he more or less equated with prose, to a kind of lyric orchestration. That was a way of trying to get more into the poem rather than less. The image poets moved in the opposite direction. It wasn't so much that we wanted to get more story in, although that was one of the methods, but that we wanted a fuller, richer, and more complete verbal experience in the poem than was commonly being written in the late sixties and early seventies, a time when Merwin, Bly, Wright and any number of others were writing a lyrical image poem that some of us didn't want to write. Not that we didn't like it, we just didn't want to write it.

To talk about narrative for me is to talk about a way of accessing experience, a way of maximizing experience. I can go a little farther and say what might begin to sound a little mystical—I resist this intensely and yet can't help myself. One of the firmest convictions that I have of what the world is all about is that phenomena, the physical world as I can present it, expresses. I need to know not only what to look at and what to hear but how to hear it, and I regard the poem as a "hearing" of something that is being said by everything that's around me, everything that's going on. I don't mean to minimize the role of the poet as maker. My experience of the poem is that at some point it's being dictated, and at some point it's being made or refined; the turning point where one shifts to the other is different in every poem. I think this is, at least to some measure, what accounts for the desire for varying forms rather than satisfaction in one kind of form. On this point, I would disagree with Richard Wilbur, a great authority who regards status of form as art's essential character. Narration or the telling of a story merely permits a way to access experience. The poet seeks to find a way not merely to manifest but to make understood the resonant layers of that experience. There's a kind of narrative poet—let's say Robert Service—who tells a good story, a story you want to hear at any bar or with friends, but he doesn't concern himself with what we might call the lyrical quality of language. That's not his primary interest. He's not particularly concerned with the resonant layers of language by which one tries the possibility of saying secondary and tertiary things with the poem; one might take a poem about one's grandmother, for instance, and write it in such a way that it is also about the larger issue of one's relationship with one's ancestors. I don't think Service is interested in that kind of thing. He is interested in story that will have you on the edge of your seat with suspense and excitement.

So you're suggesting there are several "types" of narrative poetry?

Yes. It may be misleading to assume that when one says we're talking about narrative poetry, we're talking about one thing that has the same objectives, but that's usually the case, particularly when lyric poets talk about narration. It's assumed we're all doing the same thing. People will say "all Southerners have got narrative." Perhaps this is the legacy of a rich fiction tradition from Twain to Faulkner and onward. But it's just not true. That's the reason why Charles Wright says in nearly every interview he's ever given, "I can't write a narrative." Well, that's baloney. Charles can write narrative well as most of his books will show you, but he's resisting the myths that diminish what any writer can be. I believe in the power of the tale for certain aesthetic and structural reasons. It has enabled me to do things I've wanted to do. But I don't like to think of myself as a narrative poet despite the fact that I began as a fiction writer and remain interested in writing fiction, still do write fiction, although covertly. I don't try to publish it. Nor do I pretend to have any expertise in that area. I'm very limited in what I can do in fiction. I don't work at it regularly and may not have the talent to do it anyway. It's an avocation, but it's part of my whole interest in, not what constitutes, what stories can do as a formal organizer of the poetry.

Ellen Voigt maintains—as she said in her essay in our recent "Southern" issue—that narration and poetry are contradictory terms. She wants very much to be seen as a lyric poet. That somewhat denies, not entirely, but somewhat, her book called *The Lotus Flowers*, which is clearly more narrational in shape than her other books. She says, "Well, it was just an experiment; I wanted to see if I could tell stories." I'm suspicious. She knows what she can do, and she does it very well, but it's also interesting that she chooses to go against what she does very well. Whereas, in my case, I have tried to do better what I felt I was learning to do. This is the proviso: I have tended to—insofar as my mother and two or three other people know my work—be a writer of longer poems. Recently, I determined I would not do that any more, and my new book is formed entirely of thirteen-line poems.

RC: "Terrible" sonnets?

Not sonnets. There is maybe a shadow-world of the sonnet's operation in the background. I certainly don't want to claim I'm uninformed about what the sonnet does, but I only wanted to write short poems, and I wanted to write them in such a way that they might imitate other forms in miniature as they proceed. It was an arbitrary decision. I wanted to do something different as a step. I do not know toward what exactly. I'm now tending to recover some of the earlier things I did and seeing if I can change them, but this is going into an unknown territory for a while. I've written short poems but not dominantly ever.

> *RC: One of the things you mentioned a couple of times was the formal matters of a poem. What kind of formal qualities do you give the most attention to while writing, or is that something that comes secondarily when you're crafting the poem later?*

No, well, I want to say yes and no at the same time. I think the most honest answer I can give you is that over a period of years you train yourself to respond with what might be called "literary muscles" which know what to do before you ask them to do it in the same way any athlete trains certain muscles to respond. I think my first sense, without being conscious about it, is to seek form. In this new book, once I knew that I was going to be writing in a thirteen-line form, I only twice sought a fourteen or other-numbered line poem. The form was given to me, so the arena that I would work in was set, and the decisions I had to make about form within that thirteen-line arena were significant, but they were different than the kind of decisions that you have when you see the blank page and you are aware "I'm going to sit down and write a poem here, but I don't know how long it's going to be. I have no conception about that."

People do this in different ways. There are poets who habitually write whatever first comes to them in prose, and then they shape it down into some kind of form. That's never been possible for me.

My typical pattern has been to respond to an image that forms, usually a visual image in my mind. I seek some verbal equivalent for it. The image emerging in verbal equivalence would very often be puzzling to me. This is where the shift to narrative comes in. Without knowing the rationale, the reason, the interest in something, a typical pattern for me has been to invent a story to explain it.

I can give you an example. In 1972 or 1973, an image came into my head of six men buried head-to-head in a circle, rather like wedges in pie that had been cut—they were buried that way. I knew that they were related, and I knew to me they were significant, but I had no idea who they were or what they meant to me. It was a twenty-two-line poem at that point. Short lines, short poem. I put it in the desk drawer, as I habitually will, and took it out a few days later. Nothing happened, couldn't budge it; it wouldn't talk to me. So I continued to do that periodically, shuffling through things, looking for something to write on each day, and at a certain point something else happened and I realized that this poem had something to do with softball. I can't tell you what that connection was, but once I knew that I began to realize that the poem wanted to remember an uncle of mine, who, when I was a child, took me out to play softball on occasions when my family would be back at the home area for funerals. From that came a poem called "The Roundhouse Voices," a ninety-one-line poem that, relatively speaking, would be called a narrative poem. In fact, it's a funeral elegy, a very clear and traditional form which identifies the imperatives of that poem. When I first saw it, I had no idea I was writing a funeral elegy. It evolved out of an image.

To try and come back to your question—it's a puzzle to me, how I turned to a form which had existed for centuries. Where did the narrative and my interest in that form merge? I had read such lyrical poems, of course, but in no sense was I consciously aware of attempting such a form or even the characteristics of that form. I can only speculate. I expect that my habits of reading had something to do with it. It may have even been at the time I made that first leap that I had been reading "Lycidas" or maybe Thomas Gray's

"Elegy in a Country Churchyard." Any of a number of things might have set off what led to the form and then subsequently to my own loosening of the form or forcing the form to be mine, I don't know. I think that's probably buried in biography.

To come at it another way, the existence of form is not something, even in terminology, that all people agree upon. The neo-verse writers, for instance, pretty much argue that form means verse and anything else is imitation. There's a poet named David Middleton who had a piece in a Louisiana arts journal recently. He says that there is verse and there is all the other stuff that is not poetry. He denies, explicitly, that form as a word not synonymous with verse means anything. I disagree. Whitman is a poet but not a verse writer. Dickinson is always a poet and sometimes a verse writer. And what of Wordsworth, Neruda, and Sylvia Plath? I think that poetry is synonymous with form but that there are different kinds of form and they do different things, and the responsible intellect tries to understand how form can be employed to produce desirable results. If that's true, my sense is that as soon as you put the first word on the page and add the second word, you're moving in the direction of some kind of form. It's part of the poet's responsibility to equip himself or herself with a sufficient knowledge of form to know, when the tool comes to hand, what you might do with it or might not do with it. If you can do that, then I think you prepare yourself for the opportunity to write poetry. I don't say that you can do it, only that you now have the tool and opportunity which can produce it.

The best poets are those able to make form maximize whatever is given them to write. There are no poets who write outside of form. There are some who write sloppily, poorly, but if it's poetry, it's formal in some way. If it's not, then it's not poetry. A good deal of what gets published in this country is not poetry. Looks like poetry, acts like poetry, talks like it, but it isn't. Unfortunately, we are now in such a situation in our training of scholars and writers that we don't equip them with the opportunity and tools to recognize what's a sort of false poetry from real poetry. This is one of the effects of the democratization of art, a relativism which values art's accomplishment less than a quota recognition for all who make an attempt. I think it's one of the reasons that criticism is in very bad shape, too. I mean by that applied criticism not theoretical criticism. James Wright used to say—he said it in an interview I did with him—that one of the things wrong with American poetry is that we don't have a criticism that is sufficiently helpful to us to know what our mistakes and weaknesses are. This may be truer today than in the late seventies when he said that.

You've written about Robert Penn Warren and Edgar Allen Poe—a chronologically Postmodernist poet and one who many would point to, because of his relationship with Symbolism, as a significant "pre-Modernist" poet—however, I can't recall reading anything you've written on any of the Modernists poets. I was wondering if you had any favorites or felt any particular indebtedness to any of them or if you feel your relationship with them is more antagonistic.

You mentioned that in a letter, and it surprised me because I was educated in Modernist poetry more than in contemporary. One of my Ph.D. examination questions was something like "Who is the better poet, Eliot or Williams?" My answer was Yeats. It is quite true that by and large I haven't written about Modernist poets, and I'm not sure why. I certainly feel very close to Yeats and to the Yeatsian sense of what the poet and poem are. Less so to Eliot, although Eliot stands ahead of that line; I don't think you can be close to Yeats without being close to Eliot in some respects. I don't have any interest in and have never had very much interest in Pound. So that tributary of the Modernist river I don't take; I'm just not interested in it.

Your question forces me to think about these things. I just did the 32nd Wallace Stevens reading at The University of Connecticut—it's not just a reading, you have to talk a little bit about Stevens—and it caused me to reread all of Stevens. I had never felt close to Stevens. In fact, I was on a thesis defense yesterday that dealt with Stevens. I still don't feel particularly close to Stevens.

I'm dividing the two teams up here with Yeats and Eliot on one side and Stevens and Pound on another. What do we do with Williams? Oddly enough we put him with Eliot and Yeats, although many people would put him on the other side. Maybe he's the utility man in here somewhere. But what do you do with Frost, who maybe I feel closer to than any of them? Modernist poet or pre-Modernist poet? A good argument can be made either way.

Perhaps the first question is what is a Modernist poet? It brings me back to Robert Penn Warren. Warren begins chronologically as a Modernist poet; Warren was publishing his first poems as Thomas Hardy was publishing his last. It's interesting to think of that overlapping, an overlapping in fact not that far from Gerard Manley Hopkins. With Hopkins you ask the same questions: is he a Modernist poet or is he not? *The Norton Anthology of Modern Poetry* begins with Walt Whitman. It begins in the middle of the nineteenth century; it's an arbitrary category in some respects to say what is modern poetry and what isn't, but I take it that what you mean is a kind of poet writing in the early part of this century, a poet who might be marked by contradictory or ambiguous attitudes toward form. Allen Tate says in one of his essays that the poet's problem is not that he doesn't have a modern form, but that he has too many forms and can't choose. That sense of uncertainty, if you look at the people I've mentioned and include Marianne Moore and others, that sense of range, of people going off in different directions and not finding common ground is what seems to me remarkable.

Maybe with the poets of my age that range of exploration is not as great, that there isn't as much range accessible to them. It's not that I'm not aware of the Modernists, not that I'm not interested. I don't feel any hostility or antagonism, with some exceptions. I don't buy Olson at all. I don't have much respect—well maybe some respect, but no enthusiasm—for Pound. I am not moved by Stevens; I admire him, but I don't have affection for him. I have great affection for Frost.

However, one of the interesting people that I've had reason to read in the past year is Robinson Jeffers. Jeffers saw himself as anti-Modernist, by which I think he meant a number of things, not least of which he saw himself as writing in more traditional forms, like sonnets. He coveted the sense of himself as a lingering Anglo-Saxonist. He saw himself, to some degree, connected to a tradition behind the Modernists rather than with the Modernists—all the classical connections that he felt so profoundly. But there's something even more than that, and it's hard to identify. Jeffers felt a sense of poetry as the expression of individual passion that he saw the Modernists resisting. He saw them connected to a kind of extension of the nineteenth century that he did not want to be part of, that he felt he went behind. I have some sympathy with that position. I don't know why I feel some of the same strong connections that Jeffers does. If you ask me to name a poem that immediately suggests to me a deep connection, I would say "The Seafarer." I feel acutely a connection to the Anglo-Saxon power of language. It's a line that runs direct to English Romanticism and then there's a hiatus. It begins to break off, to dissipate its focus; I mean the essential vocabulary and rhythm of English speech, the cadence of our expression. But I also mean a disposition to a core that might be called the form of poetry. Poe fits in there in some ways, although Poe for a Southerner is, as Mr. Tate said, "our cousin"; you simply can't avoid him, he's there. It doesn't have very much to do with his poetry, which is pretty bad as a rule. But then as the line fragments under the explorations of the Romantics, Whitman and Dickinson and others, you jump forward to where? If you ask me where I jump forward to, it's probably Hopkins and then Yeats. If we're going to define those as Modernists, there is my connection. If we're defining Modernism in some other way, then I'm not sure how to respond to your question. It really interests me that I might in some way be hostile or have some antipathy toward Modernism—because I never thought that I did—but your question makes me uncomfortable enough to consider it further.

I guess when I was asking about the Modernists, I was asking about the early twentieth-century group—Pound, Eliot, Yeats, Stevens, Moore, Williams, Crane—poets who generally produced their great work in the period David Perkins refers to as "High Modernism," poets who were very interested in formal experimentation, the use of the fragment, making the poem a very dense textual object.

Well, without playing psycho-critic, let me give you an answer. The sons typically reject the fathers. Bly and Wright and those working with image in the sixties were clearly the inheritors of that fragmentation, that elliptical poetry. Those choices were what I was rejecting. Not that I was rejecting James Wright exactly, because there's this other condition in Wright which is the prose lyric that he ultimately settled on. You can see the same process occurring in Robert Lowell. Early Lowell is all that heavily-embedded, literary, Eliotic stuff—and a lot of his early poems are also fragmented and elliptical—and then you get the poems of *Life Studies* which seek to be more open, narrational, and try to create "wholes," formal wholes rather than fragments. That's the Lowell I respond to favorably. Maybe what happened in the seventies when I was first learning how to write poems is that I was also responding to the fathers that were still around, selecting those that seemed to offer what I wanted and rejecting those that didn't.

But there's even a third answer to this, and that is: the Modernists I first read and was first influenced by were fiction writers. Faulkner, Conrad, Joyce preeminently. I started out trying to write novels. As an undergraduate, I would have killed to stay out of a poetry class. I was terrified of poetry. I felt that well into graduate school; I felt that I didn't understand the secrets, the arcane language that everyone got except me. Fiction was my access to all kinds of formal theory and structuring. At the point when I was able to come to poetry, I was twenty-eight years old, married, a father, in military service. I was able to look at the moderns through a formed character, with aesthetic and political values of my own. Perhaps the revolutionary impulses of the Modernists were not so revolutionary to me. Except for Yeats and Frost who I think are always there.

> *RC: It seems that Frost and in some ways Yeats are doing what you're talking about—they're storytelling, but they're not. Their work is not strictly narrative, but there often is that narrative beginning or narrative catalyst in the poems. There is, especially in Frost, that storytelling impulse, but with an attention to lyricism.*

Exactly, and I'll add one more element to it, which we can call, for lack of a better phrase, "regionalism." Both Frost and Yeats are very close to a local world. They are as good as they are because they transcend the local, but they begin in the local. From the first, that was of extreme interest to me. I wanted to write about what was around me; it took me a while to understand that wasn't enough, that one had to somehow lift the work to a more transcendent expression. You think of many of the Modernists, they have already gone beyond that. They tend to be universalists from the beginning rather than regionalists. Insofar as Stevens' poems are concerned, for example. Many of Stevens' poems don't particularly interest me because they are dislocated; they float in a kind of art world of the imagination. But this must be understood as an emphasis, not an absolute. Eliot is the poet of London, in the twentieth century, as no one else is. But where is Stevens' local place? Williams' is Paterson, New Jersey. But where is Pound's?

> *You mentioned Hugo and Wright. Their work seems very centered on specific place—Wright's Ohio, Hugo's Northwest. And I see, looking at your work, a sense of place being very important, whether it be the Virginia coastline or Utah.*

I'll tell you something of what I admire in James Wright's poems. If James Wright only gave us little vignettes of Polish drunks in bars, we wouldn't care about him. He'd be as forgotten as Edgar

Lee Masters is. What Wright does, in my reading, is transform the Ohio River Valley into a contemporary, nearly mythical equivalent of the underworld, of the land of the barely living and the dead. It becomes a human history and a myth in much the same way that Joyce's *Ulysses* is an overlay of Homer's. I think the power there is to see the same truth outside of the restrictions of time and place. But they begin in time and place. From the first this universality has been very attractive to me. If I could do that, I would be perfectly satisfied; it would be enough for me.

Richard Hugo, a poet I very much admire, did not have the success that Wright did. But he certainly was moving in the same direction. He certainly was trying to accomplish the same kind of mythical power in the local. In his case Montana, Washington, Idaho, the Northwest.

RC: What about Levine?

Well, Philip Levine is to me an interesting case. I've written about Levine, and I have great admiration for his poems. I also have some very real reservations about a poetry that my friends and I argue about. Levine is a much more formal poet than either Wright or Hugo. He has made a prewriting decision about form. He is, in my judgment, a fastidiously formal poet. Also, a religious poet. But interestingly enough, Levine's greatest strength as a poet is anger. Nobody can write anger poems like he can. This is a talent that, I think, places him in a Biblical, almost Old Testament, prophetic stance as a poet. There's nobody who can do the things that he can do. But I don't see Levine as particularly a poet of place, although there are certainly local poems in a book like *1933*, a lot of Michigan poems. But many of them are not, in spite of the rap that Levine writes about the Detroit transmission shop constantly. As if he's spent all of his life in a Detroit transmission shop. As he would tell you, he spent a couple of years there and some forty years as a professor in Fresno. This is only to say that he's made good capital out of his biographical experiences. He began with the local, but what happens in Levine's poems is astonishing. For instance, "They Feed They Lion"—a poem which is about hungry black people in an urban American city. He turns it into a Biblical apocalypse. Who in this country has the power to do something like that in poetry? I think that makes him unique.

But it may be a narrow talent, finally. One question about Levine's work is whether ultimately he may have a lot of range. This was certainly true of Richard Hugo—that his range was limited. Every time Hugo tried to get away from writing about discovering a little town and learning how miserable it made him feel, he wrote badly. I would take that one talent, though. I would say that's enough for me. Levine, a great poet of anger and intense victimization, has tried to be funny on occasion. He's not a funny poet, a poet of light moods. When he tries to be satiric, he fails. I said in *APR* that *The Names of the Lost* is very much compromised by being a book that takes such a simplistic political stance, that it's like a Clint Eastwood movie—*The Good, The Bad, and The Ugly*—if you don't agree with him, then you're the bad and the ugly. I think that's a weakness. It is a unionist mentality, divisive and violent. When he attacked Helen Vendler and Marjorie Perloff in a shameful essay in *Kenyon Review*, he revealed his anger without grace of poetic form. But again, this is maybe an arrogant position for me. I would trade anything I've done for Levine's best poems. Any day of the week.

Besides being interested in James Wright, Dickey, and Levine, what other contemporary writers do you find yourself returning to, following, or having an interest in?

My guess, Tod, is that you've probably already experienced the same thing that I and other poets have experienced, but are perhaps reluctant to say. I tend to read those poets who seem to me helpful in the manipulation or wielding of a tool in the time that I need that tool. If I were trying to write about abstraction, I might read Anthony Hecht because I think that he's a very fine poet at combining intellectual abstraction and physical reality. I never really want to get that far from the physical world, so I couldn't go to a poet of extreme abstraction. It wouldn't profit me. But I can look at something Hecht does because he can teach me.

I think of certain poets as touchstones when I'm having trouble. You come to recognize when you're having trouble, and you have a general sense of what it is, so maybe you go to a particular poet on the shelf. Certain poets I read over and over. I feel very close to Robert Lowell. Some people who have written about my poems have thought that I was influenced by Dylan Thomas. There was a time in my life when I greatly admired Thomas, but I would say that I haven't read Dylan Thomas in fifteen years. Not a word. Dickey is another part of my imagination, although I don't read Dickey very much anymore because his power is so compelling to me that it's easy for me to start sounding like Dickey. Warren even more so. Because he can frame a story quicker and more efficiently than anyone I know. He can turn anything into a story, and it will be intense because he can read the abstractions in ways that I find compelling and true. As Levine can. I keep Levine on my shelf, too. Dickey, Lowell, Warren, Wright. Wright for his tenderness, for his ability to say something that seems expressed not so much by the mouth as by the heart.

I like Kinnell. There is some Kinnell I don't like, but Kinnell has a wonderful exuberance, a Whitmanic energy in language that I like a great deal. And the last few years—and this won't surprise you, having said what I've been writing—I've been especially and enthusiastically reading Seamus Heaney. I love his lyrical feel for the world. But even more, the way he can and so often does put that feeling into language that is different in both vocabulary and syntactical expression than you or I use. For example, when Seamus talks about what he calls slub silk I love the sound. I don't know what "slub silk" is, but I love the sound of it. The feel of Seamus's language, the glide and twirl of it, became important to me. But also the way he can concentrate an image and efficiently allow it to speak.

As I've read a lot of Seamus, I've found myself reading more and more Brits and Irish poets. The Scot poet Douglas Dunn is very important to me. I like and read a good bit of the roughness of presentation of the natural world in Ted Hughes. There's a great sense of vitality in Hughes that I like. In many of the poems, Hughes is barking at the world, and I don't like that necessarily. But there's a poem in his *Selected Poems* called "Roe Deer," which is one of the most graceful and mystical poems you'll ever see. It's about a deer appearing at the road in a mist as Hughes is driving a car, and the deer seems not to be there, and then it's there, and then it's gone. Like angels. If they were in a Philip Levine poem, they would be angels. There's a way that Ted Hughes is able to manifest the natural world that I like a great deal and respond to.

RC: Stafford in that way, too?

I don't read much Bill Stafford. I did at one time in my life. I'll tell you a story about Stafford. When I was a young poet, Stafford was the Consultant in Poetry at the Library of Congress. I didn't know what that meant. I thought it meant that he was the head poet for the government, and, therefore, I could go and ask him a question. I didn't know. I was only about a hundred and fifty miles from D.C., and so my wife and I decided we'd go up and see him one day. We drove up, called him, and Bill Stafford, being who he was, said, "Sure, come on in." I took a tape recorder along and asked him a lot of questions. He was the cagiest human being you could ever meet. I said to him at one point, "Do you have a line theory?" And he paused in his grave way, and he said, "Yes, I do." And I waited and I waited and he wouldn't give it to me, so I impatiently said, "Well what is it?" And he put on this grin and he said, "Well, when I'm typing along I know I'm going to come to the edge of the page and have to start over." That was it. That was his whole line theory. Of course, I thought then and think now, that Bill Stafford is a good bit cagier than that. I learned what I think you can learn from Stafford and what, if I read him now, I still see, maybe more than anything else is an honesty of expression. Stafford keeps relentlessly demanding of himself what he really feels. And then he says it. His way of making a poem is finding an equivalent language for being in the moment.

For him, there's nothing that's too plain, too solid, too simple for a poem; anything can go in if it makes the poem seek comprehension. I think that's a great lesson that he teaches. He lowers the threshold of accessible form or makes form more usable for all of us without feeling we have to have a pedigree or arcane instruction. That doesn't mean that it's not complex or structured form, it means he insists on all of us having the competency to do it. There's a great lesson in that. If poets don't believe they can do it, they don't do it. The lesson applies to readers as well.

I once asked Bill Stafford if he had writer's block, and he said, "No, that's just because you're afraid to write, and I'm never afraid." There's real truth in that. He wasn't afraid.

RC: You mentioned some international poets—Seamus Heaney and, earlier in the day, you mentioned having seen Paula Meehan read. I wonder if any other international poets, particularly the Eastern Europeans—Herbert, for instance, or Salamun or Milosz—if any of their work is of interest to you. One reason I ask is that I don't see translations appearing nearly as often in The Southern Review *as in other journals.*

I do find some of Milosz's work dazzling. A good bit of it has remained, for whatever reason, distant from me, but many of the lyric poems seem to me transparently beautiful. Some of the poets you've mentioned have not been of particular interest to me, although there have been some that you didn't mention that have. Herbert and Miloslav Holub, whom I've seen read, I've liked very much. There was a Yugoslavian poet named Janos Pilinszky, who tends to write a more narrative poem, whom I like quite a bit. Ted Hughes is the only one who's translated him that I know of. That book is not widely available in this country, and he may even be dead now.

But, regarding translation, we don't do a lot of translations. *The Southern Review* has never printed much translation. It isn't our particular expertise or interest. We've done some as they've come along to us. Our recent special Irish issue has turned out to have a focus on the importance of translation to emerging Irish poetries in a way that surprised us. We didn't set out to discover that, but it kept coming up in essays. Particularly in the exchange, for example, between Irish and English, the relations and the hostilities, but also the ways in which non-English poetries have had an influence on emerging Irish writers and their senses of the deployment of language. There hasn't been a pronounced reason why we haven't done that many translations in the past. We may do more.

I think what Rob's speaking to is the vogue or intense interest in poetry that has come out of international contexts of oppression or suffering, best exemplified, perhaps, by Carolyn Forché's book, Against Forgetting, *and the impact, influence, and, what Seamus Heaney calls "the shadow challenge" that these poets' work have upon poets writing in the West, how this work has shaped many American poets. I guess I'm interested in knowing whether you've felt a "shadow challenge" from any of these writers or if you could offer your take on this vogue of "poetry of witness."*

I'm made nervous by it. I'll try to say what I can say, although it's a very complex issue, and I have both ambiguous and ambivalent feelings about it. Let's speak first of Heaney, who is a poet and a man about whom I have almost strong feelings. He's been a friend of mine since the early seventies; before he had a following in the States, I knew him. I would not be the first, among those familiar with his work, to raise the issue of whether there isn't in his thinking and his writing something of a naïve hero-worshipping. I have heard Seamus speak, for example, almost adoringly of Milosz because Milosz went through political turmoils and troubles that Seamus sees himself as not having experienced, thus being less tempered. He feels something of the same thing for Derek Walcott and for

Joseph Brodsky. I understand this, I think. I don't feel comfortable with it. In Forché's case, I don't know what to make of her righteous certitude, and so I prefer to say nothing.

In any American writer's case, it might be argued that we have the handicap of not having an immediate experience with some of the wide and deep oppressions in the world, as, for example, might be experienced by a Palestinian or a Chilean or a Hungarian. We haven't had those things in this country. We haven't had world wars or concentration camps, and yet having said that—and having tried to say, in some sense, that we don't have a subject such as those people—we do have the very real and abiding presence of a subjugated black population in this country, which is not merely an idea; it's around us. Here in Louisiana, we live in a half white, half black country. The horrible pain of black subjugation, of any aspect of racial relations, is as scathing and central to American culture as Israeli-Palestinian hostility is to the Middle East. I view Warren as a hero-poet, just as Heaney sees Milosz. But heroizing anyone risks a blindered reality and poets can't afford that.

There's a temptation on the part of serious-minded people, who happen to be writers, to want to take on the biggest possible human subjects, particularly subjects which engage and resist the oppressions of people. This is entirely appropriate. But the danger is one can become a "subject hunter," one can become a romantic of moral righteousness. It seems to me that it's a good thing to be careful of what subject one takes on and what moral position one takes, careful that one doesn't fall into the position of sermonizing, of simply talking from the position of righteous ideas which are not necessarily grounded in actual experience, of expressing the ideological position which is not human in fact. Seamus knows that this is a problem for him; he's written an essay about it. I can't recall the title of it, but it was withdrawn from his last book, although it was published in a journal. He's aware of the very human danger of falling into the trap of being an authority when we are all merely struggling to know simple, inevitable truths. In this country, because we don't really have the kinds of overtly political subjects that other writers in other cultures have had, we tend to feel we don't have a subject at all, and one has to tour to "take up" the victim cause.

But we do in fact have very real problems. Racial division has in fact become more openly real as we've seen violence, as we've heard from other segments of American society. All of the various ethnic components of the American society represent, in some way, their own story that needs to be addressed in the best possible ways to speak to the entire culture. This is not meant to be a multicultural hymn, which I see as New Age fool-speak.

I think the question is at root, "How do I feel about poets dealing with the largest possible moral issues?" I think it is incumbent upon the serious poet to take up the largest issues he or she is capable of dealing with, but not if it means becoming false to the issue or to his or her own experiences. There are certain things we just don't know about. My colleague Andre Codrescu, as well as Ms. Forché, perhaps with justification and experience, feel they can speak to the issues in American culture or any culture anywhere. I could not do this other than in a very general, very removed way. I don't know very much about them. I can speak about growing up in a racist white society because I did, and I still live in it. I know it in my fingertips and in my ears. But I can't speak of Chile. I just don't know of it. Nor can I speak of what's happening in Eastern Europe. If you know the prose of Mr. Milosz, you know that he's had much to say about people assuming the right to speak about the tribulations of his country. I don't think this is entirely possessive. I think it recognizes something in the validity of having had the experience that's not in the "knowing" of the experience. These are difficult subjects to talk about. The witnessing of poetry need not be international to be permanent and powerful. It may be, as Mae West said, focused on what's lying around the house.

RC: I wanted to ask about your teaching of poetry. In Local Assays *you said that you ask workshops three basic questions: What is the poem doing? How well does it do it? Is what it does worth doing? I'm especially interested in the third question of significance. I think people frequently bring poems to workshops without considering the question, "Is what I've done worth doing? Is it significant?" How do you know that the subject is worthwhile?*

From my perspective we're speaking of what is the most important thing about poetry. That is its relation to the moral existence of the individual. The answer to the question is that anything you choose to write about, choose to care about, is important. In another sense, nothing is important. It's one of those chicken and egg questions. What I mean by it—and the reason I raise the issue in the way that I did—is that it seems possible to me to learn the skills of writing a competent poetry whether verse or free verse. It seems possible to learn those skills without learning what really matters about poetry. I think we have all had the experience of reading books of poems that seem perfectly competent, maybe better than competent, but ultimately estranged or disengaged from anything we feel in crisis. The fault may have been in us, that we weren't capable of recognizing the dimensions and the quality of the poetry. But let's say that there is poetry we read in which our reading apparatus and our instincts are right; they say the poetry is trivial. Is it possible to write well-executed trivial poetry? I think the answer is yes, absolutely. There are people who write without the kind of intensity, without the kind of engagement with the most critical aspects of human living we could desire. I regard the "Language" poets as examples. Now, it isn't easy to say, "You wrote a trivial poem, now go write something that's serious." That doesn't and shouldn't prevent us from seeking to do it, however.

If you wrote what I thought was a trivial poem, I would tell you I thought it was a trivial poem. I would say, "Look, here's a poem that Eleanor Ross Taylor wrote that's really about vulnerability, and it's much more important than how many bottles of beer you drank last night." That may be an important subject, but if you want to be a serious poet, you have to up the ante, you have to put what you think and feel and are into some kind of vulnerable expression. There's a lot of jargon and has been a lot of talk about poetry in respect to "risk"—"this poet takes a risk" or "that poet takes a risk." It's not like brain surgery. It's not that kind of risk where I'm saying "Go ahead and operate doc, I won't make it if you don't." But in the long run, there is a risk. And those risks addressed are why we care about Keats and Whitman and Dickinson, why we want the new poems of Yusef Komunyakaa and Louise Glück. If the poet is not finally willing to be relentlessly honest, if the poet is not willing to fail in his or her expression, to be and appear to be silly, sentimental, wrong, then the poet is probably not going to accomplish anything other than the learning of competency or skill.

Dick Hugo told me once—we were talking about sentimentality, which is probably the singular weakness of most contemporary poetry—he said he couldn't imagine a poet who was any good who didn't risk being sentimental. I think that's absolutely true. We all develop our various guises and efforts to avoid appearing and being sentimental, but if we're not willing to risk that, the poem is probably not going to say anything that disturbs or provokes or challenges anyone. All of those things I take to be primary values of poetry.

Robert Penn Warren said that he regarded the poem as, almost literally, a laboratory for human experience in which you could watch the actions of human beings play out and see the result of values at work, and the writer could discover, by testing in that laboratory, the continuing value or lack of value in what human beings have historically cared about. To make it simple, the issue of courage: is it valuable for a man to be courageous? And if so, in what way? Test it out in the poem; show a situation where a man is put into a circumstance which might require the presence of courage and see if the poem convinces you. I thought when he first said that, "Sure, but you're writing it in advance, and so you know how it's going to come out, so how can it be a test?" But after a while, you come to realize that if you are truly risking what you know and feel, then the language takes over and it does become a test. You don't know how it's going to end. That's the surprise. That's the risk that pays off in one way or another.

Now, you can back up and take this another way. If you want to argue that poetry does not exist to identify, dramatize, and deliver, among its other functions, values that help us to know how to live, then you have removed from it the whole ethos for poetry as a civilizing agent in one's life. A.E. Housman, the great Latin scholar, has an essay called "On the Nature of Poetry" in which he says—he uses the curse of Isaiah—I won't get this exactly right but it will be close—he says that the curse is "a people's eyes shall be blinded, their mouths shall be stopped, and their ears shall be closed up" so that they can't see, speak, or hear. But they can otherwise live, if you can call that a life. What he says poetry exists to do is take the blindness from the eyes so you can see, the blockage from the ears so you can hear, and, lastly, fix the mouth so that you can speak, which is all, I take it, an emblematic way of saying that one participates most fully in living by employing the senses, by employing what we have to make expressive what we know about life—that we live it and see it and hear it and speak it. I see in poetry, as Housman suggests, a very real civic function. Not in any pollster way where the masses are moved to do anything, but in the way each of us is somehow refined, helped to know, and thereby to be better people through the agency of the most concrete and beautiful expression of our values, individually and socially.

If you accept that position, then I think you can say to students some things are more important to do than others, and part of what your education ought to be is to try and recognize what is more important beyond the individual's own interests. This doesn't mean that you won't do a little for yourself every chance you get. It doesn't mean—I have no way of knowing, but I can easily imagine— that Milton didn't like a joke every now and then, even while he was writing *Paradise Lost*, which is a pretty grueling thing to spend so many years doing, I would imagine. Still, if your eye is on being the best poet you can be, then you ought to know what being serious, the highest reaches of seriousness, might mean. I take it that it's my task to cause my students to respect their art and their potential as fully and completely as they can. That is seriousness. I have very little tolerance of people who want to fool around. I have very little tolerance of people who want to be the class clown or the class show off. We're not studying poetry for that purpose. I've been lucky. Over the years I've had a number of people who believed, as I did, that they could learn to write important poetry, and they were committed to the struggle to do that, and, as a result, I've had some wonderful experiences in classes. When you deal with serious people who are trying to know how to be artists, even if they were trying to be bricklaying artists, it's a wonderful experience. It's a way to be more fully human than you might have been otherwise.

PHOTO BY MOLLY BENDALL

David St. John was born in Fresno, California, in 1949. A 1974 graduate of the University of Iowa Writers' Workshop, St. John is the author of several books of poetry, including Hush, No Heaven, Study for the World's Body: New and Selected Poems, *and, most recently,* The Red Leaves of Night. *The lyrical possibilities of the self's encounter with the fallen world have been at the center of David St. John's poetry since his earliest collections. Meticulous attention to sound qualities coupled with a keen sense of tone and dramatic impact—the emotional weight under which his speakers sometimes sing is palpable—are hallmarks of St. John's poetry. His distinctions include the Rome Fellowship in Literature and a Guggenheim Award; he currently teaches in the English Department at the University of Southern California, Los Angeles.*

DAVID ST. JOHN

David and I spoke in Los Angeles, California, during summer 1998.

David, could you tell me what poet first introduced you to poetry? Whose work really brought you into the fold, if you will?

Well, there are actually two examples. When I was very young, probably twelve or thirteen, I just by accident happened to see an article in a magazine of my grandmother's. It was either *Harper's* or *Atlantic*, I can't remember, but it was an article on Dylan Thomas. And I remember sitting in one of her chairs, reading this article, and being astonished by the character of the language, the power of the language, the range and force of what English could do. It had a tremendously profound effect on me. It created, I think, a sense of possibility in a range of music that I hadn't understood before. I had read some poetry; I had read more fiction, even at twelve, thirteen, fourteen. I came from a household where there were a lot of books and much to be read. But in terms of poetry, it was really this first encounter with Dylan Thomas that I think set a standard, albeit an explosive standard, in my head. Then, when I was a sophomore in high school, I remember hearing a reading of *The Waste Land* by T.S. Eliot. And the man who was my drama and forensics teacher—I debated and that kind of stuff in high school— the guy who was the teacher knew I was interested in poetry and asked if I ever heard T.S. Eliot read and I said "no," and so he played for me Eliot's reading of *The Waste Land*. And for me, *The Waste Land* is still the beginning of some of the preoccupations that I have with language and poetry. And in spite of the well-rehearsed attacks on Eliot, I suppose one of my preferences for *The Waste Land* over *Four Quartets* is the fragmented sense of *The Waste Land*—the sense of echo, the sense of reverberation. The allusions don't disturb me the way they disturb others. It seems to me a poem of great psychological reckoning. And that's what interests me. And as you know, I think the poetry of the twentieth century is all about fragmentation and disjunction, and I think that Eliot is one of the places where you see this being enacted in the language—that sense of trying to find some measure of wholeness within the psyche with which to contend with these broken and jagged pieces of experience.

What of other Modernists who had a similar project, but certainly didn't pursue it in the same psychological, internalized vein? Williams captures that similar fragmentation but with a more materially-driven method. Pound's method in The Cantos *is unique. Do they appeal to you as strongly?*

They both appeal to me. Especially in all the obvious ways. Williams' sense of an American voice, a particular immediacy of diction. Pound's sense—for me, I love Pound's culling from the literatures and the thinking and the devotions and the prayers and ambitions, the verbal ambitions of the past—the sense of trying to gather and distill what he sees as the best of what the human mind has embodied in language. But along with Eliot, I suppose the one who affected me the most was Stevens. For me, the music of Stevens became an irreplaceable influence. For many years when I doubted why I was writing, I turned to Stevens for a sense of consolation. And it was really the sheer, ravishing beauty of Stevens that again allowed me to have some sense of faith in my own continuance.

The language more so than any of the philosophic dimensions of Stevens?

For me, much of what can be extracted, let's say, in terms of thematic consistencies, precepts or ambition—whether they're philosophical or something else—I always find useful but less interesting than how those very notions or concerns find their embodiment in language. In other words, those things are like topic sentences for critics to extract, but I find them reductive and not representative of the poet; much of the criticism I read I find descriptive and entertaining but not necessarily representative of the dimensions of the poet's voice which seems to me clothed in something much more subtle and soulful and less susceptible to a kind of critical outlook. If that makes any sense.

What of Hart Crane?

Well, I love Crane and it's interesting because I don't—in the past I really haven't talked about Crane's influence that much. When I was a student of Philip Levine's, Crane was one of the first poets he suggested. But I'm not as articulate in talking about his influence on me as I think some of the other poets, and I don't think I'm as articulate in talking about Crane as some of my friends. Again, though, it was the quality of the mind as enacted in this extraordinary sort of verbal carrousel that really gave me a sense of possibility. All of these poets who have influenced me, and certainly the Continental poets, I mean both Stevens and Eliot certainly threw me back to poets like Baudelaire, Valery, and Rimbaud, and of course Mallarmé, who I love. And those poets have all been spiritual guideposts for me, as well as the great Russian, Mandelstam. Coming of age in the late sixties, the poetry of Latin American and Spain, along with the poetry of postwar Poland, was the most powerful. Milosz's postwar poetry anthology was a real bible I think for many of us. The poetry of Zbigniew Herbert. Also the translations of Neruda and Vallejo. They were all beginning to appear and had, I think, a tremendously profound effect on poets, many of the poets I know of my generation. It's important to me that poetry be seen as a world activity. One of the things I want in my own poems is to try to incorporate the things I admire in the poetries of other poets from other countries and to find a way to see if I can make those things happen in English. For better or worse, I think of myself as a late nineteenth symbolist century poet trying to bring some of those things into the twenty-first century. I think it's what I've been both praised and blamed for, and I'm happy to take that responsibility.

Williams is someone that many people trot out as the primary shaper of the language of contemporary American poetry. To put it another way, the "plain speech" of a great deal of American poetry masquerades as being within the lineage of Williams. That doesn't seem to be quite accurate to me. It seems like a misreading of Williams. What do you think?

Oh, absolutely. I would say it's a reduction of certain ideas of Williams and it's using Williams as a kind of shield for banality. And I would challenge anyone to read *Spring and All,* the late Williams, and not have to contend with the extraordinary lyric complexity in that work. The poems of *The Desert Music* seem to me some of the most gorgeous and lyrically elaborated meditations that I know of. And to use its—certainly you know Williams is not here to disagree with me, so I feel funny about making any claims on his behalf, but all I can say is that the Williams many people have chosen to champion is not the Williams I love and admire. He's a poet who seems to be much more multifaceted and multidimensional, and in spite of Williams' powerful objection to *The Waste Land* and to Eliot, he still seems to be a poet of, if not similar psychological complexity, a poet who has a wide range of ambitions for his own work. And something I want to make clear is that I always have refused to make choices in these situations; for me, it's important to have what I admire in Eliot as well as what I admire in Williams. I don't see any need to align myself in any camp in these kinds of arguments. It seems to me to be antithetical to what poetry can do.

I remember you saying, previously, "We need all of poetry."

That's exactly right, and I feel that very strongly.

And so, certainly then, one of our recent most divisive times in American poetry was the eighties.

I think it's still a negative thing. I think it's not just silly, I think it's purposely divisive. I think it's antithetical to what poetry does best, which is to create empathy for what is. And if you have a poetry based on exclusion and a kind of privatizing and a kind of re-creation of another hierarchy, whether it's literary or otherwise, it seems to me absolutely antithetical to the power of poetry to erase borders and margins, the power of poetry to really deeply affect and shape a powerful empathy for other people in the world, other people in one's own community and other ways of thinking. It seems to me poetry makes possible an event that very little else makes possible and that's that you can join in the perception of the poet of the experience of thinking or perceiving something in a way that's unfamiliar to you, in a way you haven't previously experienced. And it seems to me that's the function of art—to provide us with these experiences, these reckonings with the world that are unfamiliar to us. And the more wide-ranging our vocabulary is, the less frightened we'll be of what's to come, whatever that may be. That's the reason why art always makes possible the future because it provides glimpses of these experiences before they are, in fact, necessary for our psychological survival.

George Steiner writes about art's ability to do that in his book Real Presences.

Absolutely.

How art allows glimpses of the unknown that is the absent otherness of death, and how these glimpses through the aesthetic object prepare us for death. Prepare us for closure, prepare us to invite otherness . . .

In.

In. And I think another thing connected to this divisiveness is the great deal of competition among poets. The sort of pseudocelebrity. It harkens me back to a Blake who wrote, "Among real poets there is no competition. As it is in heaven, here it is in poetry." Or something close to that.

I think that, as you can imagine, as with the sense of divisiveness in poetic camps, the kind of poetic competition that goes on is, on the one hand, natural because poets don't have the opportunity to make money the way that fiction writers do, and so they're reduced to looking at themselves through a very particular lens, which is unfortunate and it makes certain kinds of prizes and certain kinds of awards, publication in certain journals, seem disproportionately important. Anyone that writes poems because they want to be on the cover of *APR* is doomed to disappointment and frustration as a writer. I find that terrifically sad. But I'm also someone who has been incredibly fortunate, because by the time I was in my late twenties, I'd already gotten more attention for my work than I ever anticipated in the whole of my career. And whether it was deserved or not is another question. But what it allowed me to do is to really step away from a lot of these issues, and I think I've been given the extraordinary luxury of being able to pay attention to the work that otherwise I might not have been able to. It's not why poets write. Whatever the nature of competitiveness, however petty people are, I deeply believe that that's not why poets write. I think you can take the most embittered, prize-hungry poet in America and my belief is that that's not why he or she writes. I believe it comes from something far deeper and far more complicated in their own lives and experience, and I'm happy for them. I think it would be better if all those prizes just went away. I think one's attitude should be: whenever any poet wins a prize, any poet gets any money at all, that this is something terrific for every poet. And I think that the fact anybody's giving poets anything is astonishing in and of itself. And if anybody writes poetry believing they deserve something, then they're already in such deep shit that I'm not sure there's any way out.

What about your reading of Blake? Other poets to whom we usually append the title "mystic." Can you talk about that sort of work?

Absolutely. And I think that the ambition of a true mystic, if you look in different cultures, different esoteric literatures, the ambition is often a move toward silence. A move beyond language, beyond the worldly realm in which language is one of the readings which we perform.

What you're speaking to is a recognition that language is perhaps a provisional vehicle toward bringing the godliness that the mystic desires contact with into the world, but eventually the mystic recognizes the provisionality of that and moves on toward silence.

Whereas the artist or the poet, I think, is happy to remain engaged with the vehicle. Certainly I think there's a distinction to be drawn between the idea of mysticism and the idea of mystery. And the distinction for me is that all the varieties of experience which move us most powerfully, whether it's the classic preoccupation with love and death or questions of prayer and devotion, hold at their core something that wants to resist language. In other words, those things that seem to me most potent in our experience are precisely those things that most seek to defy utterance. So the poet's job is to use the beauty and music and texture of language to lure that mystery out into the light. The poet is able to do that in a way that invites this otherwise sequestered sense of our experience to join voice with us in a kind of conversation. And certainly, sexuality, certainly the anxiety and apprehension about our own erasure, the sense of what constitutes faith and experience in living—all of these things, the sense of loss of someone near us, all of these things repeatedly throw up barricades toward being exposed, and the artist's job, the poet's job, is to seduce the mystery into the open so that it can be not just honored and acknowledged, but invited into the gorgeous dance that our lives might be. And I think that mysticism, that kind of opacity suggested by mysticism, that there's a valence suggested by mysticism. But what poems can do is to go in search of unveiling of different kinds of mystery. What pleases me is the sense of that mystery as a very visceral, sensual body of being and something to be touched and touched upon by the works of art I admire most, whether music, painting, or poetry.

Poetry, of course, has language as its medium, something that is in some ways accessible to everyone.

Okay, this is an important point because people sometimes come to poetry assuming that because they understand the mechanics of the mechanism, they think they understand the workings of language. But in fact they don't. I don't believe people come to poetry any more equipped to understand the workings of poetry than they do when they come to paintings or music. They believe they should be able to apprehend a poem immediately. But once, especially with students, once you begin to ask them to look at poems in the same sort of sculptural way, the same sort of painterly way, the same sort of musical way as they would come to other arts, then they're able to understand the uses of many languages around them that they encounter in their daily lives are pragmatic uses. They're uses of language to get things done. They're necessarily reductive uses of language. What poetry does is to complicate and enrich the dimensions of language. And it takes a while, I think, for the reader to accept that, to come to terms with that, and to understand in fact how to read the poem. And the other thing that is important to me is that people understand poems as experiences.

Poems are not these little objects; poems are the experiences of someone else's perception, the movement and construction of that person's mind and sensibility. That's what you're experiencing. Whatever the content or nominal concern of the poem, what you experience is someone else's sensibility and it is *an experience.*

You mentioned, early on, Dylan Thomas as a poet whose use of language invigorated you. What other poets from that mid-century generation do you return to? Berryman, Lowell, Bishop?

They've all been important poets for me. Schwartz is another that I point to. In fact, I wrote the *Oxford Companion* entry on Delmore Schwartz, which really pleased me. Lowell, certainly. Lowell and Berryman, because I was a student of Levine's, and Levine had been a student of both Lowell and Berryman. From the time I was eighteen, I had a heavy dose of both. And obviously *The Dream Songs* were poems that seemed like revelation to me, and, I think, to all of us at that point. Lowell's *Life Studies*, of course, were also significant. Again, all of these poets provided me with a sense of possibility. And maybe none of them as much so as Bishop. And that's something that a couple of people just noticed in recent reviews, which surprised me. After my first book, *Hush*, when I was floundering around trying to decide what to do next, I really began to read Bishop exhaustively for a couple of years. And the book that emerged was *The Shore*. And I'm not sure that other people can see Bishop's hand in there as much as I can see it, but there are three women whose writings stand, for me, behind that book. Most dominantly Bishop and then the writing of Elizabeth Bowen and then the writing of Jean Rhys. They were the writers whom I was able to look to . . . They were the writers who instructed me in a kind of style that I wanted. I wanted to find a certain kind of transparency in the language, and they were the writers that influenced me most of all.

What about Ginsberg? He's usually connected to the lineage that goes all the way back to Crane, Whitman, and Blake.

Ginsberg I always found entertaining, and certainly he is someone, since growing up in California, I was able to see read several times. And it's hard to be coming of age in the sixties without having a heavy dose of the Beats, especially Kerouac and Ferlinghetti, but what interested me most, in fact, was that he did send me back to Blake and Whitman. And I suppose I loved the idea of Ginsberg, and I think he's an important figure in terms of the use of voice, a kind of muscular spontaneity, but I didn't find him as compelling as I found other poets—say Vallejo or Miguel Hernandez; there was something always a bit too self-conscious about Ginsberg's performance. I always felt that Ginsberg, much like Robert Frost, was positioning himself in front of whatever camera was available. "Wichita Vortex Sutra" is the poem I admire most in Ginsberg. "Wichita Vortex Sutra" was the culmination—*Kaddish* is a great poem, *Howl* is great poem—but it was "Wichita Vortex Sutra" which I read first on an airplane, and I remember thinking this has a kind of swirling, passionate, inclusive energy that very few poets can embrace, and that's the Ginsberg that really thrills me. I admired him personally for lots of different reasons. Maybe most of all his generosity to other poets. But the work affected me most in the way that it echoed other poets I admired.

Coming to consciousness in the sixties and seventies, you saw many poets turn their energy toward connecting poetry to the political sphere. How is poetry connected to the political?

I find any kind of poem with a particular kind of didacticism to fall into the realm of essay. And the poems that have political concerns that are the most powerful are the poems that enact a revision of sensibility. It seems to me that this sort of revision is a truly political act. To paraphrase a concern, to use a poem to mirror an issue, to be a ventriloquist, to note a kind of injustice that belongs to someone else: these dynamics are troublesome. I think a lot of political poetry is appropriation of someone else's political concern. And the poets whose poems I admire that have political content, whether Herbert, Neruda, or someone else's work, are the poets that allow the reader into a new way of seeing their world. And that kind of very radical revision of consciousness seems to me quite extraordinary. Unless one's agenda, one's concerns, are embodied and enacted within the poem, then the poem becomes the voyeur commenting upon the political staging that they see in front of them. And that seems to me too easy a solution to the dilemma, self-satisfying, and it seems to me much harder work to engage the reader in an experience within a poem that may alter how they see themselves, how they might see their own relationship to what is other. Every great poem is a profound act of empathy with what is not oneself. Many of the poems that have an overt political content, in fact, invite a response from the reader that leaves the reader outside the event, that leaves the reader as a voyeur and invites a kind of simple acknowledgment of the injustice of the subject or the kind of disturbing quality of the event.

One of the great dilemmas of contemporary poetry is that there's a kind of reliance on reportage. Whether it's domestic or political, there's a sense that the illusion of truth, the illusion of a particular journalistic truth necessarily occasions great consequence, and that's just not so. Many of these poems simply invite the reader to congratulate the writer on his or her own sensitivity, having observed whatever injustice they've observed.

Or if it's in "the domestic or personal" category, then it congratulates the writer on their endurance, perhaps.

At their having survived. It's the kind of congratulations that occurs on talk shows; it's the Oprahfication of American poetry. And it's been going on for a long time. Certainly one of the things it provides us is a number of voices or kinds of experiences that may not have been included in poems of the past, which is always good, but it also invites this kind of voyeurism I've been talking about.

I guess the name that people trot out is "Confessionalism." But that's not a real useful term. It's interesting that some of the work that you're describing perhaps claims lineage back to Life

Studies—or at least that's one of the prevalent literary historical narratives. Because it seems what Lowell's doing in that book is very different from what I see in many other poems.

In the same way you were noting a kind of misunderstanding of Williams, I would say there's a similar misreading of Lowell.

Or Plath.

Or Plath.

And I've always found that troubling because the use of language in her work is nothing short of stunning, amazing.

It is amazing. And Plath is one of my favorite poets, I have to say, too. That sense of power and the luminous glory of the language. It was Levine who gave me Plath to read. And then I went through a period where I didn't read Plath for many years. About eight or nine years ago, my wife, Molly Bendall, who often teaches Plath, would ask me, "Oh remember this poem of Plath's?" And I realized that I didn't remember those poems of Plath's as well as I wanted. I went back because of Molly's love of Plath and discovered all over again not only how great the poems are but also how important those poems were to my idea as a young poet of a poem's construction and what a huge influence she had been when I was in school.

It seems to me that Plath is a poet whose work is, for many, inseparable from her life. And yet, if we didn't know a whit about her life and we looked at her poems, we could certainly see the pain quite vividly.

Oh absolutely. And I think it's part and parcel of something you noted earlier. And that's the importance of a certain kind of not just celebrity in the world of poetry but an attention to biographical aspects of poets as a way of trying to decipher the poems. It seems to me inevitably reductive, and it seems to me one writes in order to escape one's self as well as to voice who one is. So I think that it's an unfortunate dynamic, but it's not limited to the world of poetry. It's a reflection of what's going on in the culture. I mean it's the *People* magazine idea of poetry.

So, then, how would you describe the speaker in your own poems?

I think that the speakers are often men and women who are searching for some sense of psychological peace in a world that is moving at a kind of kaleidoscopic pace. They're looking for moments of connection. They're looking for moments of reprieve and sanctuary as they somewhat restlessly move through their lives and their experiences and cross both real and figurative borders. They're men and women who want to risk a kind of nakedness that's both metaphorical and physical. They're people who have given up on faith but have not given up on hope and, as such, are still open to some notion of belief. In other words, however spiritually disappointed these figures may be, they remain questing in their own idiosyncratic ways.

So, "No Heaven—but this" is how it is?

It's because these people are living at the margins of their own lives, and they're looking for moments of companionship and moments of recognition they find in each other and the world. And yet, as in the end of that poem, even though there is this sense that there is no heaven, there is the sense there is "no heaven *but this.*" *This* can constitute its own sense of peace and reflective quiet.

It's an optimistic note.

Absolutely, it's meant to be an affirming gesture.

Is your vision of human essence optimistic like that?

It still is. It's interesting because my ambition has always been to be thought of as the most decadent poet in America, but as I read each new book of Frederick Seidel's, I realize he's gone there before me and also with a kind of extraordinary ferocity of nihilistic power that I'm still not capable of. I'm young, you know, so I'm still hopeful that I can obtain his dimension of savage realism. But I'm afraid it's probably not in my future. There's still something too nineteenth century and romantic in my view.

That sort of nihilistic, ironic, jaded, cynical pose is such a part of our moment; it seems to me that your poems are declarations against that.

You're absolutely right; finally, that's exactly what they are.

What shapes a poem for you formally? How do you know what constitutes any given poetic line?

Well, one of the things people tend to forget is that many poets of my generation, even though we may not be part of the New Formalist revival, have a strong education in traditional meters and rhyme, in traditional forms of every sort. I came of age reading Wilbur and Merrill and Hecht, and when I taught at Johns Hopkins, I taught a poetic forms course every year.

I'll even occasionally write with more overt formal dimensions—sonnets or variations on sonnet forms or ballad forms. The Pasolini poem obviously is in terza rima except in the end of the section with the villanelle. But people don't usually think of me as a formal poet. And that's fine with me. I prefer to be a poet for whom the traditional aspects of poetic form remain absolutely important and essential, but that's not the way I want to be identified. And you can look at any of my poems and see a way in which a certain rhythmic closure and often a secret rhyme are employed to give the sense of completion. It's one of the things that's become a tic in my poem—too much reliance on a kind of obvious yet "hidden" closure. So, all of those elements of form that would be regarded as traditional form are important. At the same time, every poem needs to have its interior form, which is the form that the imagination and perception give it. It's the form of sensibility and movement of that particular mind. And don't forget that I believe the poem is a little model of consciousness and the poem enacts the sequence of perceptions in language and that language itself is performative in that way. And so, the other thing, if you look at the poems as early as "The Poem of The Remembered," "In the Shore," or "No Heaven," you find poems that use a kind of broken field in the line—unpunctuated, italicized, language that's used in high relief. Spacing between the words. But that's as much a formal choice as opting for the sonnet form. It's also a decision to use a certain type of line, a certain type of broken field at that moment of the sequence.

> *I recall those poems and that your use of columns is almost dialogic. Although Olson isn't someone that comes immediately to mind when I think of your work, I can't help but flash on the projectivist project. But not in any sort of programmatic sort of way.*

I'm happy to hear you say that because what I hope is that whatever happens in the poem, it doesn't seem schematic or proscriptive. I don't want to appear to be writing out of an assumed set of precepts. I want the poems to discover their form within my imagination. To come to a poem knowing already that it will fit the kinds of mechanical directions of a certain set of aesthetics seems to me dangerous, and in my experience it certainly hasn't worked. I continue to write simply to discover what I have to say and how I might say it. If I know too much beforehand what any of that might be, then the poem becomes a little poetic essay of very little interest.

> *Robert Hass writes, "Desire is full of endless distances." Is there a goal for the desired "connections of consciousness" that you talk about? Is there an ultimate vision in your work?*

Take pleasure in the process.

There is no Paradiso, then?

I would not be disappointed to find that there is one, but I don't go forward with that conviction. I go forward with the hope that one can move beyond the Inferno and beyond the Purgatorio, and I think many of the figures in my poems are moving across the landscape of the Purgatorio with some mirror in their pockets in which they hope to see the Paradiso. But I think that, for me, what's interesting is what men and women do, how men and women behave. The choices they make or don't make in the face of situations and conditions of not simply stress and extremity but of both sexual and psychological complexity. So I'm less interested in the happy ending than I am in the struggle, the process. That seems to me really worth looking at. I trust that all the figures and characters that populate my poems will find their own ways and directions. What interests me is to try to talk about these moments and these windows. I greatly prefer pieces of the story to the whole story. I'm not deeply concerned about how the story ends, because it ends differently with different people. I'm not even that concerned with how it will end for me. But I am concerned about the kinds of specific and particular acts and choices, the acts people choose and the choices they make in response to the events and dilemmas in their lives. That seems to me endlessly fascinating. I just read at the Ropewalk Writer's Conference. And someone who knows my poems pretty well came up afterwards and said, about the poems of this new book—which is called *The Red Leaves of Night*—they said, "These are the same characters that appear in *No Heaven*, only ten or fifteen years later." They're still searching, they're still looking. A little sadder, a little wiser, but they're still looking.

*Nance Van Winckel was born in Roanoke, Virginia, in 1951. She received
an M.A. degree from the University of Denver. Although her earlier poetry
frequently relies upon a strong narrative thread, her recent poems have a
more ruminative, lyrical quality. To put it another way, she tends to use
narrative to center a poem around an event rather than give poems a story-
like quality. She has published three collections of poetry,* Bad Girl, With
Hawk; The Dirt; *and* After a Spell, *as well as three collections of short
stories,* Limited Lifetime Warranty, Quake, *and* Curtain Creek Farm.
*A recipient of National Endowment for the Arts grants, the Washington
Governor's Award for literature, and other awards, Van Winckel currently
teaches in the M.F.A. programs at Eastern Washington University and
Vermont College.*

NANCE VAN WINCKEL

Nance and I conducted this interview in Spokane, Washington, during winter 1995 and summer 2001.

You've written many poems that use voices, that speak through different personas. From where do you think these voices come? Do you receive them? Or perhaps "retrieve" these voices that guide these poems?

I think about it more as finding an attitude or a certain tonality through which the poem originates—a kind of verbal posturing I hear from the speaker in the poem. And then I just try to hear that more closely. More intensely. Of course, though I realize any poem's speaker is partly me, what I'm interested in are the voices that aren't as familiar to me, that aren't as recognizable.

I have a theory about where this comes from. I think as we mature we try on various personalities to figure out who we're becoming— as children evolving into adults. But, as we try on these new personalities, we also cast them off just as quickly because maybe they feel uncomfortable on us or maybe we don't know how to express ourselves inside of them. But perhaps what really happens is that we don't entirely cast them off. Instead, we bury these selves inside us. For instance, when I was growing up, say about age twelve, I had a tomboy personality, and it manifested itself in a lot of ways.

I was sarcastic to adults; I played football and hung around with the boys. But eventually I began to leave that self behind and started perceiving myself in a more feminine way. Still, I think I never really left that tomboy self; I think it just went deeper down, and certainly that's a self that comes out from time to time in poems, a sort of sassy imp. Sometimes when I look at her, I see someone talking with a hand on her hip—a whole attitude and gesture. I see her still as more boy than girl. I suspect there's some anima/animus idea connected to this too.

> *Theorists talk about feminine versus masculine discourse. Do you think such theories apply to what you're saying? Are there strictly feminine voices or attitudes that inhabit your work? Or masculine? And do you think you can clearly distinguish between them?*

That's one of the things I try to find out in the drafting process. I try to see how the consciousness reveals itself. Partly that's what a poem is to me, an act of exploring what this consciousness is and where it psychically hails from, and, in a more physical, concrete way, where it's located in time and space. So, yes, it does seem as if it's one or the other, male or female, but it sometimes takes a while for me to figure out who it is, and when I do, the poem usually opens up; that's where the narrative begins to open up. Whoever is talking often has a story to tell.

Czeslaw Milosz has written about this in his collection of essays; in the "Essay in Which the Author Confesses That He Is on the Side of Man, for Lack of Anything Better," he says: "Every man and woman I pass on the street feels trapped by the boundaries of their skin, but, in fact, they are delicate receiving instruments whose spirituality and corporeality vibrate in one specific manner because they have been set at one specific pitch. Each of them bears within himself a multitude of souls and, I maintain, of bodies as well, but only one soul and one body are at their disposal, the others remain unliberated."

You're also very attracted to the work of Wallace Stevens. Yet out of all the Modernist poets—I'm thinking of H.D., Pound, and Eliot especially—Stevens seems the least interested in personas; that is, he seems most interested in exploring his own mind, his own imaginative, epistemological relationship with the world. Could you talk about your attraction to Stevens' work and perhaps what you've learned from him?

Stevens went on his ear. I think that's first and foremost what's hooked me to Stevens. Lately I've been looking at how he uses diction, levels of diction. Many of my favorite Stevens' poems have this odd duality of diction. For instance, in "Academic Discourse at Havana," he has this really funky mix of academese and also a wonderful, lush aristocratic diction. Then there's the diction of decadence, of Florida and Cuba, the tropics; I call that Stevens' guilt discourse. I think he had a bit of guilt for being an aristocrat, trafficking in so much money. A lot of that flows out in his poems in a certain tongue-in-cheek way. I like how he puts these different dictions together, bounces back and forth between them. I'm thinking of these lines:

> The toil of thought evoked a peace eccentric to
> The eye and tinkling to the ear: Gruff drums
> Could beat, yet not alarm the populace.
> The indolent progressions of the swans
> Made earth come right; a peanut parody
> For peanut people.

There's a little nuttiness in this juxtaposition, a kind of self-effacement about where he is, how learned he is, and the way his relationship to the poetry world keeps creeping on this lush world of the concrete, the physical. The dictions keep crossing over on each other. I think it's this tonal play I'm attracted to; he played tonalities like his own invented notes on a language scale. And the poems are so rich in other sorts of music as well, wide deep vowels and clackety consonants like castanets.

> *"The Comedian as the Letter C" is probably a prime example of that type of play: "Nota: man is the intelligence of his soil, / The sovereign ghost. As such, the Socrates / Of snails, musician of pears, principium / And lex." The poem is, throughout, such fun; he makes fun of the pedagogue . . .*

Possibly he was a bit chagrined that he was so smart.

> *Rilke is another Modernist who is very dear to you. In your second book of poems,* The Dirt, *one might even call Rilke a sort of guiding angel. What interests you most in his work? Is there a particular period of his work you're most attracted to? Which poems do you return to most often?*

Well, of course I love the *Elegies*, but I also like the poems that come just before the *Elegies* or, I suppose, in the middle of the *Elegies*. He'd written a few of them when he'd begun suffering from writer's block and he couldn't get any more of the *Elegies* out; that's when he went back to these other poems that are sort of prayer-poems. I think that's what appeals to me—the permission he gives himself to offer prayers. He seems to demand of himself that he stay connected to something bigger than he is; to call out toward the spiritual plane, and to recognize that whatever he does in poetry has to have a foot—even just a toe's penetration—into that plane. I'm touched by the way he bolstered himself and kept reminding himself in various poem-mantras that the spiritual world existed as much as the physical world; his poems were his way of putting feelers out there.

> *In Robert Hass' essay on Rilke that introduced Stephen Mitchell's translations, he talks about Rilke's disdain for this world, the physical realm, and how he attempts to distance himself from it, and you talk about your attraction to his supplication and his attachment to an idealistic realm, yet in your book where we find Rilke as an epigraphical-angel, so many of the poems are so physical, so "of this world." Could you talk about that tension?*

Your question takes me back to Rilke's "Spanish Trilogy." I think what we see there was how he believed we get to the spiritual through the physical. That poem talks about looking at a landscape, at sheep "penned in the fold at night /enduring the great dark absence of the world." For me, that's it: the spiritual has to somehow be pulled up through the physical. That's a way we recognize it. I think, too, it's got to have the physical presence of the people, the folk. That's one of the good things to look at in this particular Rilke poem: "old men left alone at the asylum / who cough in bed, importantly, from children / drunk with sleep upon the breasts of strangers." They're just ordinary people, and you have to surround them with . . . I don't know what to call it . . . your humanity perhaps, and take them through you, and that's how you arrive at the spiritual, by always internalizing what's around in the physical world.

> *And somehow that internalizing elevates things toward the ideal,*
> *the beautiful?*

Well, I guess that's where I don't feel very Rilkean as a writer myself; I don't feel it has to be beautiful. But maybe that depends on how you define beauty. I simply have to feel that the poem can finally exist outside me, be shared, that the story that's told, the landscape it's from and the consciousness we've entered, are shared.

> *One thing that Milosz talks about that is in a similar vein—one*
> *thing that saved him when he was experiencing a crisis—was*
> *thinking and meditating on a scene he had witnessed in the*
> *postwar years of a peasant family sharing tea in a train station*
> *amidst an incredible chaos of relocation, sharing a fundamental*
> *human gesture that he saw as more "real" than anything else that*
> *was going on around them. Is this more in the direction of what*
> *you're implying?*

Exactly, yes. I think what you've described Milosz talking about is supremely beautiful, people trying to maintain, amidst their poverty and desperate circumstances, some element that, for them, contains what is beautiful in life. This makes me think of Elizabeth Bishop and a poem of hers that I love, "Filling Station," where she buzzes by in her rich-person car for a fill-up, and she, in typical Bishop fashion, just describes the filth of this gas station. But then, as she's looking at it, she starts to notice all these little elements that the people who work there have set around themselves to give their lives beauty. Small things. They've put a crocheted doily under a half-dead begonia. Others might call this tacky, but these people live in an ugly place full of oil and grease and the smell of gasoline, and doilies are what they do to bring beauty into their lives.

An empathy that embraces more than just the stereotypes, that is actively interested in all the little ins and outs of other individuals.

The ability to project into an otherness is what we need to do more of as a people. It's an act of the imagination, and lately I've been worried that it's exactly the sort of imaginative acumen the Newt Gingriches of the world are trying to shut down. They try to reduce everyone to clones of their own values and social mythology. People who cannot imagine other people's lives in specific detail, but only in generalities and types, tend to huddle together in fear of a type, say of illegal immigrants. They're only viewed in the most general way, as a cliché. I think when people reduce their world to clichés in this way—and this seems so much the mindset of many of our elected officials—such clichés foster hysteria. It's the easiest kind of comfort to drift toward the mob mentality, where everybody is right and good except those who don't think exactly like you. Our whole culture was built on the values of multiplicity and diversity. We can't suddenly decide that's not what we're about, can we?

Several contemporary poets have argued that the art of poetry needs to be repopularized, that, in the formulation of Joseph Brodsky, it needs to get on the checkout shelf at supermarkets. How do you understand poetry's role in culture?

I think poetry is, right now, at odds with culture. I think that—as you say—a lot of people have been talking about this so what I'm suggesting isn't new; it's what Whitman was getting at, what he was saying when he described himself as

> Walt Whitman, a kosmos, of Manhattan the son;
> Turbulent, fleshy, sensual, eating, drinking, and breeding,
> No sentimentalist, no stander above men and women or apart
>   from them,
> No more modest than immodest.

And see, there's that passion, that grand stance of the work being bigger than the man. He's its mouthpiece. I feel that many poets today feel that they're apart from "ordinary folk," and in turn, many so-called ordinary folk feel that we as poets don't have anything to say to them. Sadly, we all deserve the divorce that we've gotten from each other. We're all responsible for it; I think poetry does have a lot to say to ordinary folks, but one needs to say those things in a language that is both comprehensible and endearing. For most people I know, there's precious little time for anything else in their lives that takes concentration and emotional or mental energy but work and family, and I suspect that's why the arts in general and poetry in particular are neglected—because poetry does take a lot of energy.

Earlier you talked about "attitudes" or "consciousnesses" that you pursue or follow in the writing of the poem as, at a certain point, turning into narrative. Do you see your work as primarily narrative or lyrical or meditative-lyrical? Or do any of these descriptive titles work?

That's a good question. Lately I seem to be fishing out of several different streams. Some poems—I've recently published several, for instance, that are in the voice of Jonah speaking from the belly of the whale—seem to get by with less dependence on narrative. But of course, in the case of this Jonah series, the "story" is already contextually in place, so the poems can, I think, get by more solely on voice, that is, as lyrics. For these I want something as akin to pure musicality as I can get, but for this Jonah voice, it's an awkward, jarring, discordant "music." He's pissed. He hates his situation.

At the opposite end of the spectrum, I'm working on narratives that feel absolutely labyrinthine, and I like that too: this sense that I'm going in to a story that twists and loops me around so far that I might never find my way out. Stories open into other stories that open into others, and so on, like rooms explored in a dream. I love that "lost" feeling—as a reader and as a writer. The journey is itself the adventure as much as what's discovered along the way. Last year when I was a visiting writer for a term at another university, some students there informed me that narrative poetry was dead. This made me react as my former twelve-year-old tomboy self: I suddenly had to do whatever I'd been told I shouldn't. And I did it that much harder, stronger, deeper.

Often, though, to come at your question more broadly, the type of poem will depend on what, exactly, those voices want to deliver. Sometimes they've got their little stories to tell, by God, and sometimes it's a quiet lullaby, a prayer, or a song. I write what they say. That's my job.

Lately you've been writing a great deal of fiction. In Limited Lifetime Warranty, *your first book of fiction, you wrote a series of interconnected stories. When you wrote that book did you have any models in mind? Anderson? Joyce? Dos Passos?*

Well, Sherwood Anderson's *Winesburg, Ohio* is a book that I've discussed with classes many times. I think I've been very influenced by what he did structurally in *Winesburg*, but also by his idea of the "grotesque"— those people in his book who believe one thing above all others and block out all else, all other possibilities, from their lives, because of that.

Do you work on the two genres separately? Do you have a "fiction mode" where you just work on your stories for a few weeks and then come back to the poems? Or do you just tinker with both simultaneously?

I'm still figuring this out. The first few years I wrote fiction, I'd move back and forth—practically day to day—from poems to stories. It felt very schizophrenic. But just in the last few years I've been working with a bit more regularity: a few months primarily with the prose, then back to poems for a while. I do pick up and do a little revising on the poems, even in my primarily-fiction mode, though. The poems call to me. I can't seem to step away completely. But I like taking these breaks from each. I find that after I've stepped out of fiction land for three or four months and then gone back, I'm so happy. Rejuvenated. It feels like a new play toy; I've just discovered it anew.

Also, I remember those first few stories I wrote. After each one, I'd think, "Okay, that's it; that's the last story I'll write." I never thought I had any more stories in me after I got each one out. I felt this way even after my second book of stories, *Quake*. But now, after this third book of fiction, I guess this is something that's changed for me too: I'm coming to believe that the fiction well may not run dry. I've always trusted that about poems, and now I'm coming to trust the fiction too.

I heard Rick Bass say once that reading poetry is good for a short story writer because it's like lifting weights. I like to flip the simile and say that writing fiction is good for a poet because it's like loosening up and going out for a nice, easy jog. Do you feel a different attachment to the language when you're writing in one genre versus the other?

Definitely in poetry I feel language is what I'm hearing and attending to most. Other things, like structure and attention to image, often seem to be on autopilot in poems. But I'm such a newcomer to fiction that I still have to focus a lot of energy on that thing they call "plot." It's a challenge for me to find the right structures and chronological movement to contain the drama that's drawn me into a story in the first place.

I've brought a lot of techniques I know and use frequently in my poetry to fiction, too: moving quite liberally around in time and space, for instance. And, as in poetry, in fiction I also feel guided by the whole persona idea we spoke of. But I recall that the first thing I had to learn about fiction—and this was so different (for me) than for poems—was that it was all right to know a little more in advance than a single line or image. It wasn't going to kill a story or steer it too hard to have a bit more of an initial "plan."

How has it affected the new book of poems?

The new book of poems I've been working on is constructed as a series of small lyric poems, but together they convey this larger "mural-like" story. And so this mosaic structure that I found myself using to create this new book of poems, I find myself now bringing from poetry into the fiction I'm working on. I see that same structural principle at work. I'm thinking of the thing as an extremely large tiled mural. I'm seeing the pieces of it as small tiles that go into place. Not chapters. You get a view of what the whole thing is only when you stand back and can view several pieces together.

You've told me that you're writing a novel now. Looking at your three collections of interconnected stories, how do you distinguish between such a book and a novel?

I think that in a novel, collectively the chapters have to work to answer a question or a set of questions. There are ongoing problems to be addressed. And in a collection of interconnected stories, the overall questions and the ways they're worked through get to be more like variations on a theme. Symphonic. Also, it's wonderful to be able to introduce characters in, say, story number three and have them reappear in story number seven, and nobody seems to mind that they were absent through stories four, five, and six. Basically what you're doing in interconnected stories is creating this world, this landscape for the stories, which serves as a kind of backdrop, and you get to step in and out of it in different ways. You can be dreamy in one story and straight-forward in another. The backdrop is the same, so there's a sense of cohesion. I felt the interconnected stories allowed me more tonal variation than maybe a novel could. But a novel allows so much more . . . hmm . . . what to call it? Depth? Largeness? Complexity of intertwined forward trajectories.

Do you think in your future writing you'll turn even more toward prose or do you think you'll continue in this schizophrenic state?

I'm not sure, but I remember something my friend Lisel Mueller told me several years ago: she thought that perhaps what literary culture was evolving towards was one genre, something that would be a kind of cross between poetry and fiction. There's been, for instance, such a resurgence of interest in the prose poem lately, and the short-short is becoming quite the mainstream genre. I'm interested in seeing the connections between the two genres, places where they intersect. And although I suspect because fiction is taking control over more and more control of the literary marketplace, it's come to seem an act of faith to write poems. It's probably an act of faith to read them too. For those who can make a space in their lives for this sort of thing, they're meditation tools, a way of asserting some quietude and contemplation into the chaos. For myself as a writer, I don't worry too much about what exactly I'll be writing in a year or two. It's enough to feel fairly confident now that I will be writing: that something will call to me and I'll answer.

*Carolyne Wright was born in Bellingham, Washington, in 1949. She has
masters and doctoral degrees in English and Creative Writing from Syracuse
University. Her books of poetry include* Premonitions of an Uneasy Guess,
A White Woman's Journal, *and, most recently, the American Book Award-
winning* Seasons of Mangoes and Brainfire. *She has also written a
collection of essays,* A Choice of Fidelities: Lectures and Readings from
a Writer's Life, *and three volumes of poetry in translation from Spanish
and Bengali. A widely traveled writer, Wright has also won a National
Endowment for the Arts grant for her translation work which demonstrates
the same acuity of vision and deft musicality found in her own poetry.
Currently, Wright is Visiting Associate Professor of Creative Writing at
the University of Oklahoma.*

CAROLYNE WRIGHT

Carolyne and I conducted this interview in fall 2001.

Translation has played a very important role in shaping twentieth-century American poetry. How do you understand the vitalization translation has brought to American poetry? What poets would you point to as significant in this regard and how would you characterize the impact of their work?

Without the influence of poetry in translation, American poetry of the twentieth century would be a much poorer medium. It has been greatly enriched by voices from Latin America, East Asia, Eastern Europe, as well as the usual suspects from Western Europe—much more recent are voices from the Middle East, Africa and the Caribbean, in both colonial and indigenous languages. American poets who read this work in English translation have been affected to some extent by these other rhythms and referential matrices, because they have become part of the body of work we read to feed ourselves poetically, the influences we seek out and willingly absorb.

Some would say too much influence. I remember an essay in *APR*, of all places, years ago, in which the writer of the essay—I don't recall who it was—complained that too many contemporary American poems sounded as if they were translations from other modern languages! He felt that there was too much influence from traditions not properly pertinent to English. What was this writer's blind spot? So much of what we regard as part of the canon of our literary and poetic tradition is translated from ancient Hebrew, Aramaic, Greek, Latin: the Bible, Homer, Sophocles and Euripides and Sappho, Virgil, Catullus and Ovid, just to name a few. Even Chaucer, whose English is different enough almost to be another language—its Anglo-Saxon structure and Norman French overlay of new vocabulary and verbs are not as fully merged as they are in contemporary English. And classics continue to be rendered into English by major poets—think of two recent poetry best-sellers, Robert Pinsky's translation of Dante's *Inferno* and Seamus Heaney's of *Beowulf*. Most Americans are not reading these classical authors in the original languages, as did Milton, and Donne, and even Shakespeare as a Stratford-upon-Avon grammar school pupil! This reminds me of the standard joke about the English-only movement, whose adherents seek to make English the official language of the United States, who seem to have no idea that their Good Book is a translation. "If English was good enough for Jesus," they declare, "it's good enough for me!"

And what of the actual process of translation?

That's the most interesting aspect of all. To me, the closest of all possible readings of poetry from another language is the practice of translation itself. As one who started translating poetry at about the same time that I started writing it seriously, I have learned a great deal about my own language by trying to render another language's poetry into English as fluent and graceful as if the poems had been written in English in the first place—a tough goal, but worth the effort. My first translations—from Spanish, which I had studied for six years in junior high and high school, and then some more as an undergraduate—are from the year I spent in Chile on a 1971-72 Fulbright Study grant. As part of my project for the Fulbright, I proposed to translate contemporary Chilean poets, some of whom I had read in a small volume, *Chile: An Anthology of New Writing*, edited by Miller Williams, which contained a few translated poems by each of several younger Chilean poets. Professor Hugo

Montes of the Universidad Catolica in Santiago, who was teaching a course in Latin American literature which I audited in late 1971, suggested some additional names.

Pablo Neruda won the Nobel Prize for Literature that October. The morning after the announcement, windows of every bookstore in Santiago were plastered with banners proclaiming "PABLO NERUDA PREMIO NOBEL 1971"—and the prices of all volumes by Neruda had doubled. (Neruda himself was in Paris, as Cultural Attaché for the Chilean Embassy to France; he did not return to Chile until after I departed, so I never met him.) Despite guaranteed publisher interest for any volume of Neruda translation, I had already seen enough of these dominating the Poetry-in-translation shelves of bookstores back home. If Neruda was already over-represented even before winning the Nobel Prize, I thought, how many more translators would now descend upon the body of his work? I didn't want to find myself duplicating the efforts of others.

I had read Neruda as rendered by these translators, some of them more skilled and reliable than others at approaching the monumental richness and elementality of the Chilean poet's work. The pioneering early efforts, particularly those by Ben Belitt and Robert Bly, were commendable for their energy and enthusiasm, but tended to be overly turgid and subject to numerous errors and mistranslations. Other poet-translators have done excellent work— W. S. Merwin, Alastair Reid, Jack Schmitt, Mark Strand, and Nathaniel Tarn, to name several; and (for Neruda's prose) Magda Bogin and Margaret Sayers Peden. All of these were active at the beginning of the "Boom," as critics called it: the sudden surge, in North America and Europe, in the popularity of Latin American literature in translation.

What other Latin American poets are important to you?

Other Latin Americans whose work has been particularly seminal for me and for many other American poets are César Vallejo , Jorge Luis Borges, Gabriel Garcia Marquez, and more recently, Isabel Allende. These last three are known for their fiction, but even though I usually read their work in the original Spanish, I have done enough comparative reading of the originals with the principal translations to be aware of the quality of their work available in English. Elizabeth Bishop's translations from Brasilian Portuguese, especially of Carlos Drummond de Andrade, have been important to me, though I have read less poetry in that language.

The Chilean poet I decided to focus on was Jorge Teillier, whose work I first encountered in the bookstore of the Universidad de Chile in downtown Santiago. He was a living poet whose work was substantial but not yet well represented in English translation, and whose idiom was contemporary and compatible with my own. My own poetry was in its fledgling phase at that time, and I wanted to translate the work of someone from whom I could learn more about the writing of it—much as I did from simply reading Neruda or Vallejo or the contemporary North American poets—and someone with whom I might be able to correspond. The dreamlike, small-town, rainy ambience of Teillier's poems appealed to me, a young poet from Seattle whose earliest contemporary poetic influences were Madeline DeFrees, Hugo, Carolyn Kizer, Roethke, Stafford, David Wagoner, and others of the "Northwest" school. And my own travels to the South of Chile, regions similar in geography and atmosphere to my native Pacific Northwest, made Teillier's poetic world very familiar.

And you've been interested in what some might think are even more exotic traditions.

Perhaps. Between 1986-1991, I spent a total of four years on fellowships in Calcutta and in Dhaka, Bangladesh, collecting and translating, in collaboration with native-speaking colleagues, the work of Bengali women poets and writers, for individual collections and for an anthology of this work for eventual publication. I was fortunate to be able to live for two years on each grant, for a total of nearly four years of linguistic and cultural immersion in greater Bengal: such immersion permitted me to enter more fully into the world out of which the poems emerged, and to gain substantial fluency in Bengali, able to carry on fairly complex conversations, read literary texts, and write letters and other basic narratives.

While in India and Bangladesh, I worked with my collaborators in both poetry and prose, but I focused more closely on poetry, partly because poetry is more elusive, harder to render successfully in the target language, English. I wanted to complete all poetry translations while I was still in Calcutta and Dhaka and able to meet in person with poets and collaborators. I preferred to have each translator concentrate on the work of one poet at a time, so that we could both familiarize ourselves with her sensibility. After selecting a group of poems, the native-speaking collaborator produced a first version in English. This was not exactly a prose trot, but more like a preliminary sketch: its object was to convey accurately the sense of the original Bengali, even if the phrasing was clumsy in English. Whatever their awkwardnesses, though, these first versions were the essential raw materials from which I would fashion the finished poems in English. The next phase was to sit down with the collaborator and go through the Bengali poem word for word. I copied out by hand the precise literal word order, noting such subtleties as idiomatic phrases, multiple entendres or word play, and level of diction: the formality or familiarity of verb conjugations, pronouns and other forms of address, and of nouns and adjectives—whether they were standard or colloquial Bengali (more or less analogous to common English words of Anglo-Saxon origin), or of "high" Sanskritic derivation, similar to words of Latin or Greek origin in English. My native-speaking collaborators also supplied cultural information built into the poem's language through proverbial expressions, allusions to Indian and Bangladeshi history or mythology, and references to customs and traditions the poet would expect Bengali readers to be familiar with.

The next step was to combine elements from the collaborator's draft with the word-for-word literal version and the relevant cultural information, to create an English version that was as faithful as possible to the original in meaning and tone, and also successful as a poem in its own right. At this point I worked alone, thinking and creating as a poet. My poetic raw materials, though, were not my own experiences, ideas and imagery, but those of the Bengali poet as glimpsed through the sensibility of the Bengali translator. Having immersed myself as best I could in the life and prosodic nuances of the original poem, I tried to write as the poem might have been had the poet been writing in English in the first place. It was advantageous at this stage that I, the native English-speaking translator, was a poet myself—responsive to the original Bengali poem and also sensitive to the various possible translated versions of any given line that would work best as poetry in English. It was also helpful that I grew increasingly fluent in Bengali, as a result of living so long in the culture and speaking every day with native speakers, as well as from the concentrated focus on the language that the translation process elicited. When my tentative final version of a poem was finished, I showed it once again to my collaborator, and to the poet herself if she happened to be fluent in English. If there were any remaining inaccuracies, they were cleared up here. At that point, the translation was essentially complete.

Can you trace the effects that such translation work has had on your own writing practices?

This extensive practice of translation over the years has had a pervasive effect on my own poetry—from a fresh approach to imagery similar to that of my own geographical origins in Teillier's work; to a deep-imagistic entry into the elemental world of Anuradha Mahapatra's Bengali poetry: vast, rural, isolated, full of disturbing visions and surrealistic juxtapositions at the edge of myth; to the hard-hitting, uncompromising, and sometimes provocative directness in the poetry of dissident Bangladeshi poet and columnist Taslima Nasrin. These poets, in my and my collaborators' translations, have each appeared in individual collections. This concentration on and influence from their work derive from the fact that theirs have been some of the most compelling voices from among the many poets I have worked with.

Many established American poets have translated for their own practice, or to bring certain poets' work into English—I've already mentioned Pinsky and Heaney. Most of these newer translations are also retranslations, not the work's first appearance in English, and they are very responsible: faithful to the original language but also graceful and natural-sounding in English. Such was not always the case with first renderings. Pound's pioneering versions from classical Chinese were not really translations in the strict sense, but versions he created from Fenollosa's prose trots. And yet readers fluent in Chinese have said that his versions, "The River Merchant's Wife: a Letter," for example, are very true to the spirit of the original Chinese. Arther Waley's all prose *Tale of Genji*, however, makes Lady Murasaki sound like a rather fussy-nineteenth-century-British gentleman; in Edward Seidensticker's rendering, Murasaki Shikibu speaks to her readers like a Heian era lady, with a highly nuanced medieval Japanese aesthetic sensibility, and when her narrative pauses for an interlude of poetry, the lines break into poetry in Seidensticker's text. For careful, accurate, faithful translations from East Japanese and Chinese, I turn to Kenneth Rexroth, Paul Hansen, Carolyn Kizer, Gary Snyder, Sam Hamill, and Jane Hirshfield; for more recent translations of Vietnamese poets, Kevin Bowen, Martha Collins, and Bruce Weigl.

In the last several decades, there have been many pairings of well-known American and British poets with European poets: Bly translating Tomas Tranströmer and other Swedish and Norwegian poets; Galway Kinnell translating François Villon; John Felstiner and Michael Hamburger rendering Paul Celan; Marilyn Hacker translating Claire Malroux; Ted Hughes and Assia Guttman, and later Chana Bloch and Chana Kronfeld translating Yehuda Amichai; Charles Wright translating Eugenio Montale; Robert Hass working collaboratively with Czeslaw Milosz; Edmund Keeley and Philip Sherrard translating Odysseus Elytis and Yannis Ritsos; James Wright rendering Georg Trakl, as well as some Neruda, Vallejo, Juan Ramón Jiménez, and Jorge Guillen. These few examples demonstrate how essential an activity translation is for modern and contemporary American poets, and how closely identified, for

English-language readers, certain poets from other languages become with their translators. There is also a small army of excellent poet-translators, most of them members of the American Literary Translators' Association, some of whom do not promote or even write their own poetry, but who have produced and published consistently excellent translations of poetry. Among younger American poets, translation is another form of practicing one's craft, of learning another language from the inside.

*Many of the poets you've mentioned are considered "political poets."
How do you understand the relationship between poetry and
politics? What do you think of "poetry of witness?"*

Carolyn Kizer indirectly commented on this issue in a recent interview, remarking on North American poets' lack of tragic sense, a tragic sense possessed by many of these Latin American, Eastern European, South and East Asian, African and Caribbean poets whom I've mentioned, many of whom we read in translation. What is this tragic sense? I would call it a sense of the profound imperfectibility of humankind, as manifested in our deeply flawed personal and political relationships with each other, the recognition that we have all failed each other—that no matter how good and idealistic our intentions, we cannot help but fail each other—in large and small ways, because of our shared, inescapable human condition, in all its tragically flawed beauty. The "poetry of witness," as it's now called, emerges, I think, from direct experiences of war and dictatorship and famine and disease and civic chaos on the soil of these other poets' countries, all of which serve as graphic empirical evidence of human folly and frailty. Most American poets, at least after the Depression and World War Two, have been buffered by middle-class affluence—good nourishment and access to health care, lots of consumer goods to make our lives comfy and convenient—and the deeply-ingrained optimism of our manifest-destiny, can-do, silver-bullet-solution, fast-fast-fast-relief, macho-heroism-will-save-the-day, technology-will-solve-all-problems culture.

But perhaps some of the more shallow, unexamined aspects of American optimism will now be transformed, following the horrific events of September 11, 2001—a monumental, politically-motivated and sensational destruction of human lives and major governmental and economic structures on our own soil. September 11 is the closest the U. S. has come, since Pearl Harbor, to the graphic evidence of life's inherent dangers, the vulnerabilities that most of the rest of the world has always known. Perhaps more Americans, poets among them, will now evolve a tragic sense. In fact, an entire literature of witness in response to September 11th is already evolving and beginning to emerge in memorial readings and journal issues, and no doubt, anthologies, novels, and eventually films. One aspect of American optimism is its dynamism—the literature of witness for September 11th is already well into production! (Curiously coincidental—September 11, 2001, is also the twenty-eighth anniversary of the military coup in Chile. I am finishing an essay about this, called "The Other September 11," for one of these special journal issues.)

With respect to the shallowness of some American optimism, I am not speaking of poets who have emerged from the working class or from minority groups or who happen to be women. Most of us have had personal experiences that demonstrate that life is not fair or free of politics, that intractable social problems and attitudes which have direct negative bearing on our personal lives cannot always be solved by good will or even by concerted community effort (not even by a macho heroine of color!). We know that certain options have been restricted or rendered unavailable to us, no matter how hard we have tried or how good we have been, simply because we are not male or white or upper-class or heterosexual. Like the tragic figures in Greek drama—not that our lives take place on such a grand scale, but we can claim lower-level parallels—we cannot alter our circumstances by our personal goodness or positive thinking or sincere efforts. One poem much read aloud in the weeks since September 11, 2001, has been W. H. Auden's "September 1, 1939," partially, I suppose, because the title is a date so uncannily close to this most recent one, but also because the poem is a meditation on events leading up to the outbreak of World War II. Auden was a poet with a powerful tragic sense of what he called "human folly." He knew that he had nothing but "a voice / To undo the folded lie," that he, like everyone else at the end of that "low dishonest decade" of the thirties, felt "uncertain and afraid" now that that decade's "clever hopes" had expired. He knew that for all our "accurate scholarship," our understanding of the sources and causes of war and cruelty—even the most basic schoolchildren's understanding that "Those to whom evil is done / Do evil in return"—we are still powerless to prevent the "error bred in the bone" of every human being, our own deep-seated selfishness and lack of love for others. "We must love one another or die" is the ultimate graphic truth, even if our desire "Not [for] universal love / But to be loved alone" prevents such an "affirming flame" of love ever to shine forth. No more profound sense of humankind's inescapable nature, "composed . . . / Of Eros and of dust," has ever been expressed in poetry as by this British poet turned American, and the parallels between that poem and our own circumstances on the eve of . . . what? our own era of all-encompassing warfare and negation and despair? are pellucidly clear.

And surely your time abroad has informed these attitudes?

My own feeling about the tragic sense and the poetry of witness derives in part from my having lived for significant lengths of time in the capital cities of two small countries (a year in Santiago de Chile; and two years in Dhaka, Bangladesh), and two years in Calcutta, in West Bengal, one state in the huge, diverse nation of India. These are all countries where larger public events, political events, have direct bearing on the personal lives of the citizens— such events turn everyone into witnesses, participants, victims, even victimizers. In Calcutta, I worked on several occasions with Mother Teresa's Missionaries of Charity, at the Refuge for the Destitute and Dying at Kalighat, not far from where I stayed. In Bangladesh, I experienced the anti-dictatorship movement and consequent fall of the military regime of Hossain Mohammad Ershad, followed by the country's first free and fair democratic election—and I was sequestered in my house against possible anti-American reprisals at the start of Desert Storm, the Gulf War air campaign against Saddam Hussein's forces. I also witnessed some of the influence that Saudi-based Islamic fundamentalist organizations were trying to exert in Bangladesh, a matter of great concern to independent-minded educated Bangladeshis. Those years in India and Bangladesh were most wonderful, but (besides the massive translation project I undertook there) I have hardly yet touched on Bangladesh or India in my own poetry, mainly because I have not yet finished with the monumental effects that that first experience abroad in Chile has had on my writing.

In Chile in 1971-72, for example, most new policies or political actions had immediate, visible effects. There were no other power centers outside of Santiago, no widespread sheltering affluence (as in the U.S.) to diffuse public attention or provide economic buffering devices. Any major event swept over the country in one big wave—the scary unravelling of the national polity during Allende's brutally truncated presidency, and the subsequent violence of the U.S.-supported military coup and seventeen years of repressive dictatorship under Augusto Pinochet.

At that time I was in Chile, I had just left off marching in Seattle and Berkeley against the Vietnam War and also in favor of the environment and of civil and women's rights issues; my friends back home were still demonstrating. Allende's presidency was as immense and divisive a national event in Chile as the Vietnam War was in my country. Perhaps it was even bigger, because the marches in the streets, the battles in the countryside, were not televised from distant cities or from across the ocean, but often from right around the corner. And certainly the Vietnam War was the defining political event of my generation, all of us in our teens and early twenties during those years. At least it was for the men of my generation: much of our own American "poetry of witness" comes from Vietnam veterans—Kevin Bowen, Yusef Komunyakaa, and Bruce Weigl—all of them young men from working-class backgrounds who didn't obtain or didn't seek college deferments, as did middle- and upper-middle-class young men, from whose ranks most mid-career American male poets have emerged. Some women poets of my generation, including myself, have been affected by being in close relationships with Vietnam vets—Carolyn Forché and Linda McCarriston also come to mind. Forché, through her massive anthology *Against Forgetting: Twentieth Century Poetry of Witness*, is the American poet who has brought that term to prominence. Many of the poets represented in that anthology are the same ones I've mentioned whom we read in translation, and who have the tragic sense that Kizer has talked about.

Poets who have written out of extremity.

Yes. I suppose that Chile was my Vietnam, my pivotal political experience. I had already been to Chile and back, and was beginning, in my first semester at Syracuse University, to translate Chilean poetry and to turn some of my 1971-72 journal notes and drafts into lyrical-narrative poems about the Latin American experiences. These experiences were not easy to assimilate with the self-absorption in American public life that I perceived on my return. I was disheartened by the massive indifference to Chile that I encountered in 1972 and 1973, when Americans were preoccupied (if they had any political preoccupations at all) with the bitter final years of the Vietnam War and the scandalous proceedings of the Watergate affair and could not be persuaded of the importance of events in a narrow shelf of a country nearly a hemisphere away. I showed a few of my early attempts at poetry set in Chile to my Writing Program poetry workshops; perhaps the ho-hum response these received from fellow students and teachers said more about the clumsiness of their execution than the insignificance of their subject matter, but I didn't know this at the time. In retrospect, I see that I shouldn't have been discouraged by American indifference to Chile, and my poetic peer group's lukewarm reception to those early poems about Chile. Had I been more mature, more confident, further along in my writing life, I might have completed my Chilean poems within the year after I returned, and assembled them in a collection that could have been published in the wake of the 1973 coup. That was when politically liberal Americans—who had been distracted by their outrage at Kissinger and Nixon, Vietnam and Watergate—suddenly rediscovered Chile, now in the death-throes of its socialist experiment. They belatedly elevated Chile to the status of a *cause célébre*.

But at the time of the coup, I was in the first weeks of my first semester as a Poetry Fellow in the Creative Writing Program at Syracuse, and I had just been in a bicycle accident that knocked loose two of my front teeth and required emergency dental surgery and root canal work. I watched the fuzzy black-and-white television news footage of the coup through a haze of painkillers. In September 1973, I had already produced early drafts of some of what would later be my strongest poems, but I didn't know this at the time. I was published author of only a handful of clumsy, earnest verses in mimeographed and hand-stapled journals with names like *Ab Intra*, *Gato*, and *Crawl Out Your Window!* It would take years of poetic apprenticeship, through several other manuscripts and earlier book publications, before I developed a voice sufficiently nuanced and consistent, mature enough to confront the complexities of international events as they impinged on individual lives, to sustain the narrative momentum of the Latin American poems. By the time I had developed such a voice and was able to reshape my early drafts into workable poems, as well as draft new ones, the Chilean coup was long past.

But it still became part of your poetic sensibility?

Yes. *Seasons of Mangoes and Brainfire*, the book containing those poems, as well as several others dealing with the speaker's experiences with marginal conditions and people in her own country—on reservations, in small towns, among Holocaust survivors and victims of the Iran-Iraq War—was published in 2000 after winning the Blue Lynx Prize from Lynx House Press. I have been most honored by the book's having won an American Book Award for 2001 from the Before Columbus Foundation, one organization of writers that recognizes and encourages the literature of witness and stands for the multicultural diversity at the core of such literature.

I have been asked why so many of these poems are about political outsiders and dissidents, and if such figures are essential to the poetry of witness. Some of these figures are not outsiders exactly, at least in the poems in *Seasons of Mangoes and Brainfire*, but highly principled idealists such as the murdered and exiled Brasilian activists in "Wander Luis," or Victor Jara, the Chilean folk singer and composer arrested and murdered after the military coup. These were people whom I met in Chile and Brasil and elsewhere, whom I admired at the time, and for whom I then mourned when I learned later of their disappearances or brutal deaths after the Chilean military coup in 1973. The work of these artists and activists stood for everything that their countries' repressive military regimes hated and tried to destroy. To me, such heroism and ultimate sacrifice make these figures consummate insiders, inside the great circle of the blessed way-showers of the human race. Such a degree of giving of self is hard for many North Americans to understand, I think—until we look at our own way-showers: Dr. Martin Luther King, Jr., John F. and Robert Kennedy, a few of recent memory—and any of countless ordinary and extraordinary individuals who have given themselves to purposes higher than their own ambitions and personal gratification: in civil rights, the curing of disease, education, the environment.

But there are outsiders besides those exiled by political circumstances.

Yes. The speaker of many of the poems of *Seasons of Mangoes and Brainfire* is in some sense self-exiled, impelled to enter into cultures not her own and come to understand these cultures and countries on their own terms, in their own languages and with their sets of references and stances toward the world. Why? She's not a tourist, or a cultural dilettante, but someone from outside that culture who needs to be inside it, as best she can, somehow to bridge the gulf of incidental differences to touch the common humanity that unites us all. This speaker (as in "My Last Night in Bahia") finds herself in awkward situations, sometimes abandoned or stranded, but never for long, because people, often the most unexpected people, surprise her with acts of kindness and generosity.

And sometimes the experiences leave the speaker disappointed—with those who pretend much but live at less than their self-declared principles. Sometimes she goes almost too far, almost losing herself in this merging with another culture, but so far she has not lost her life—either literally or figuratively. This sort of risk-taking is what makes this woman speaker feel most fully and deeply human—I guess that is one of the thematic threads that runs through most of the poems in *Seasons of Mangoes and Brainfire*. Of course, when she goes home, she can perceive all that makes her own country a strange and uncanny place; I'm thinking of "The Retarded Woman on Cooper Street" or "The Grade School Teacher During Recess," or "The Peace Corps Volunteer Goes Home," all that makes her distinct and different among her supposed own kind.

What other literary developments or developments in the other arts have shaped your understanding of contemporary poetry?

Developments in other art and literary forms that have shaped my understanding of contemporary poetry—or at least some of the other influences upon contemporary poetry—involve pop culture, which includes the advertising industry, TV, Hollywood movies as well as independent and art films, classical as well as popular music, and what's been called America's own classical music, jazz. In most cases, the influences of these other art forms seem to manifest more in terms of subject matter than of form, though some who have written jazz-related poems have tried to reflect or recreate jazz improvisational structures. Poets like Ai, Michael Harper, William Matthews, C. D. Wright, and Al Young have written series of poems about rock 'n' roll artists and blues and jazz performers. There are *The Jazz Poetry Anthology* and *The Second Set*, edited by Sascha Feinstein and Yusef Komunyakaa, to which dozens of American poets contributed; Feinstein now edits the jazz-related literary journal, *Brilliant Corners*. Poets such as Wanda Coleman, Jayne Cortez, Komunyakaa, Sonia Sanchez, Ntozake Shange, and Patricia Smith have recorded their own poetry to jazz, or move in that fluid area encompassing jazz and blues, rap, and performance/slam poetry, as well as more conventional published texts. Some poets, Thulani Davis and Komunyakaa among them, have recently been commissioned to write libretti for operas; Richard Wilbur has been doing the same for decades, as well as translating operatic libretti from French.

Can you explain specifically how you see jazz reflected in poetry? Are they poems about jazz or poems with jazz-like formal qualities—which would be what?—or both?

Poems with jazz musicians or specific jazz pieces as subject matter are quite common, as in the work of Hayden Carruth and the poets I name in the previous response; in these poems, jazz often serves as a trope or metaphor for the human condition in Western culture, as a modal backdrop to the poem's dramatic situation, as in work by the lamentably short-lived Lynda Hull. These poems may be in any form or free-verse structure. Some jazz-related poems, such as work by those I name above who do performance poetry, attempt to reflect or recreate jazz improvisational patterns, using formal strategies such as anaphora, syncopated rhythms, varied meter, refrains, big tonal and typographical gestures to capture the edgy energy and excitement of the best sessions (lots of words in CAPITAL LETTERS, w/clipd fonetic speling& many exclamation marks!!!), jazz- and blues-derived terminology and slang, a fair amount of virtuosic ranting and celebratory effusions—often with political content that subverts majority-culture assumptions—and poems that are nothing but insistent lists of musicians' names or tunes or recordings.

The best introductory selections of such work, in my view, are the Feinstein/Komunyakaa anthologies I mentioned earlier. Carruth, whose recreation of a 1940s-era recording of Albert Ammons's "Bottom Blues" (the final sections of his poem

"Paragraphs") is included in this anthology, has said in interviews that he doesn't try to imitate the formal properties of jazz, because he doesn't think it can be done in written language. Nevertheless, if you read those sections from Carruth's poem, you may feel, as I do, that it certainly captures the profound thrill, the humor and sorrow-laced energy of that recording and of much of the best jazz being performed today. It seems to me that jazz music's emphasis on improvisation within and around set melodic and rhythmic patterns is having an effect on American poetry. At least for those poets who have been writing about jazz and in the spirit of jazz, there is a greater exploratory quality, a more compelling energy to their work, as well as a wealth of distinct imagery, lore, story, and political edge.

Okay. And other media and mediums?

Many poets have written about TV, film and movies, poems with TV shows and characters, movie stars, and film story lines as subject matter. Lawrence Goldstein recently edited an issue of The *Michigan Quarterly Review*, and later an anthology, on writing and poetry about film. It could be said that the intense visual descriptiveness of much American poetry is related to many poets' childhoods with TV as babysitter, with our well-cultivated tendencies toward consumption of kinetic visual media as popular movie-goers and film buffs. How many of us who teach workshops have also given related exercises to our classes: write a poem with a film or TV character as persona; write a narrative poem which follows, or ironically fractures, the plot of a film or play or TV show.

One medium that has influenced me a good deal is visual art—painting, printmaking, drawing—in part because I have done a good deal of all three, drawing and printmaking especially. Like many American poets, I have written poems that describe paintings or photographs, and I have also assigned this exercise to students in workshops. I often guide students toward some of the "New York School" poets, particularly John Ashbery and Frank O'Hara, both of whom moved in the milieu of contemporary art—action painting, abstract expressionism, neo-realism—so were surrounded in their professional and personal lives with New York art and artists. Ashbery wrote art reviews and criticism, and was editor of *Art News*; O'Hara was a curator for the Museum of Modern Art and also an editor for *Art News*. Though neither of them writes much about specific paintings or works of sculpture, they both cultivated a playful and ostensibly arbitrary poetic strategy, much like the methods of the abstract expressionism that was in its heyday in the early careers of both of these poets. Ashbery's poetry especially moves through seemingly random, montage-like, experimental or surreal imagistic juxtapositions that stop just short of logic and meaning, rather like conversations overheard as we're falling asleep. O'Hara is more accessible, more topical—we generally know what's going on in his poems, and pretty much to whom ("Lana Turner has collapsed!" and "It is 12:20 in New York a Friday / three days after Bastille Day..."), but the turns and twists of his speaker's thoughts are equally whimsical. By appropriating the tactics of the painters who surround them, these poets enact a painterly methodology that can be quite freeing to one's imagination.

Are there any "older" poets that you can think of in that regard?

William Blake has been an inspiration for me in this regard—in his lifetime he was known primarily as a commercial artist, "Blake the engraver," a painter, printmaker, book illustrator and designer. He was also a cantankerous and eccentric autodidact, especially as a poet, who worked in isolation from the genteel, university-educated circles in which his literary contemporaries moved. During his lifetime, he was an obscure and impecunious lower-middle-class tradesman who self-published his brilliant, incomprehensible poetic epics on plates hand-rendered in his crabbed script and illustrated in corrosive acids with his own "infernal" visions. Blake's presence had been brooding behind my own work since I was an undergraduate, when I discovered him in the full-color facsimile edition of his *Songs of Innocence and Experience*, a volume which my mother gave me for my birthday while I was still a student at Seattle

University. In graduate school, I devotedly copied many of his drawings and prints, part of a determination to continue what I thought of as a dual vocation as poet and visual artist. For the Blake seminar in which I enrolled for the master's degree, the difficulty of Blake's hermetic poetry inspired and awed me, and I read almost his entire oeuvre, far more than the course required.

The first sestina I ever wrote, now called "Another Look at 'Albion on the Rock': Plate 38 of Blake's *Milton*," started as a description of one engraving he created to illustrate his long visionary poem, "Milton." Previously entitled "Sestina After an Etching by William Blake," it was a serviceable enough exercise, as I taught myself to work in the sestina form, and it was even published in that version. But after I returned from several months in Europe in the mid-eighties, including visits to the Tate Gallery and the British Museum, I looked up and studied more closely the etching, informally called "Albion on the Rock of Ages." The dramatic situation I had read into the postures of the lovers on the rock had originally prompted the poem—the active, still-alert female, the indifferent, drowsing male—had figured all too frequently in scenes from my own life, especially during graduate school days. But the objective correlative, as Eliot has called it, provided by Blake's etching enabled me to speak of private circumstances in public terms, those of the Blakean couple Albion and his consort, and to enrich and complicate those tedious personal occasions with all the literary and mythological resonances of Blake's work. I revised this poem into its present form in light of what I hope are deeper insights into, and greater aesthetic distance from, the conundrums of the human nexus. The poem pokes fun at the poses lovers unknowingly affect in the absolute sincerity and, for them, absolute uniqueness of their passion—or lack thereof.

Other recent literary developments that have influenced some American poets include traditional forms introduced from other cultures, just as the sonnet was introduced into England from Italy after the Renaissance, or the sestina from twelfth-century Provençal. I have found certain non-Western forms such as the Malaysian pantoum and the Persian-Urdu ghazal particularly useful, both for my own work and for exercises that elicit some fine accomplishments from students. The interlinked, repeating lines and rhymes, and the cycling back at the end to key opening lines—formal features that characterize the pantoum—can create a hypnotic lyricism, even in rhyme-exhausted English. And Agha Shahid Ali's new anthology, *Ravishing Disunities: Real Ghazals in English*, is quite illuminating. Besides a few traditional examples by Faiz Ahmed Faiz and Mirza Asadullah Khan Ghalib, translated from Urdu, Shahid has collected ghazals which, though written in English, observe the structural beauties of the form: rhyme, refrain, end-stopped couplets, the final signature couplet—all the hallmarks of this thousand-year-old tradition of which he himself, immersed in this poetry since his Kashmiri childhood, is a consummate master. In light of the horrific events of September 11, and the ongoing global repercussions thereof—among which is a new-found awareness in this country of Islamic-influenced culture—who is to say what further resonances and relevance such forms as the ghazal and pantoum will have upon poetry in English?

Charles Wright's "The New Poem" claims that the new poem "will not be able to help us." What do you think?

It would be interesting to hear what Charles Wright thinks of this line now, after our recent crises. I like what the late Al Poulin, Jr., wrote about this poem in his anthology, *Contemporary American Poetry*. He proposed that, in light of Wright's entire oeuvre, the desolate view of poetics represented in "The New Poem" ("It will not attend our sorrow. / It will not console our children. / It will not be able to help us.") could be read as a sort of "antipoetics, perhaps even as a parody of a certain modish aesthetic." So perhaps we don't have to regard it as a grim provisional prophecy of our literary future.

Of course, we do know that poetry cannot help us in the practical senses of providing food and medicine to refugees, like the Red Crescent in Afghanistan; or of assisting with mortgage payments or burial money for those who lost loved ones in the terrorist attacks of September 11, like the Red Cross and other charities in this country. Poetry cannot strengthen the security at airports, or grant jobless benefits to minimum-wage workers laid off since September 11, or resurrect the Clinton-era economic boom and the 11,000+ Dow Jones industrial average. Yet since September 11, poetry has been the language to which we have turned for solace more than to any other medium or genre. As William Carlos Williams wrote, "It is difficult / to get the news from poems / yet men die miserably every day / for lack of / what is found there." Our new poet laureate, Billy Collins, was quoted in *The New York Times* saying that in times of crisis "people don't turn to the novel or say, 'We should all go out to a movie.'" He said that in these recent days, people are turning to poetry for consolation: "What we want to hear is a human voice speaking directly in our ear." Dickinson, Neruda, Rukeyser, Yeats, the aforementioned Auden: poems by these and many others have been read on the radio and television, and have appeared in newspapers and websites devoted to healing from the September 11 tragedy.

With its sonorous and imagistic beauty, poetry is also a medium of communication which can reach across cultural and linguistic distances to create a context for understanding. I've already mentioned the poetry of Islamic cultures—what we know of as the poetry of Sufism, the mystical aspect of Islam. This poetry, known in the West primarily through translations of Kahlil Gibran, Omar Khayyam, Kabir, and Jalaluddin Rumi, presents a world entirely different from the austere, joyless, politically and socially repressive, Saudi-based "Wahabi" Islam that predominates among the bin Laden terrorists. Sufi poetry is full of yearning and love for the Friend, the Beloved, the Being in the Heart—names for the earthly lover, the spiritual teacher, God, or all of these at once. There is physical as well as spiritual love in these poems, and wine, and singing, and worldly pleasure; and the search for an earthly beloved becomes symbolic of the quest for submission to and union with the ineffable Divine. Certainly the West can identify with the warmth and humanity of Islamic culture as represented in this poetry. At this time, when so many people worldwide are grieving for loved ones lost as a result of September 11, and those who have suffered other losses can empathize with the September 11 mourners, we can all identify with the human voices speaking directly to us in this poetry, as well as in the poetry of our own culture. So I continue to hope that poetry, the genre to which I and everyone else interviewed here have dedicated our imaginative energies, our caring and concern—our hearts and lives, if you will— I hope that poetry can help to console and inspire all of us.

Robert Wrigley was born in East St. Louis, Illinois, in 1951. In 1976, he earned an M.F.A. degree from the University of Montana, where he studied with Richard Hugo. The author of five books of poetry, including Moon in a Mason Jar, What My Father Believed, In the Bank of Beautiful Sins, *and* Reign of Snakes, *Wrigley is a celebrated and original poet. The recipient of Guggenheim and Kingsley Tufts awards, as well as many others, Wrigley writes a dramatic and musically propelled poetry, combining narrative threads with a percussive attention to the sonic texture of words. Rooted in a firm sense of place—whether the Midwest of his origins or the Idaho of his mature life—his poems articulate the visions of a life lived with awareness and passion. Wrigley is currently a professor in the creative writing program at the University of Idaho.*

ROBERT WRIGLEY

Robert and I spoke in Lewiston, Idaho, during spring 2000.

What do you see as the story of American poetry in the twentieth century—does it begin with Pound? Williams? Frost? Dickinson? Who do you think is the most important American poet of the early part of the twentieth century?

It shifts. It changes. I'd say Frost. I'd say Frost for reasons of—I'm going to call them reasons—of complexity. I think Frost is one of those poets who manages to be complex in ways we are mostly not able to grapple with. His poems are so much about the unsayable, which is why I believe a poem so apparently transparent offers more. Take a real chestnut like "Stopping by Woods on a Snowy Evening." It's so delightfully bottomless. You can never get to the end of it, though "the end" is right there where you start. But then there's Eliot whose *Four Quartets* I go back to and read all of the time. I don't much go back and read *The Waste Land*; I've done that; I passed the exam the first time, and I don't really want to hang around with it much anymore. After Frost and Eliot, I go back and read *The Bridge*. I love Hart Crane. Just for the sheer exuberant, craziness of it. That is, I don't think I could explicate *The Bridge* with a pistol to my head, but I don't care. Crane is getting at something, through language, that is not attainable any other way. Same way with a lot of Stevens, a lot of Roethke, a lot of Thomas.

354 RANGE OF THE POSSIBLE

Frost, Eliot, and Crane are three poets who emphasize the ineffable—Crane and Eliot especially. And have a desire to shape the ineffable into a great cultural edifice.

I think that my whole notion of ambition is aimed in a different direction. I don't have any problem with making a "cultural edifice"—if it should turn out that one makes that. But it seems to me that if you set out to make such a thing, you're likely doomed to fail. What you really need to do is mind the poems, mind the lines, mind the language itself, and eventually that edifice will either come to be over the course of many years—as you've built something— or it won't.

Maybe Stevens is interesting to examine in that respect. *Harmonium* is a collection of poems that doesn't look as if he's assembling this great cultural product. But by the time you get to the late meditations—"Credences of Summer" and "Auroras of Autumn" and "Notes Toward a Supreme Fiction" (I love that poem)—then you get the sense that now he's honed the tools, and he's ready to make that thing that's going to be, well, supremely powerful, just in terms of size and scale. I think that he had to work his way to that. That many, if not most, of the poems—the anthology pieces, I guess—he is known by are from *Harmonium*: well, make of that what you will. It either supports my point or it doesn't.

Frost I don't think was ever much concerned with the great cultural statement. That sort of thing, I think it didn't matter to him. Ironically enough, he may have made the most significant cultural statement, affected the larger culture most profoundly. Perhaps it's just that Frost was too sly to speak of such a lofty sort of ambition. For me, there's a way in which "shaping the great cultural edifice" seems more the sort of aim of Newt Gingrich. I prefer my ambitions to be connected to the page and thus to the individual reader. This is not necessarily more modest either.

I remember reading in a critical work that "Directive" was a reply to Four Quartets.

Yeah, maybe. Among the many wonderful things you can say about Eliot, there's the fact that he commanded so many "replies." I admit, I have a hard time separating Eliot's politics from his work, and that bothers me. I mean, I insist that one must separate the art from the artist, as *much* as possible, but that sort of latent fascism gives me a terrible set of the creeps. Really, it's too bad.

It sounds like you're interested in poets that are firmly tied to the nineteenth century Romantic tradition. Stevens and Frost, certainly. When I think of your work that makes sense. What's your understanding of Romanticism?

Well, I don't know. The lyrical impulse affixed to the individual soul? I know that I can't really go six or eight months without reading the odes of Keats and making myself feel miserable about my life as a poet. Christ, he wrote those before his twenty-sixth birthday. I love *Don Juan*; that's the kind of poem I love to go back and read just for fun because the extraordinary way that he controls lines. It's so self aware—*Postmodern*, even. I love certain parts of Coleridge; I read his *Rime of the Ancient Mariner* again a few weeks ago; I hadn't read any poems by Coleridge in a long time because I hacked my way through *Biographica Literaria*; I felt like I ought to have gotten a medal for it. It made me go away from Coleridge for a while.

I certainly consider my work in the Romantic tradition. I think that for a lot of poets it's a very alive tradition, especially the American notion of Romanticism and the Western American notion. The idea that this place, this landscape, as something alive in a way that Keats had never imagined it—if only he'd survived and moved with his brother to Kentucky, American poetry might be an altogether different beast. Though probably not American Romanticism, which was necessarily less domesticated, I suppose. This was a much wilder continent, this American landscape, this new world of ours. This place.

Many contemporary writers put a great deal of emphasis on formal experimentation; what's your take on formal experiment?

I'm all for experimenting, though I'm not especially experimental myself. Right now, I'd love to get my students experimenting by writing pentameter lines; that may not sound very experimental, but I tell them that they really ought to learn to do it just to see what happens. There's a way in which the experimentation of Postmodernist and what gets called post-Postmodernist verse is not much more than the logical extension of Modernism; in my less congenial moments, I'm inclined to say that it's just warmed over Modernism, that that wheel's already been invented. This may just be a function of age, mind you. I test myself against earlier models—things like the pentameter line, like the Sicilian quatrain: what will this approach do to me? What will that make me say? I'm not going to abandon my late twentieth century, early twenty-first century view; I'm not going to change my syntax radically, but I am going to count syllables, and I am going to write in this rhyme and see what happens. I hope always to be writing a poem I'm not quite able to write: I guess you could say that's my ambition.

Much of contemporary poetry has been shaped more by the poets that reacted against Modernity—in the fifties, for instance, the shift toward a "more personal" poetry guided the Confessional poets away from High Modernism, which greatly shaped contemporary American poetry. Which poets of the mid-century are most invigorating for you and why?

It's hard to say who the mid-century writers are. The one poet I want to mention most of all is James Dickey. And I think that he qualifies as a mid-century writer: *Poems 57-67* is a masterpiece. I think that it's a monument in the language. I came to Dickey sort of backward; when I was an undergraduate student, Dickey was big; there were all of these people with Ph.D.'s who had written dissertations on James Dickey, and they were all in love with his work, and I wasn't. I couldn't figure out what was going on there.

Twelve years later I had an epiphany. Dickey's enterprise, what he's getting at in terms of intensity—those incantatory anapests, those beautifully cadenced, relentlessly drum-pounding poems made my head explode. I just went at Dickey with a vengeance and became absolutely devoted to that particular volume and to his legacy as a poet.

After that, Sylvia Plath, who, ironically enough, it seems to me is very much connected to Dickey. They both bring that same kind of extraordinary, powerful passion to the page; it's no accident that one becomes a feminist icon and a martyr, and the other becomes an unfortunate symbol of machismo. I think that he's been crapped on; I had a tough time getting through the Henry Hart biography; I didn't like it much. I think that Hart's either missing a lot or his distaste for the man colored his reading. Dickey is about more. I don't think, for example, that he was into building a cultural edifice, but I think he was very much committed to stretching the boundaries of the art, of challenging the art and the reader. I do, incidentally, like Christopher Dickey's book about Dickey, about his father, but I think that's also a real complicated matter. It's a memoir about the complex relationship between father and son. I think in some ways that Dickey is overlooked, and Plath has been coopted in a lot of ways for political purposes. I just finished Jacqueline Rose's book, *The Haunting of Sylvia Plath*, and it's really a pretty remarkable analysis of the ways in which Plath has been misread, censored, and even cravenly edited.

Speaking of those two poets, I once had a phone conversation with Dickey, during which I told him that I was teaching a graduate seminar at Montana. I was going to cover him and one other poet, and I was reluctant to tell him who the other poet was because I knew what his reaction would be, but he pushed me, and I told him that it was Sylvia Plath, a seminar called "Dickey and Plath," and he harangued me to no end about that. I didn't really know him that well, but he was both put off by that and intrigued by that.

Why was he put off?

Well, he was very dismissive of Plath, as were a number of my teachers—those teachers from the same tradition Dickey came out of. They thought that she was just spilling her guts. In my way of looking at it, however, I'm not even sure that she even qualifies as a Confessional poet. I don't see her poems as being confessional in the way that Ann Sexton's poems are. It seems to me that what really works in Plath is the way that she is under the spell of the language. Her miracle months—if you want to call them that, near the end of her life—when she was under the spell of the language. It was as if the language was as much telling her what to write as she was telling it what to do. I love that passionate engagement. That's how you get where you need to get. And I see that same sort of headlong, perhaps heedless, passion in Dickey.

That is quite a pairing.

It's unlikely, but it works very well in the classroom. I've actually taught that class a couple of times, and the students enjoyed it both times. They found it imminently possible to link them, as different as they are. Both poets are so relentlessly exhilarating.

What about Berryman? He also put heavy emphasis upon the workings of language, but moreso in terms of syntax rather than the percussive sounds.

The Dream Songs—there are so many of them! And there are so many of them that are wonderful and delightful, but I think that you're right, his working of the language is more syntactical, rather than a sonic delight. It's also more voice or persona driven, I think. It's oddly more like highly torqued vernacular. You hoot at the cleverness when you get to the end of a passage in Berryman, and that's a different dynamic. "Homage to Mistress Bradstreet," though, is exquisite. It's my favorite Berryman. It's still "Henry," in a way, the voice, now and then. It's still resplendent with character, but that voice is rendered with a kind of high seriousness, without so much miring in the wit and sweat of the self. I do know that there is something about the quality of the language that knocks me out, that seems to me to be of the same cut of cloth as Plath at her most impressive, Dickey at his best.

The other mid-century poet that I wanted to mention was Roethke, who is enormously important to me. There's a way that you can look at Roethke in the early books—say *The Lost Son*—and it seems to me his weird playfulness— "It's sleek as an otter / With wide webby toes, / Just under the water / It usually goes."

Yes, it sounds like Edward Lear.

Like Lear and even a little like Dr. Seuss. It also sounds a bit like John Berryman, too, in a way, though not so bawdy. Those poems, though—the earlier Roethke—don't really move me; what really does it for me in Roethke are the late meditations, particularly *The North American Sequence*, which I think is a transcendently beautiful piece of work. As it is with all the rest of these mid-century poets, if you want to call them that, my attraction has to do with the quality of their engagement with the language. The sound of the language and it strives toward a new kind of truth. In my mind's ear, I hear a voice, when I read all of those poets, that I find mesmerizing. I want to tap my foot, I want to cheer, I want to plunge my fist into the air.

Bishop is someone I thought that you might mention.

I do love Bishop, but she doesn't do the kind of brass band effects I prefer, I suppose. She's so quiet in some ways, but I think that in a poem like "The Moose"— and I go back to "The Moose" and take my students to "The Moose," in that poem, and "Crusoe in England," and that perfect "Sestina," the equally perfect "One Art"—well, she breaks my heart. I take my students to "The Moose" just to talk about the opening sentence. It's thirty-six lines long! Granted, she uses a few semicolons, but it's stunning. It's beautiful.

And there are passages in Bishop that I think are as good as anything. The problem with naming names is that now I haven't talked about Lowell. As far as I'm concerned, if Lowell hadn't written anything else other than "Falling Asleep Over the Aeneid," I'd still find him a major poet. I think that's one of the most astounding poems that I've ever read. In pentameter couplets. It's amazing.

I'm not a New Formalist; I don't have a membership in that club. I don't really want one. I think, though, when those poets are doing what they're doing, at their best, everything is fine. I don't find anything particularly new about Formalism, though. Wilbur and Hecht and Hollander and a lot of other people had been doing that work when many others weren't. I love craft. I love to see how people have manipulated both the traditional elements of poetry and devised new ways of seeing through craft. It's like Pound saying, "Make it new." But don't throw away any of the old tools either. Use them all.

When I use the phrase "mid-century writers," I refer to the writers who came of consciousness beneath the shadows of the moderns to whom they almost invariably reacted in their poetics. There were also a number of writers who began a reorientation from the urban to the wild world at about mid-century; I think of Snyder, Levertov, Brother Antonius, Bly, and others.

Kinnell. One of my favorites.

Sure. I wonder if you could talk about—and this is connected to the desire to write out of a specific place you mentioned earlier— poetry and nature. What is nature poetry for Robert Wrigley?

I've been called a nature poet of late, and I'm not fond of the moniker. I'm not fond of any other way of modifying the word poet, either. (Well, maybe "living.") I don't really want to be an Idaho poet, though I am an Idaho poet, to the extent that I am a poet who lives in Idaho, but an address is a strange kind of definition of what a poet's enterprise is. Or a Western poet or a nature poet.

I guess what I'm getting at is that there are a variety of different ways that poets depict the natural world. In your work, it's a natural world with a propensity toward the violent, the broken, a "wilder" nature than in some poets' work.

There's an essay by Joyce Carol Oates, "Against Nature," in which she complains about nature writing and concludes that finally there's only one response for nature writers—to look at nature and express awe. I want the nature I look at to be not so much awesome as awful. Not because I think that it's dangerous or hideous; I think that it's dangerous *and beautiful*. Much of that comes from living where I live; I live at a place called Rattlesnake Point, and it's not an inaptly named place. Quite simply, I live in a place where nature is writ large and lives loudly and immensely among us.

I think nature is the stage on which human actions, certainly the ones in my poems, occur. I like to believe that what's different in my poems from other poets who work predominantly on the stage that is nature is that my stage also involves people. I'm not into simply looking at nature registering my awe and its grandness. How boring. Far more often than not, my natural world has characters, a list of dramatis personae. I believe that there's a way in which nature can be said to get at the most human parts of human beings—even "civilized culture" or urban life.

I want to return to this discussion of the natural world in a moment, especially in connection with your book, Reign of Snakes, *but your comments raise a question about poetics. In many contemporary poems, the narrative elements that you're speaking about have fallen by the wayside—we frequently don't get a speaker, let alone a dramatis personae—especially in what some would say is the most avant-garde of contemporary poetry. How do you react to these poetries?*

There are kinds of poetry in this country that strike me as privileged. That strike me as the playfulness of the leisure class. That seem to me to want to make no attempt to get at people, to reach people, to move people who do not come to the page with many advanced degrees. If I ever wake up in that situation, I'll give up writing. One of the best experiences of my life was being poet laureate of Idaho. Actually, I was what was called "Idaho Writer in Residence." One week in 1988, I read in Preston, Idaho, population several hundred, ten miles from the Utah line, and later that same week I read at the Library of Congress. Believe me, reading at the Library of Congress was a snap. It was a very sophisticated, savvy, well-read audience, easy to read to. Well, try reading to an audience of thirty or forty or fifty in Preston, Idaho, at the community center, and consider the fact that most of the audience has never been to a poetry reading before. Read to them but do not leave those people bored or thinking that poetry is not something that should matter to their lives because they're not smart enough or educated enough. I mean, we might send Charles Bernstein to Preston and see what they think. But these are fine, intelligent people, and there is some shit they will not eat, to steal a phrase. If I had taken on the task of being Idaho Writer in Residence, and walked away from those small towns, those places, leaving those people feeling less than satisfied about poetry, I think it would have been a terrible malfeasance. That gig taught me more about audience and what I wanted to do with my work than almost anything else has. You can see the logical connection which goes back to Frost.

Pound's "punch the reader in the face" line from a letter is not relevant here.

Or the whole notion that for the poet to be any good—Eliot's phrase, "The poet must be difficult in a difficult time." Frost is difficult. But he also allows almost any reader to walk into a poem and look around and walk away affected in some way or another. In fact, when you start looking hard at Frost, you start to see how challenging his work is. This is not to say that there aren't very difficult and challenging poetries being written today that disallow any kind of engagement by readers who aren't tenured, as it were, but it sure seems that way. That's what I mean by privileged. It seems like a kind of art through which their aesthetic cues the professional commentators to make a living and earn tenure by observing their poetry and not much else.

I see your point. Apparently, after Hugh Kenner came out with his book about Pound in the early fifties, as the critical machine got cranked up, so to speak, Pound realized license to make The Cantos *even denser and more congenial to academic explication.*

That's funny. And sort of a literary Murphy's Law, perhaps.

"I prefer something instrumental, wordless, that is no distractions from the provinces of whats; I prefer something mournful. Letting the music wash over me, I enter into it, and I envy the musician's utter abandon to sound. It's a kind of ache I feel. I wish, I wish . . . I want to be able to bring forth the very kind of exquisite sadness the music proffers without the vast complications that attend when one cannot simply say but must of course say something." I thought that your essay, "Making Music of Sense," from which this comes, was engaging. And yet, it's a real difficult line to walk between the desire to be absolutely musical and the forfeiture of meaning. Some poets seem to compromise one or the other.

You bet it is. Frankly, it's not possible, which is why it is to be sought. Dylan Thomas, for one, certainly slid over into the overly musical. I'm absolutely taken with him anyway, even though I have no idea what's going on with a lot of those poems, and I don't love them nearly so much reading them as I do listening to tapes of Thomas reading them. That's special; it's extraordinary. There's a way in which those poems are a kind of aural part of the art. My old teacher, Dick Hugo, used to say, as a kind of bromide in class, and he said this in more or less the same way in *The Triggering*

Town: "The poem is a struggle between music and meaning that should never be won." Like most things Hugo, as well as Madeline DeFrees and John Haines, my other teachers, told me—even insisted upon—when I was a student (and I remain a student; I will never not be a student of this art) that particular line from Hugo started making sense after about twenty years of writing. When I say that I want to let the music wash over me, I want to put forth that same kind of exquisite sadness that the musician can without lyrics, I mean that absolutely, but I mean that more in terms of a kind of atmosphere of music. You can't say it without meaning, though. Pure poetry is an impossibility. What I want to do is get myself to that place from which I can sing most meaningfully. That has as much to do with how I *feel* the language as much as how I say the language—ahh, that sounds incredibly silly or—it's not easy to talk about. I want to trust the words to take the poem where it ought to go.

At the end of your poem "A Capella," you write, "to make my peace with music," and it seems like that is what you're speaking toward, a way to make one's peace with the desire to sing and yet recognize that notes aren't enough.

Yes. When I was a kid, I wanted most of all to be a musician. But by adolescence I knew I'd have to go another way. Music was too hard, I thought. You had to give your life to it. So what do I do? I become a poet? Oh, that's rich. That'll be much easier. The fact is, poetry has to dispense something like wisdom; it has to dispense something like a new way of seeing, in addition to a new way of hearing. The language, the connotative qualities of the language are what bring forth that new way of meaning, of seeing, it seems to me. I've decided that I'm better off letting the language tell me where it needs to go. By that, I mean that I see music not as something that gets brought to the poem after the fact; it's something that helps create the poem. I'm trying to write as musically as I can line by line, phrase by phrase, as I compose the poem from draft one. How you string a set of consonants together can affect what word comes next, what word pops into your mind; if it comes into your mind only because it sounds like a word you've already used, there's some sort of connection intellectually between the words you've just used that wouldn't be there if you hadn't been trying to make as much noise as you possibly can. It seems to me that what I'm talking about is a way of getting inside the language, of falling into the spirit of the language. I love that phrase—"falling into the spirit"—which is an old Holy Roller term when people, such as the ones in my wife's church, for example, when she was a kid, used to fall on the floor and roll around on the floor. The holy rollers. They'd thrash about and speak in tongues, glossalalia. They were said by their fellow parishioners to have fallen into the spirit. I believe that that's exactly what happens to me when I'm at work on a poem. If the poem is going to turn into something that's going to matter to me, that's going to make me want to keep on working at it, at some point in its composition, I have to feel as if I've left my own body for awhile.

But the composition process is frequently long. You're talking about an ecstatic state with the Holy Rollers.

But those folks learn to cultivate the state. They learn to go in and out of it. It didn't always happen for them, just as it doesn't always happen for poets. In the essay you mentioned, when I talk about that process I go through, what I'm trying to do is cultivate that state. The thing that happens when you cultivate that state enough it becomes a kind of muscle that you work. It gets a little bit easier to cultivate, and it gets a little bit easier to approximate. There are passages of my poems that I think—I hate to use this word—but feel to me almost inspired, that feel to me as if I was working inside the spirit of the language. I had to find a way to connect them by coming back to them and imposing the intellect, but the intellect has to be filtered through the same lens, the same tools worked by the same muscle that shaped the musical part.

This seems connected to the juxtaposition between narrative and

*lyrical poetry. When I think of your work, I feel as if there's been
an attempt to integrate these two modes. I feel that even moreso
in the last two books.*

Absolutely. I was pretty much a plodding, straightforward narrative
poet for a while. I'd have my flashes of musically-turned phrases
here and there—and don't get me wrong, I love narrative, and I
love music: you've got to figure out a way to make those things go
together. We all know about the theorists who would tell us that all
narratives are corrupt, there is no storyteller, there is no author, it's
all a competing set of constructed narratives, blah, blah, blah.

Well, okay fine. I guess my response to that has always been,
"Well, no shit." That's obvious really. Do we think that Shakespeare
didn't know that? Surely he did. Surely he understood those kinds
of things. I think that if you try to go through life without stories
and you actually believe that narrative is gone or dead or no longer
operational, you're going to be proven wrong every time you turn
around. We are ourselves narratives. We are ourselves little stories
we are in the process of enacting. Telling. But at the same time, you
can open a lot of little magazines and see these little poems that
sort of look like narrative poems, and they tell stories, frequently
vignettes, but they are dull; the language is dull and conversational,
more than conversational, flat. That doesn't do it for me. I believe
that poetry is heightened language, heightened speech. The best
storytellers, of course, have a way of heightening speech as they tell
their tales.

Everything I can muster: I want to use all the poetical properties
of poetry. Alliteration, that ole worn out song, assonance, internal
rhyme: I want my poems to go thump, thump, thump with rhythm
every now and then, in order to make that narrative propelled,
something that you want to hear, even in your mind's ear.

*Another convention that has been interrogated is the idea of the
speaker. Who do you consider to be the speaker in your poetry?*

Ron Carlson said, "All of my stories are based on personal experience whether I've had it or not." It's true. All the speakers in my poems are me or someone I imagine myself to be. I find that it's not possible for me to be a terribly different voice. I can be a different person, and I have a number of poems written from the point of view of women, but I can't leave my voice, my way of saying, behind. It would be foolish, though, to go through all of my poems and decide that every one of these poems is autobiographical, that every one of these poems is about something I've done or lived through.

That seems an important issue in contemporary American poetry—the amount of emphasis put upon the speaker, especially in terms of suffering the speaker has apparently gone through. Trauma X, Y, or Z somehow seems to elevate the poetry in many people's eyes. What do you think about work that focuses on suffering in that manner?

Some of it makes for wonderful poetry; some does not. Once again, it's got to do with craft. If the craft isn't there, no matter what kind of hell you went through, it's not going to turn into poetry. Craft is a catch-all phrase; I mean the art of it. I think of a poet like Sharon Olds, who sometimes writes what you might call very simple, conversational poems; I think her poems aren't lavish with music and noise, the way that I think mine are, but I find her poetry extraordinarily admirable. I love what she does with craft. I never have any doubt when I'm in a Sharon Olds poem *that I'm in a Sharon Olds poem*. A poem in which the saying matters as much as what gets said. I think that it's a familiar place. Not just because of what she's writing about, but also because of how she's writing about it. That has to do with her weird line breaks—in some cases, they really are weird—and ending so many lines with conjunctions and prepositions which more often than not strikes me as a terrible sin; I do it myself, but in the case of Sharon Olds, it turns out that you can see reasons for doing what she did. It may be that she just stuck to her guns long enough, but I think that she has found a way to craft the poems in a way that they are well made and not just maunderings. Naturally, she gets imitated, and sometimes none too well.

> *Reign of Snakes wrestles with what it is to be human in a natural world of which we are a part and from which, in some ways, we are apart. Instinct versus intellect might be another way to put it.*

That makes sense, and it bridges back to the idea of the poem as being a struggle between music and meaning. On the one hand, the intellect is in charge of meaning. On the other, instinct seems much more connected to the dance or the pulse, the way the blood moves through the body, the heartbeat and the cadences of life.

> *The people in your poems moving through this violent entity which is the natural world—whole and beautiful and unified— sometimes seem out of place, as if they don't belong. It harkens to mind Robinson Jeffers.*

I do refer to Jeffers in the book; that is, I make reference to a line in his "Hurt Hawks," but I'm not nearly the misanthrope that Jeffers was. I hope. I do think that it's not the intellect that gets us in trouble in the natural world; it's that sometimes our intellect doesn't really matter. You can be a whole lot smarter than a mountain lion, but that doesn't mean that you're going to survive the attack of one. That doesn't mean that he isn't going to dispatch you and make a meal of you. I think that we go through life as human beings cutting ourselves off from the essentially important part of ourselves because we do not see ourselves as part of nature; we do not see ourselves as part of this great scheme where violence is in fact ordinary life.

There are a people who maintain that cars and pollution are, for example, perfectly organic things because, after all, we are creating them. That seems ludicrously extreme to me. At the same time, I guess I feel most alive in the natural world; my intellect seems most alive as well. It's a violent and exquisite system that we're talking about.

In writing a book that revolves so much around snakes, some might think that it would be a risk to take such a familiar symbolic entity; your book reinvigorates, remythologizes the creature, though. Can you talk about snakes?

I love snakes. They are beautiful animals and so vilified. People despise them; people are terribly frightened of them. I didn't want to deal too much with the snake as archetypal villain; I didn't want a Miltonic snake in this book. He's there; he's more there as the offspring of Satan, as we are there as the offspring of Adam and Eve—the offspring of God and God's image. In the way that the snake is both a beautiful animal and a peace loving animal and a deadly animal, so are human beings. We are snakelike. There's a poem in the middle of the sequence *Reign of Snakes* that—I finally had a student come up to me and say, "There's that one poem in that sequence where there aren't any snakes"—has no snakes. It's the poem where Big Joe Truccano is ultimately executed by the gang he works for. His arms and legs and genitals are cut off; he's left in an abandoned orchard—possibly an apple orchard, wink-wink, nudge-nudge. Of course, the student picked up on all that and wanted me to make connections, and I'm not trying to be coy now, and I wasn't trying to be coy then, but I don't have much inclination to offer up an official way of looking at that poem or any other poem of mine.

I remember in Dickey, in *Self Interviews*, in the part "The Poet Turns on Himself," he basically explains a half dozen of his poems. That has always struck me as a mistake (though it's a useful one for his readers perhaps). He offers up "the official interpretation," which draws a little line around that poem and says no one else can enter—or if they enter, it's entering it for completely wrong reasons.

How has your role as a teacher affected your work? That's how many contemporary poets pay the bills.

There are an awful lot of us doing this, and you wonder how many more can keep on doing it. It does, after a while, begin to feel like a kind of industry. But as I once heard James Tate say, "They're not hurting anybody." I don't hear anybody complaining about all of the M.B.A.'s and all of the business administration majors that are getting jobs flipping burgers. The fact is that there is a demand for poetry. That's what's interesting. Why do so many people want to write poetry? And you can take that and run with it and you can make something negative of it if you like; I mean, you can say, "All these people, sure, but are they buying books of poetry? Uh uh." Well, they are buying enough. My books don't sell tremendously well; they aren't best sellers. But they sell well. My last four books have all sold more copies in the first year than *Harmonium* did. So things, I think, are better than they used to be—there are readers out there. And I think that there are more and more readers out there.

Why do you think that so many people want to write poetry?

It goes back to Williams, I'm sure. Every day there are people who die miserably for lack of what is found in poetry. When was this not true? People are beginning to recognize that—and part of it is because of creative writing programs, part of it is because of poetry slams, because of literary magazines, because of National Poetry Month. In a way, National Poetry Month is absurd. As I heard David Baker point out, it's also National Lawn and Garden Implement Month, April is. What a ludicrous thing, but at the same time, some people, some entity, some businesses pay a little bit more attention to poetry than they might have. That ultimately has a cumulative effect. I think that more and more people are interested in poetry. This is not bad news. Unless you really want to be Ivory Tower guards and you want to keep the unwashed out— and keep the unwashed from writing poetry. In some ways, that day is here already.

The effect that teaching poetry has on a practicing poet is also a serious question. Right now, the control group would be to find enough poets who don't teach in order to discover the effect on those who do teach. But I enjoy teaching immensely. I remember the first time I had to teach a composition class; I knew how to write, and you sit down the first day of class, and a hand goes up, and a student says—this actually happened to me: I'm twenty-three years-old, I'm a T.A., I'm a graduate student—and a student raises his hand and says, "What's the difference between affect and effect?" My mind goes completely blank. I knew that I was going to be a teacher, though, because I turned it back on him—"Why don't you look it up in this handbook here? Give me a report on Wednesday about the difference."

I mean, my point is this: if you want to know something, try teaching it. Teaching is excruciatingly difficult. Sometimes making yourself sit down with another batch of student poems is very hard, and yet, every time I do, there are these flashes of things that are amazing. Sometimes they don't know that they are doing it; sometimes they do. I find it exhilarating. After a good class or a good conference, there's usually not much else I want to do besides go write. I don't know that there are a lot of other things that I could do for a living that would make me feel that.

Partisanship in contemporary American poetry is a very real issue; it's a very real issue connected to poetic practice, careerism, awards, and the critical industry. What do you think about the fracturing connected to various schools and movements, as well as the politics of awards and such?

It's certainly a problem if you go out and start picking your students all the time to win prizes. You certainly open yourself up to the charge of nepotism. You shouldn't do that. When Hugo became in charge of the Yale Series, he more or less served notice that if you were a graduate that worked with him, no dice; he would not pick his students' poems. A couple of us actually got into a heated discussion with Dick about this; not that we were advocating our books but that what if the best book is demonstratively one that happens to have been written by your student. He said, "Fine. But if it's the best book, and it should have won the Yale, then someone else will publish it, but I can't." I think that took enormous integrity to stand by it, which he did.

The same people judging contest after contest is also idiotic; at some point, you'd think that these people would say, "I've done this enough." You begin to wonder what their motives are. I don't care what their motives are. I don't care about partisanship; you want to write "Language" poetry and dismiss every other kind of poetry, fine. You want to write narrative poetry and dismiss every other kind of poetry, fine. You want to maintain that if it doesn't scan, then it's not poetry, fine. I think you're all wrong. Ten years ago I would have been a lot angrier about this and a lot more dismissive about people I didn't figure fell into my camp, but I've been trying through my forties to be inclusive. I don't want to throw away any of the tools as a poet; I don't want to throw away any of the possibilities as a reader. I recently read some poems written by a student who was emulating Charles Bernstein, and so I read some of Bernstein's work, and he's a very intelligent man; there are some things going on in those poems. I was glad to have read them. I won't go buy a book, I bet, but I was glad to have read them. I encouraged the student to read more of them; if he wanted to write like Bernstein, I probably wasn't going to be much help to him. I don't see that the axe grinding gets anybody anywhere. I mean, I don't think he's got much to say to folks without the kind of education and training he himself possesses, and that makes the sort of work he does, in my mind, of little significance. Finally, I think that it's probably fine for poetry. Just as cowboy poetry is wonderful. I don't think that much of it is going to find it's way beyond cowboy classrooms, but cowboy poetry gatherings are jubilant, wonderful things. We should all be so celebrated. At it's best, it's a lot of fun.

You seem to be optimistic about the lot that poetry has been given in contemporary culture. From slams to education workshops to M.F.A. programs, you recognize the community interest. A more cynical outlook might say that poetry is an absolutely inconsequential, marginalized art in the days of the internet, tv, etc. What do you think about poetry's role in popular culture? Or in politics?

I don't know that it has a role in popular culture; I just think it's there. Poetry's role may be the same as music, as painting, or song writing. I try not to worry about what the role of poetry is in the culture. Or ought to be in the culture. It's there, and it matters to people. If the poet has any responsibility to the culture, it's to make the best poem he or she can make.

I suppose I believe that there are probably some political roles that poets might play. What I love about Yeats is how he can deal with terrible political realities of his time. One of our greatest living American poets, Philip Levine, is a poet who is decidedly political, of course, and a great poem, a masterpiece poem is his "A Walk with Tom Jefferson." It's a highly political poem.

My third book, *What My Father Believed*—I guess that's my most overtly political book—was a book I had to write, a book I had to get past. The fact of the matter is I think that to write a poem is an essentially political act. It's an essentially political act because poetry slams and cowboy poetry and continuing ed classes—none of those things can change the fact that poetry is something that the American poetry capitalist system has never learned to make big bucks off of. Poets write poems and would write poems even if they got no money at all. Not much of our culture works that way, does it? Therefore, it's a political act; it's a way of actually challenging the validity of the capitalist system, the whole profit making system. I am optimistic. Let's hear it for lack of profitability!

I remember once listening to a poet who had imitators. He had gotten to the point where he had imitators, and he was laughing about it, and he said that he felt that they were climbing the ladder behind him, and he felt that he should stop and kick down at them to keep them away from there. I remember being amused by that at the time, but I think about that now and wonder why? It's okay. None of this really matters. What really matters is the engagement with the page. With the poem. All the stuff about factions, about prizes, about poetry's role in culture seems to me to be distractions from that essential relationship between the poet and the language and the language's ability to plumb the human enterprise.